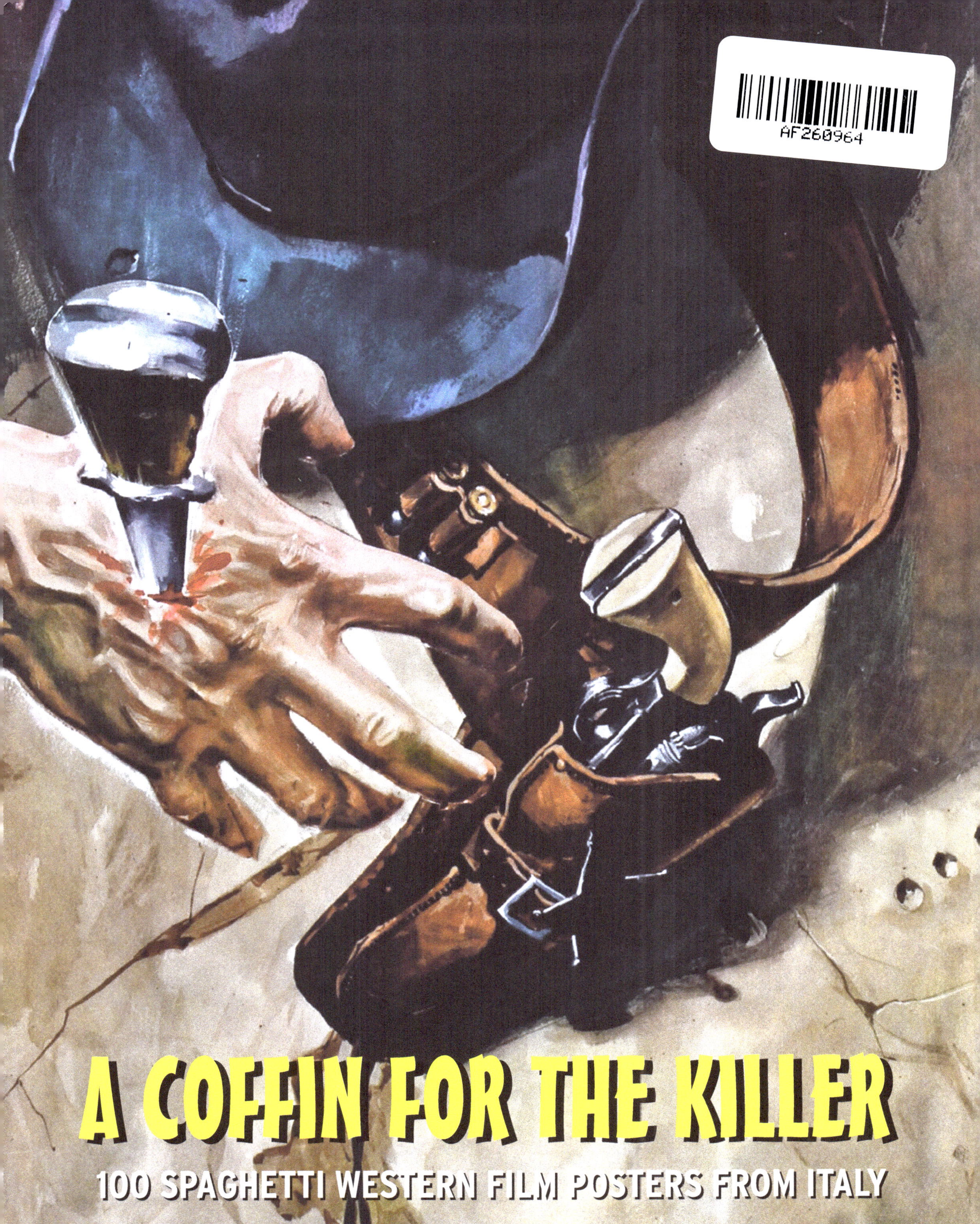

AF260964
A COFFIN FOR THE KILLER
100 SPAGHETTI WESTERN FILM POSTERS FROM ITALY

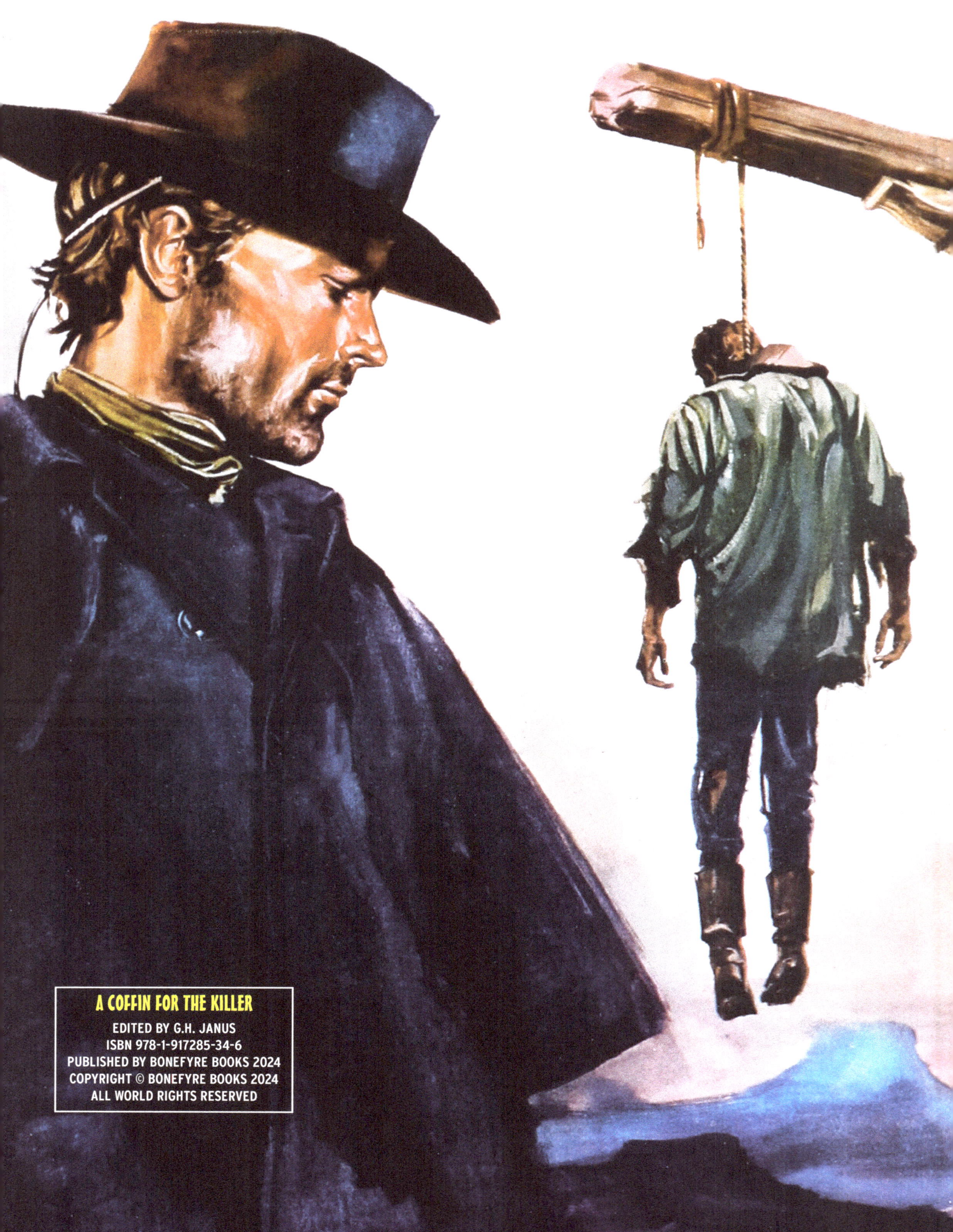
A COFFIN FOR THE KILLER
EDITED BY G.H. JANUS
ISBN 978-1-917285-34-6
PUBLISHED BY BONEFYRE BOOKS 2024
COPYRIGHT © BONEFYRE BOOKS 2024
ALL WORLD RIGHTS RESERVED

POSTERS

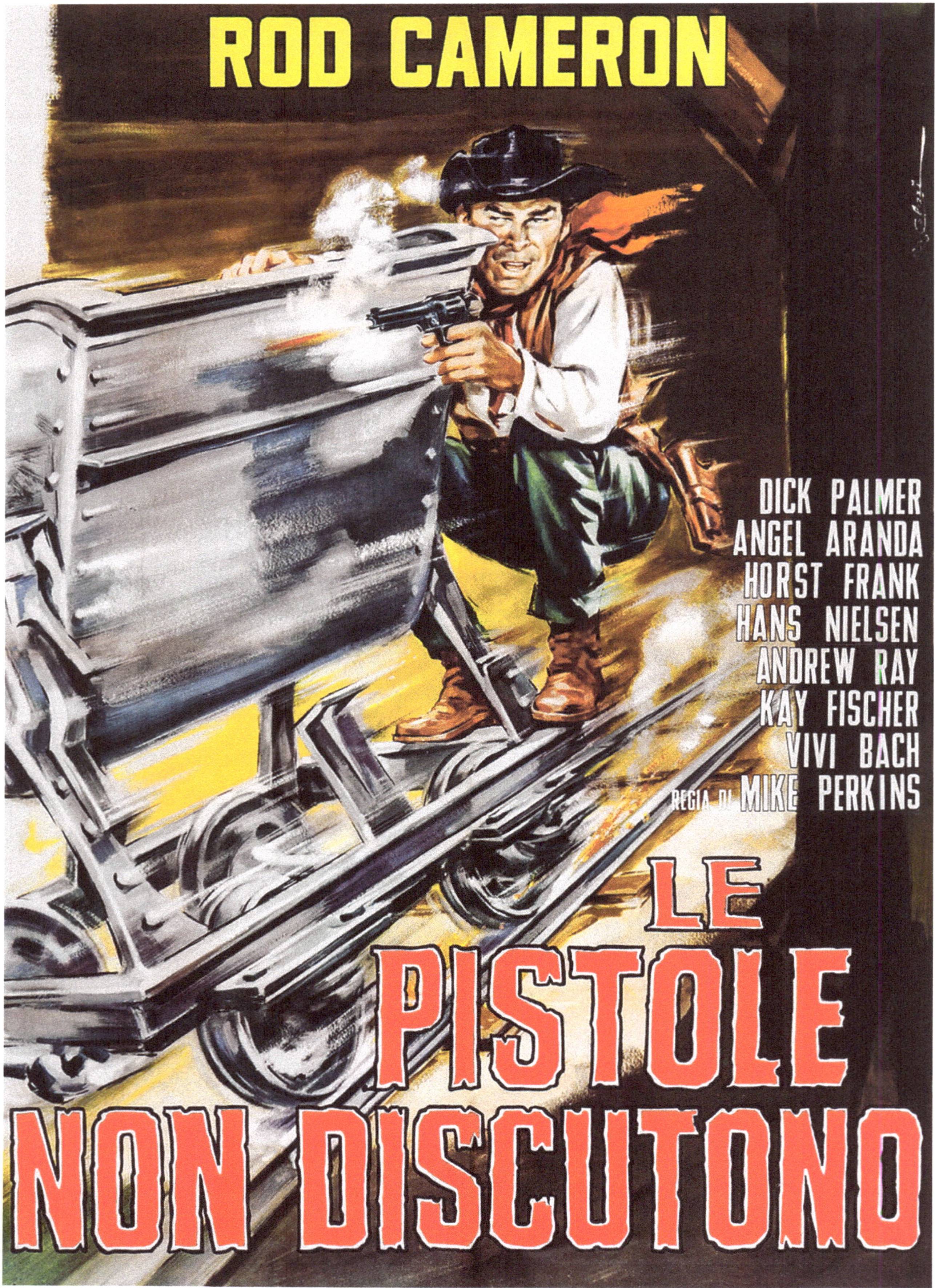

LE PISTOLE NON DISCUTONO

(''Guns Don't Argue'', 1964, Italy/Spain/Germany). Artist: Mauro Colizzi.

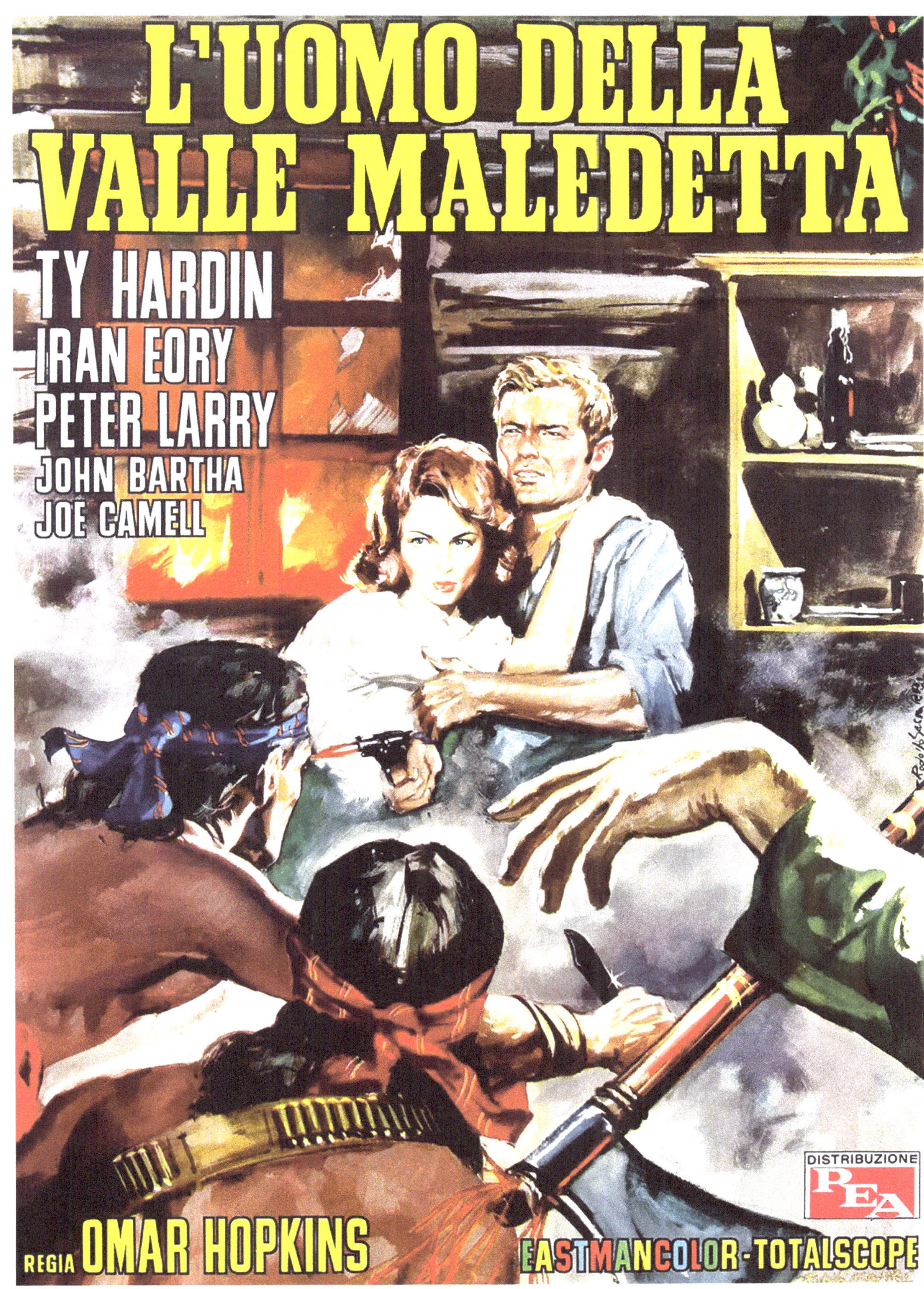

("Man From The Cursed Valley", 1964, Italy/Spain). Artist: Rodolfo Gasparri.

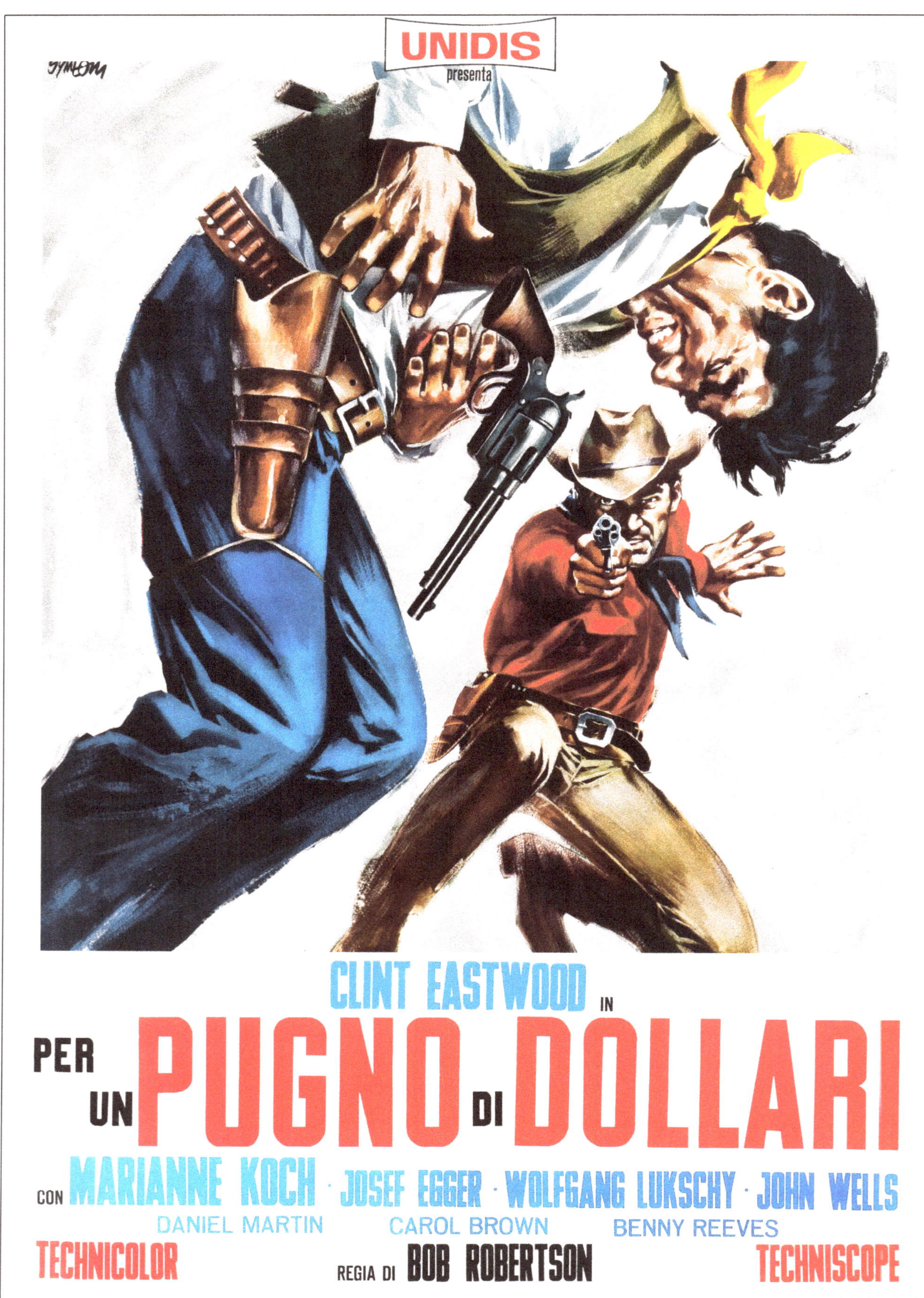

PER UN PUGNO DI DOLLARI

("For A Fistful Of Dollars", 1964, Italy/Spain/Germany). Artist: Sandro Symeoni.

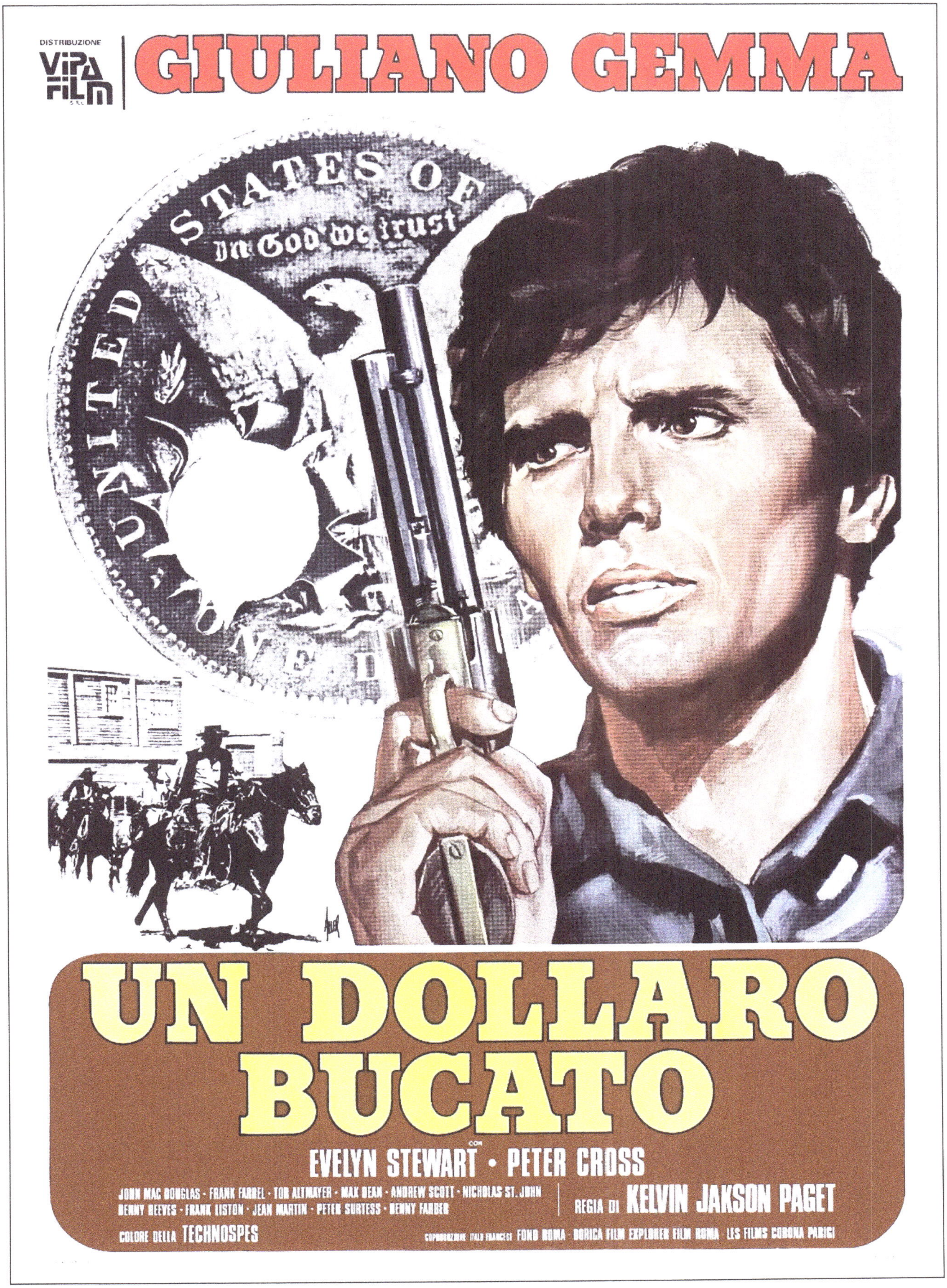

("A Punctured Dollar", 1965, Italy/France). Artist: Carlo Alessandrini.

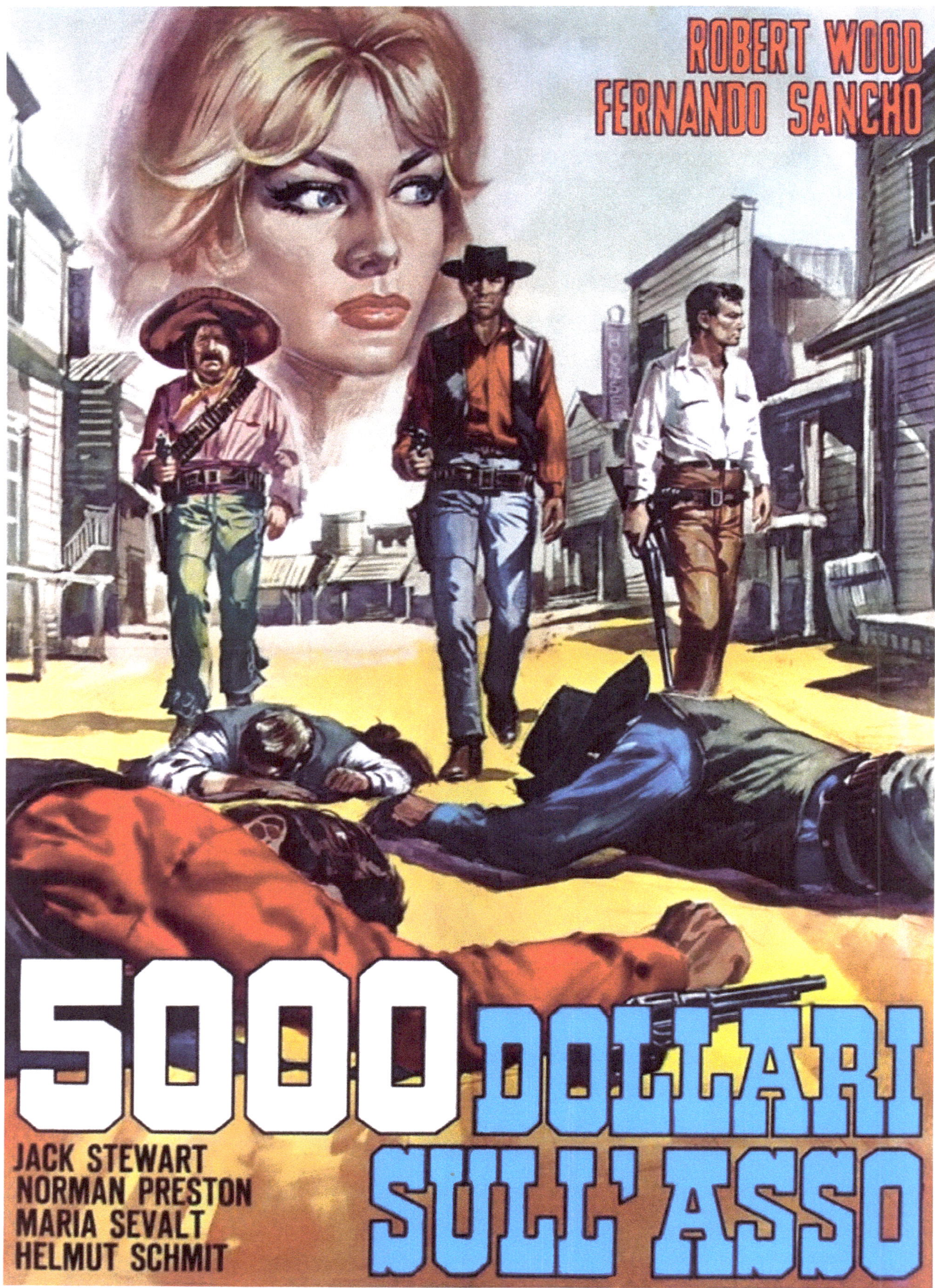

("\$5,000 On The Ace", 1965, Italy/Spain/Germany). Artist: Renato Casaro.

8

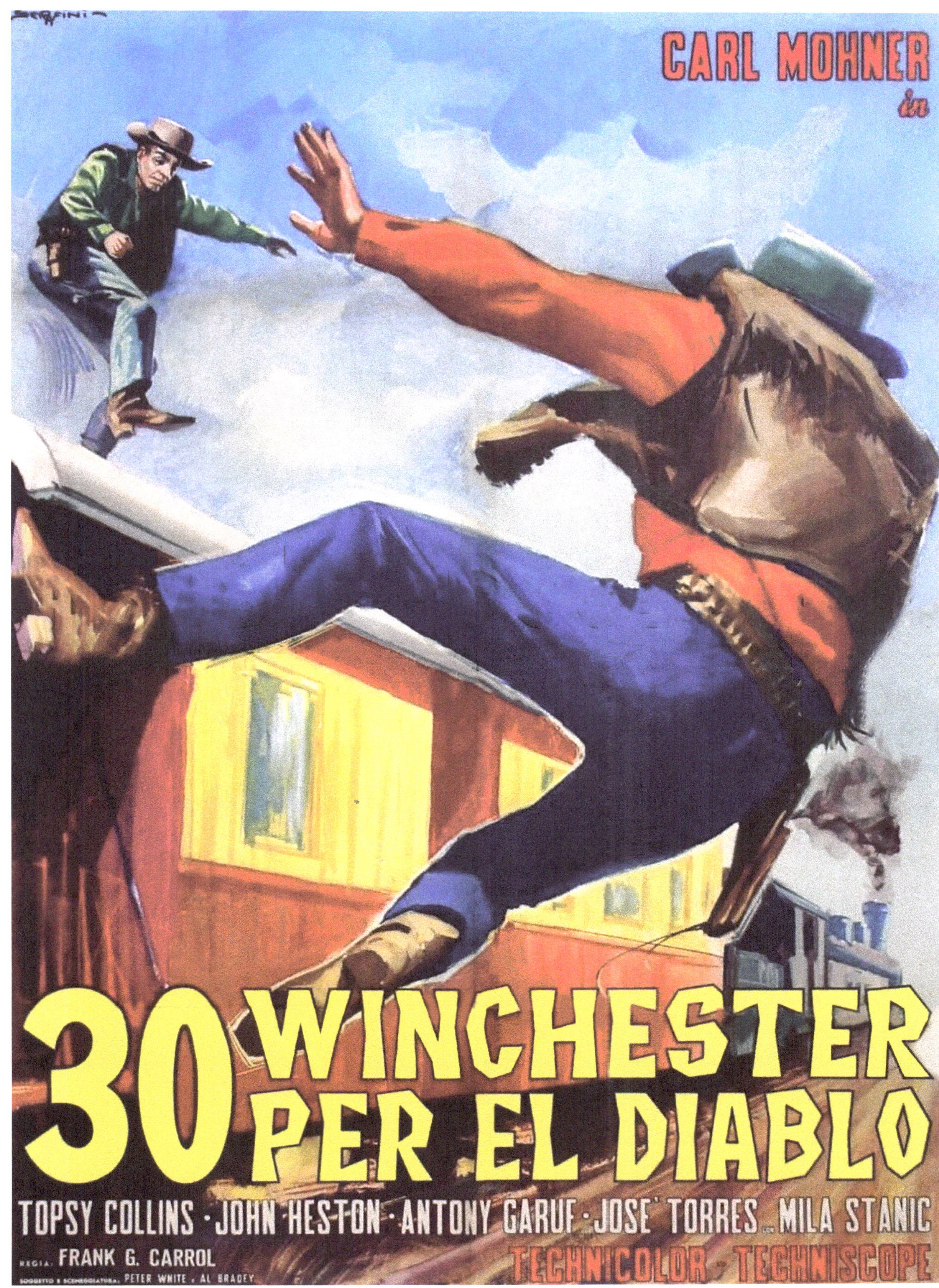

(''30 Winchesters For El Diablo'', 1965, Italy). Artist: Serafini.

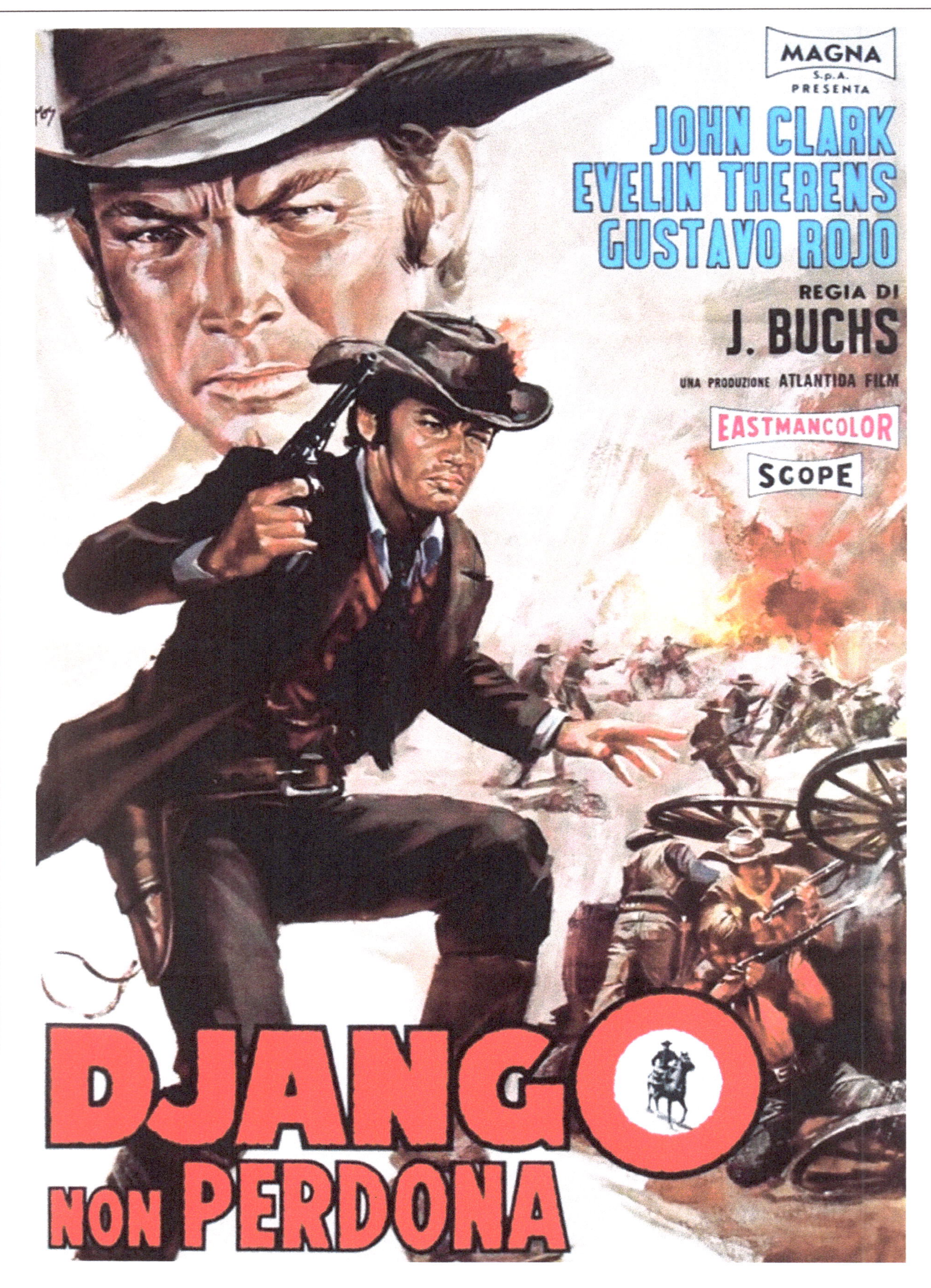

DJANGO NON PERDONA

(''Django Never Forgives'', 1965, Italy/Spain). Artist: Moz.

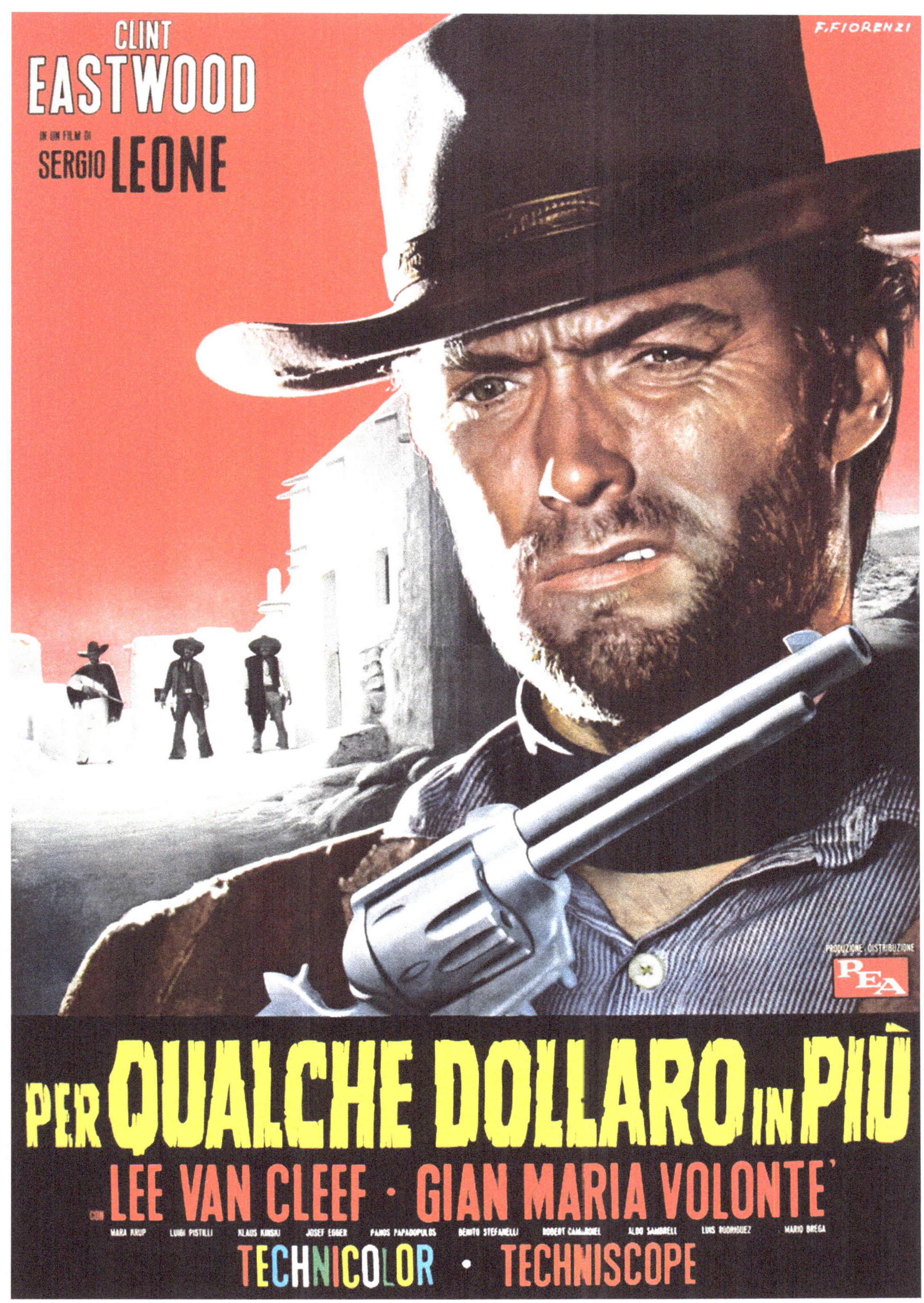

PER QUALCHE DOLLARO IN PIÙ

("For A Few Dollars More", 1965, Italy/Spain/Germay). Artist: Fiorenzi.

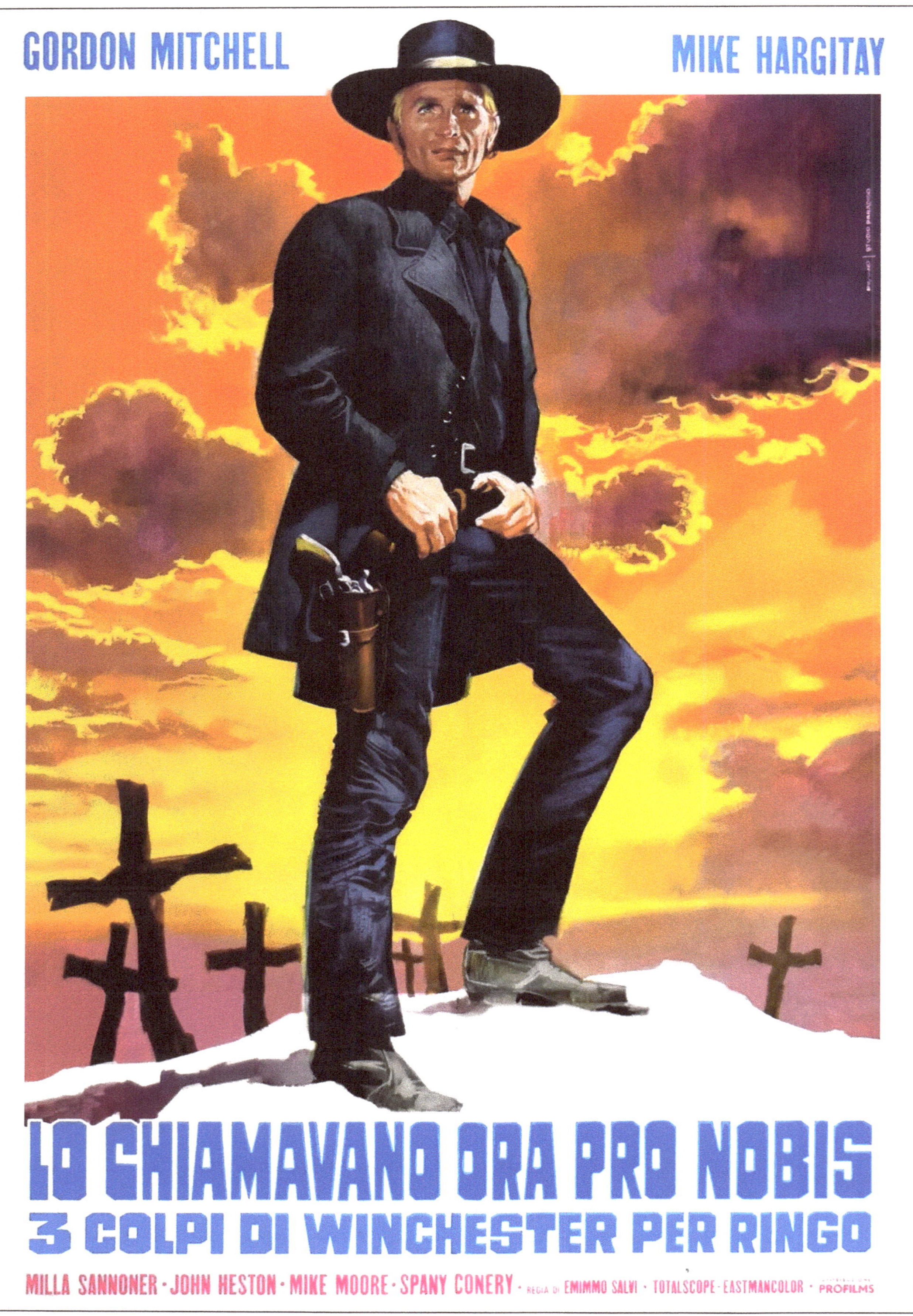

LO CHIAMAVANO ORA PRO NOBIS

("They Called Him Ora Pro Nobis", 1966, Italy). Artist: Mario Piovano. Original release title: **3 Colpi Di Wichester Per Ringo**.

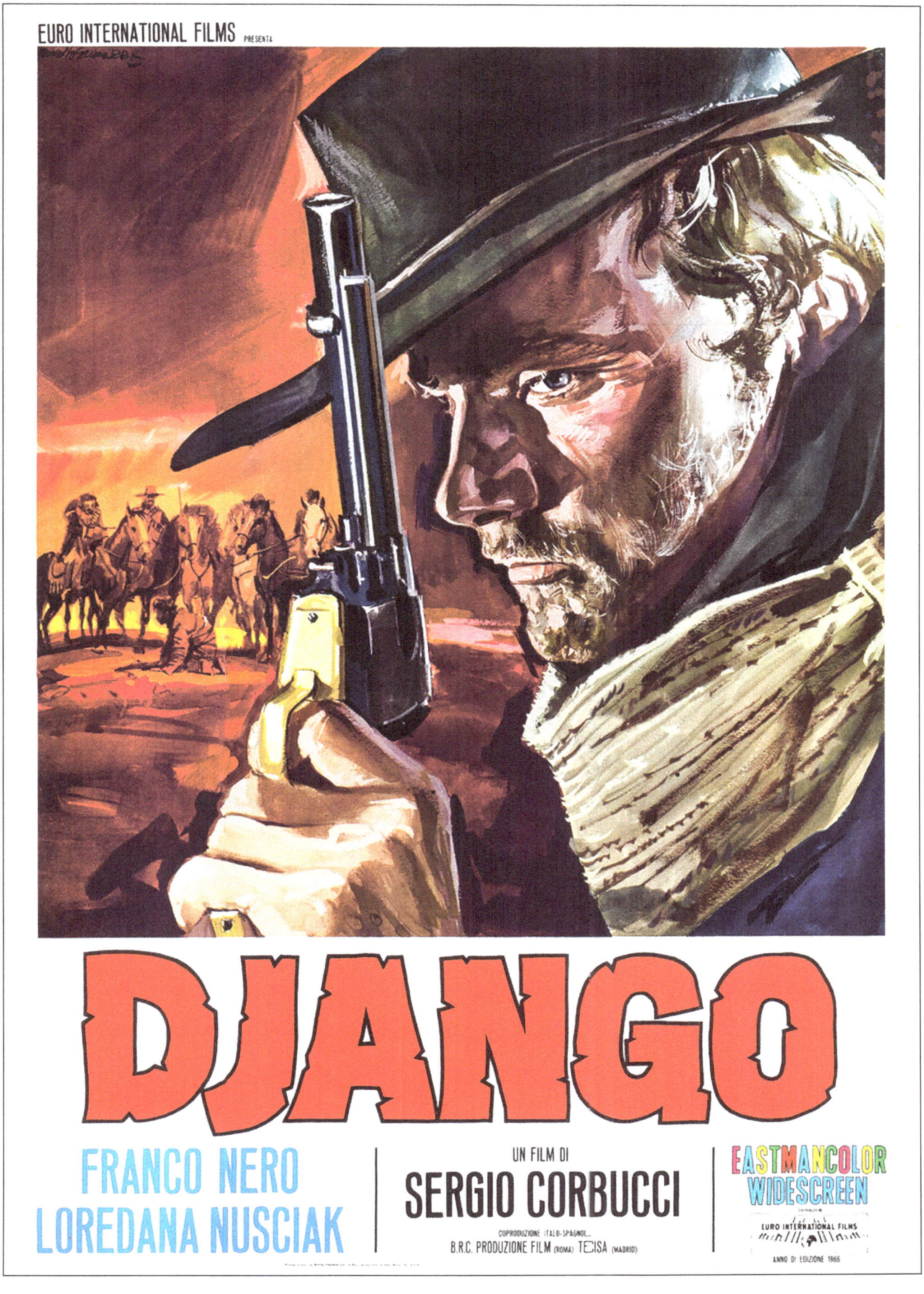

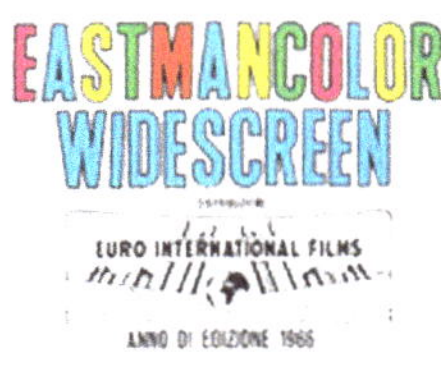

("Django", 1966, Italy/Spain). Artist: Rodolfo Gasparri.

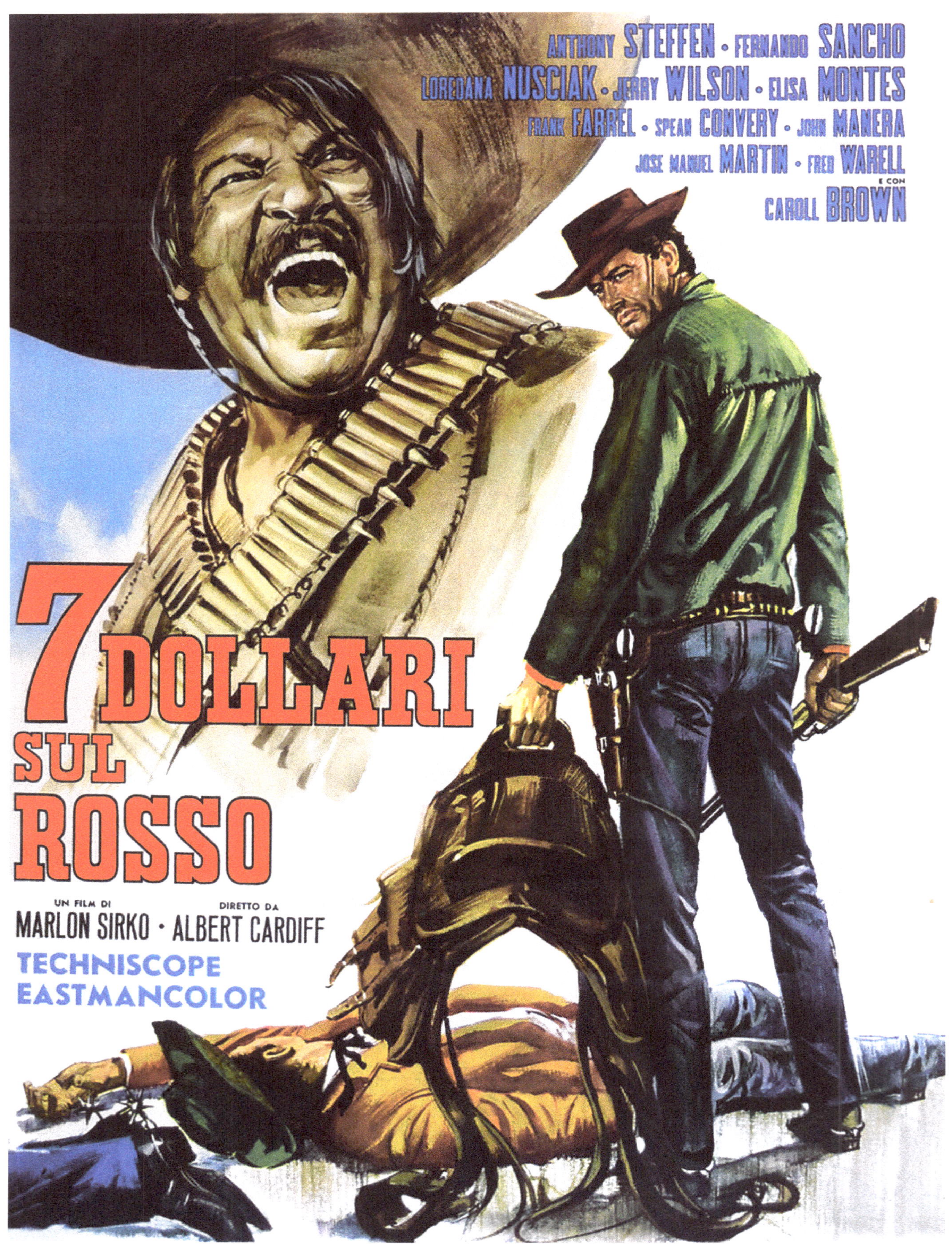

7 DOLLARI SUL ROSSO

("$7 On Red", 1966, Italy/Spain). Artist: Renato Casaro.

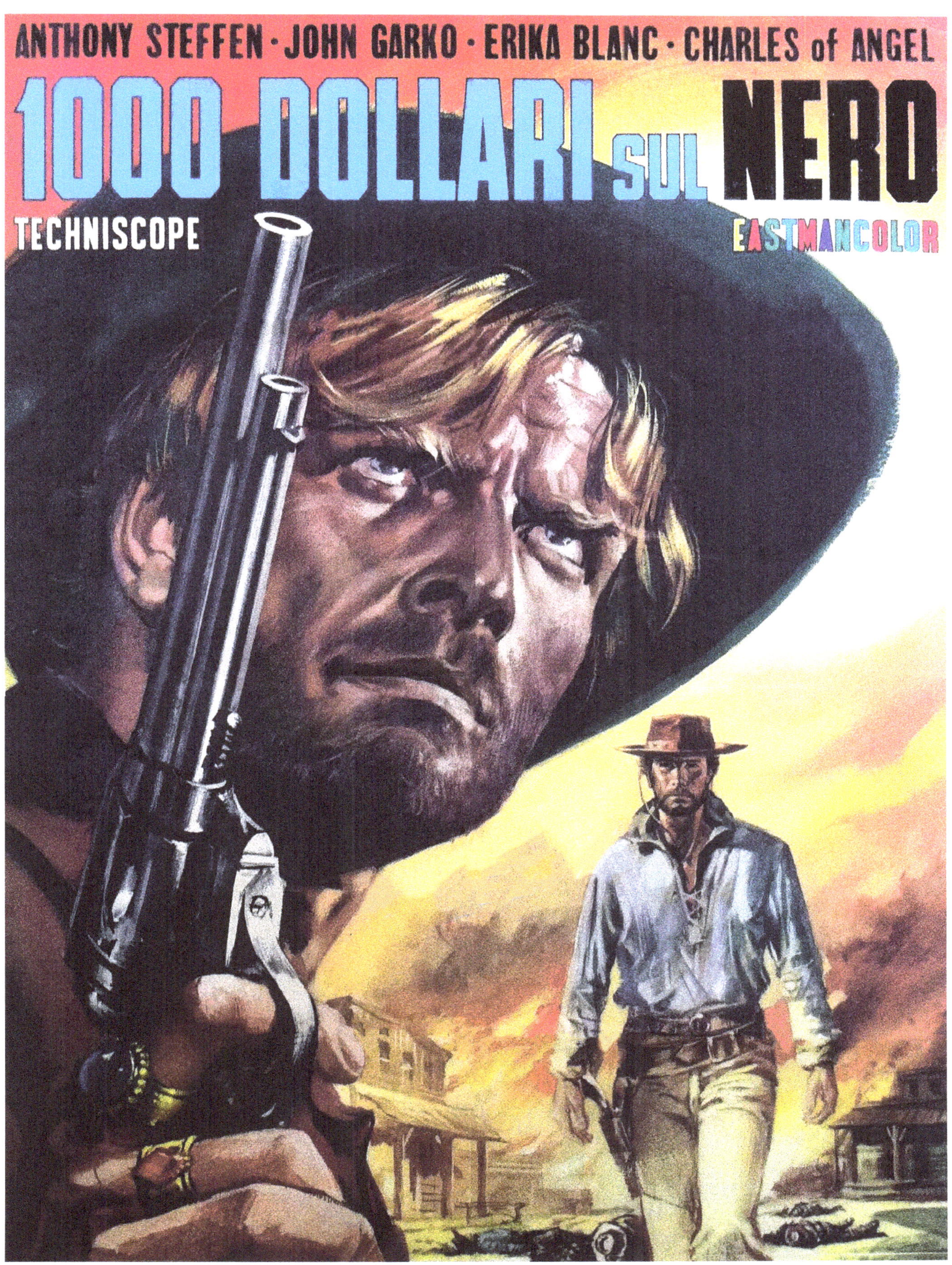

("$1,C00 On Black", 1966, Italy/Germany). Artist: unsigned.

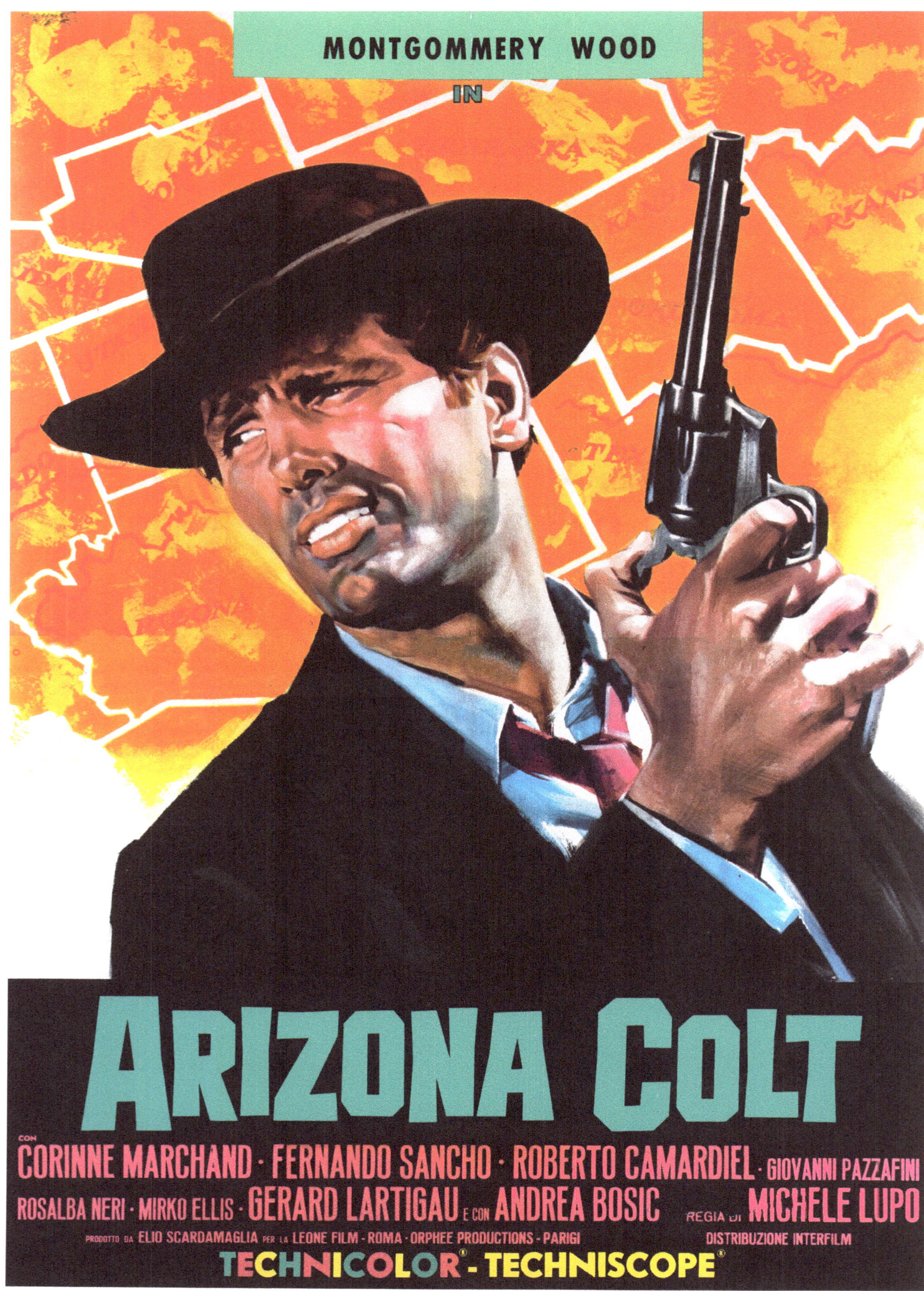

ARIZONA COLT

(''Arizona Colt'', 1966, Italy/France). Artist: unsigned.

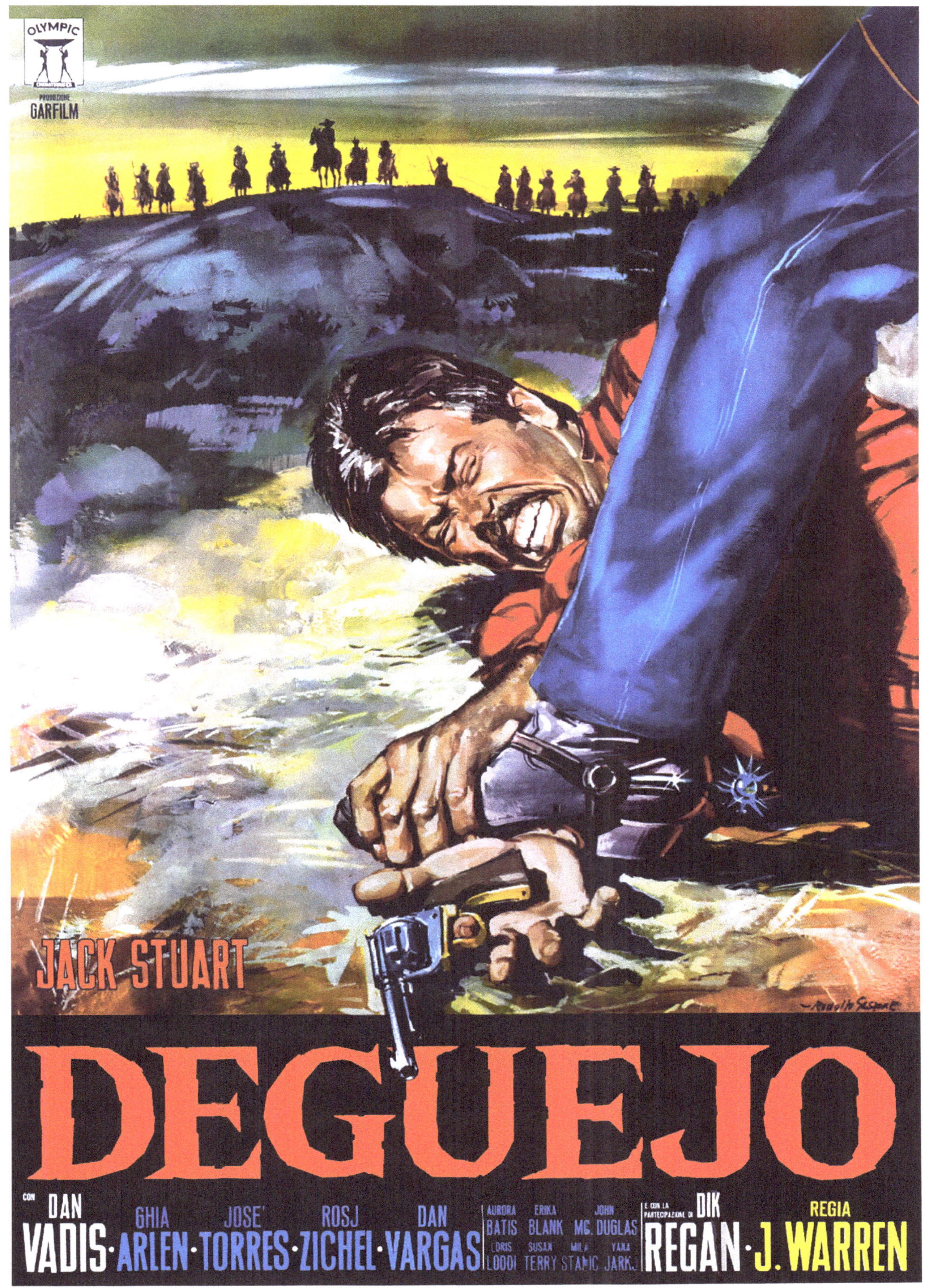

OLYMPIC
PRODUZIONE
GARFILM
JACK STUART
DEGUEJO
CON
DAN VADIS
GHIA ARLEN
JOSE' TORRES
ROSJ ZICHEL
DAN VARGAS
AURORA BATIS
ERIKA BLANK
JOHN MC DUGLAS
LORIS LODDI
SUSAN TERRY
MILA STANIC
YANA JARKJ
E CON LA PARTECIPAZIONE DI
DIK REGAN
REGIA
J. WARREN

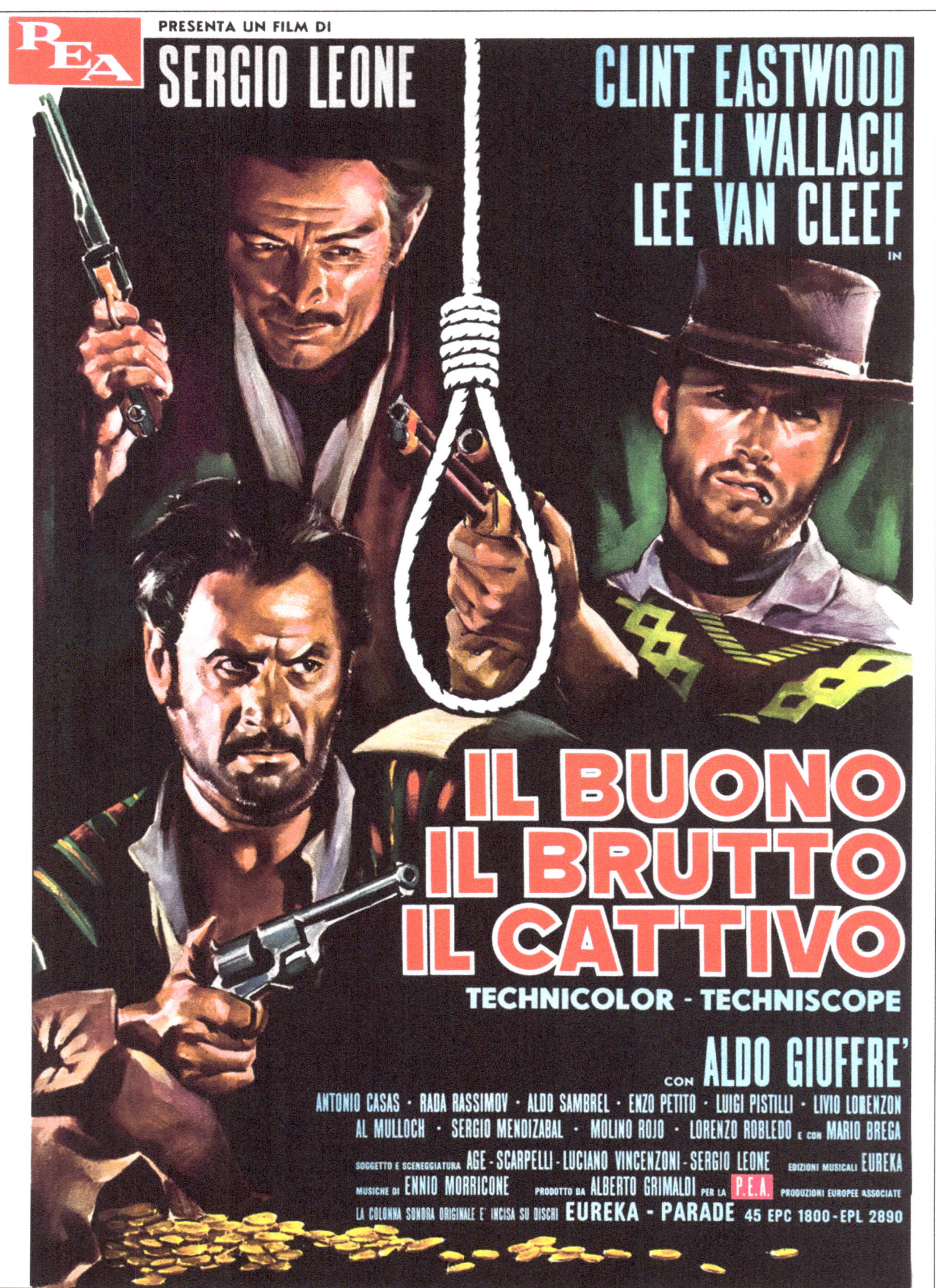

IL BUONO IL BRUTTO IL CATTIVO

(''The Good, The Ugly, The Evil'', 1966, Italy/Spain/Germany). Artist: unsigned.

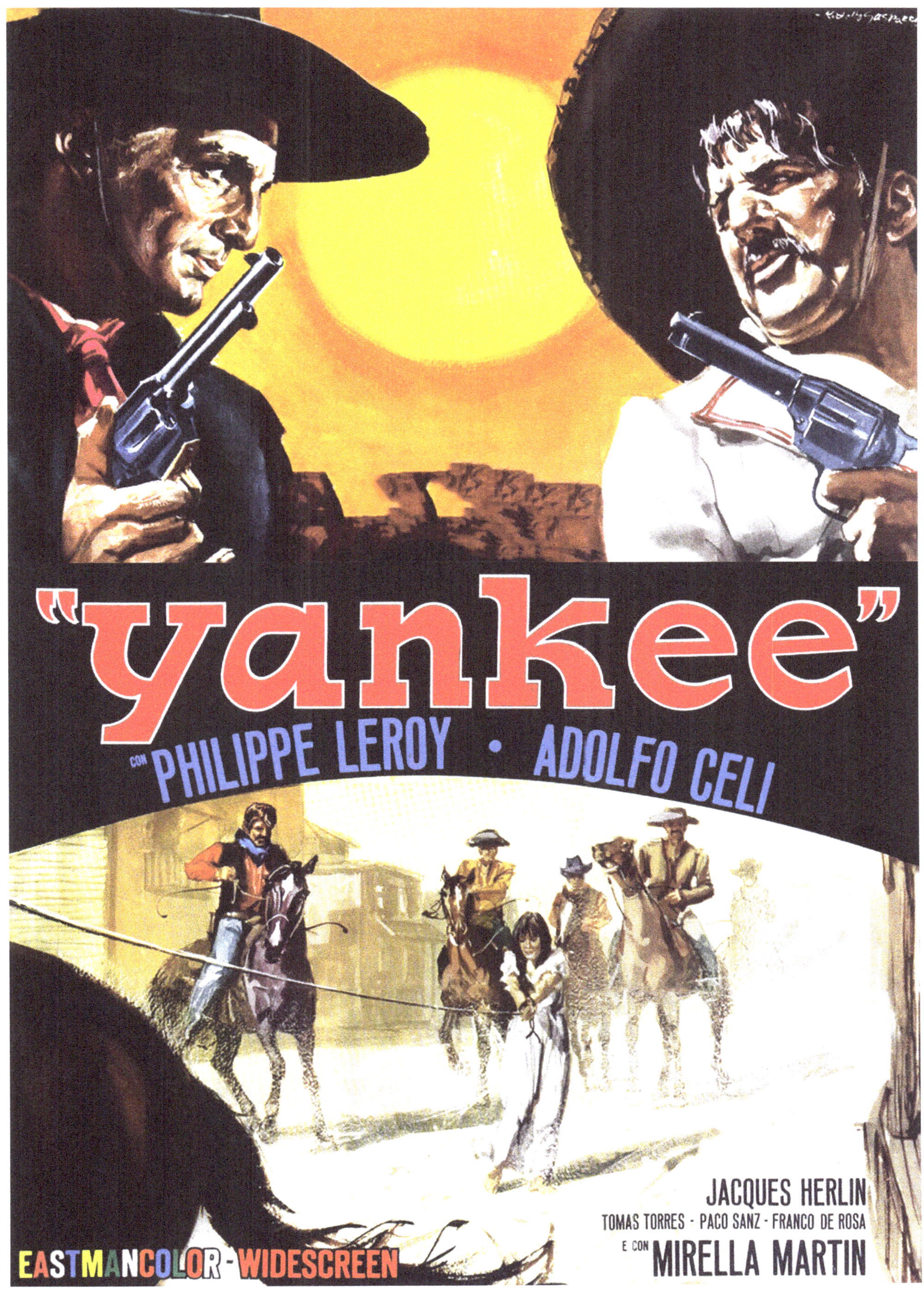

YANKEE

("Yankee", 1966, Italy/Spain). Artist: Rodlfo Gasparri.

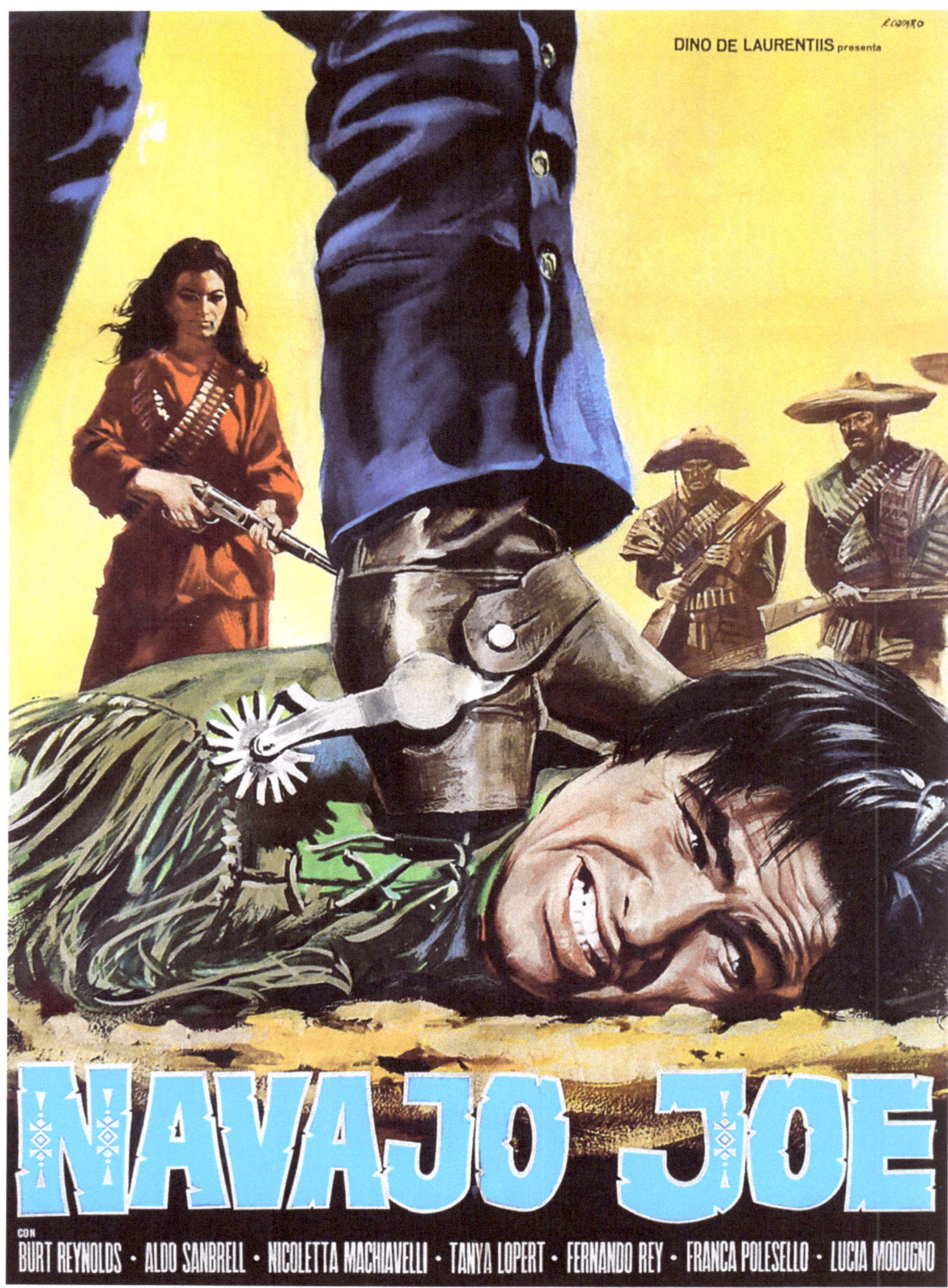

NAVAJO JOE

("Navajo Joe", 1966, Italy/Spain). Artist: Renato Casaro,

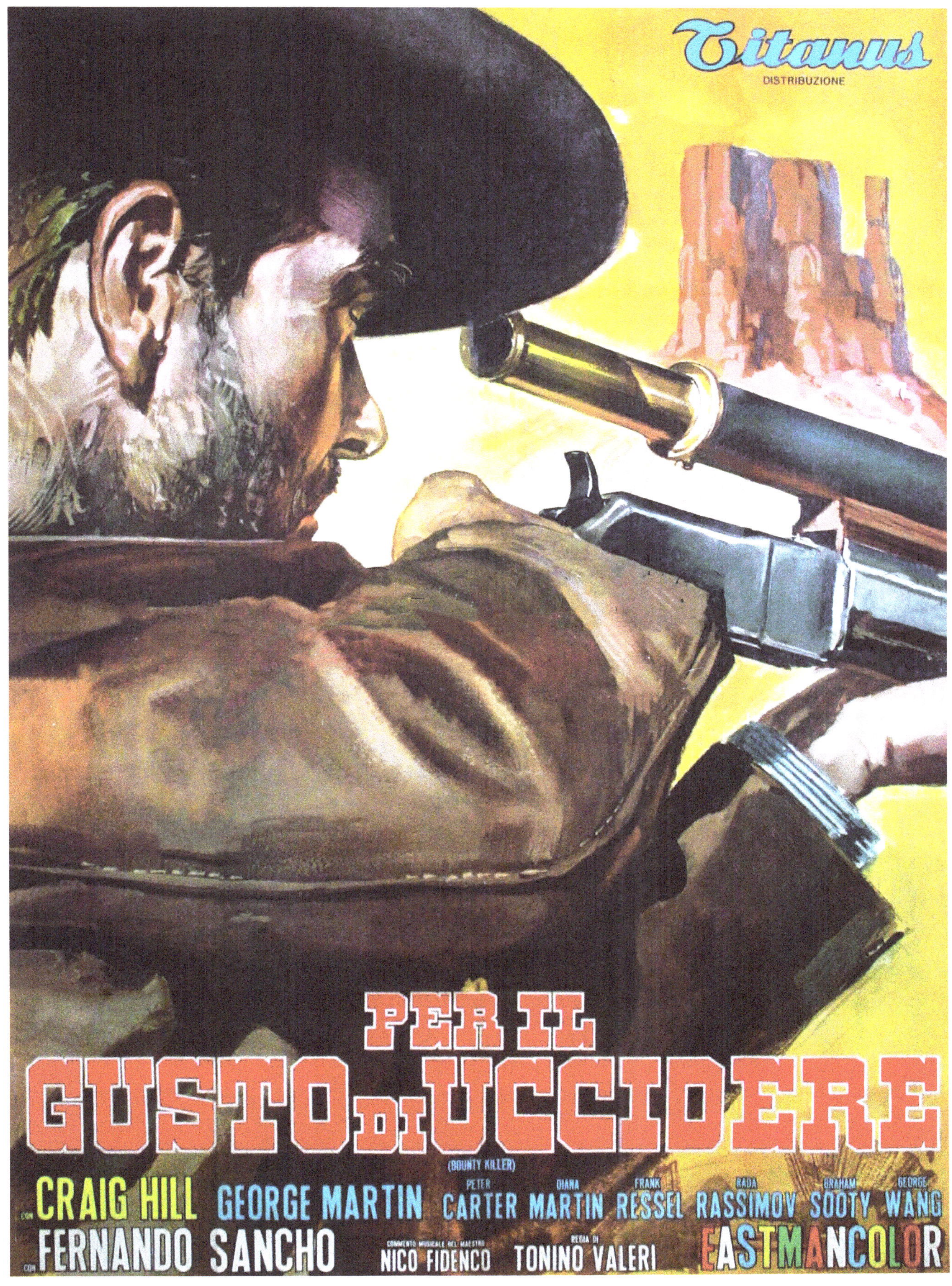

PER IL GUSTO DI UCCIDERE

(''For The Taste Of Killing'', 1966, Italy/Spain). Artist: unsigned.

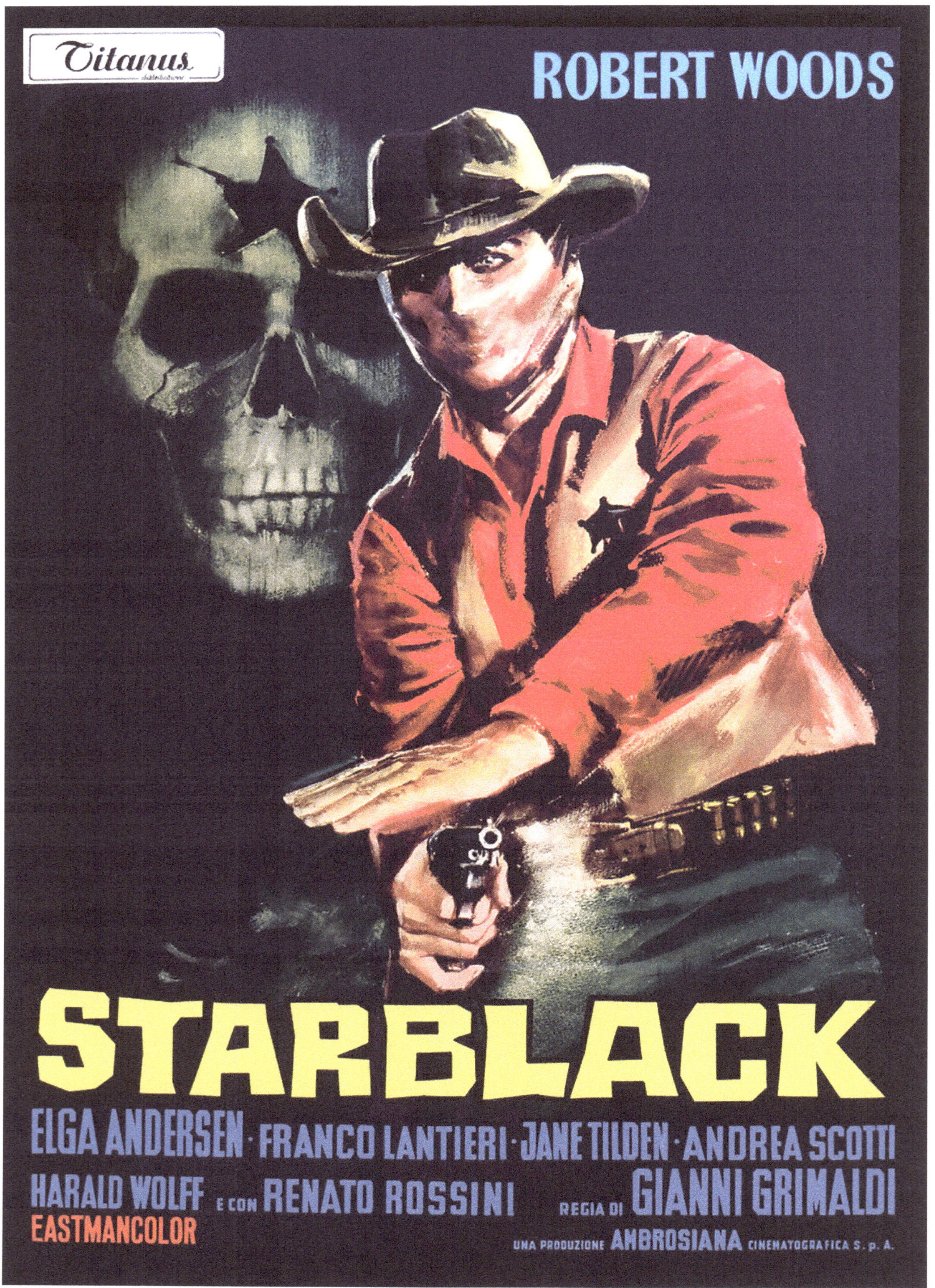

STARBLACK

(''Starblack'', 1966, Italy/Germany). Artist: unsigned.

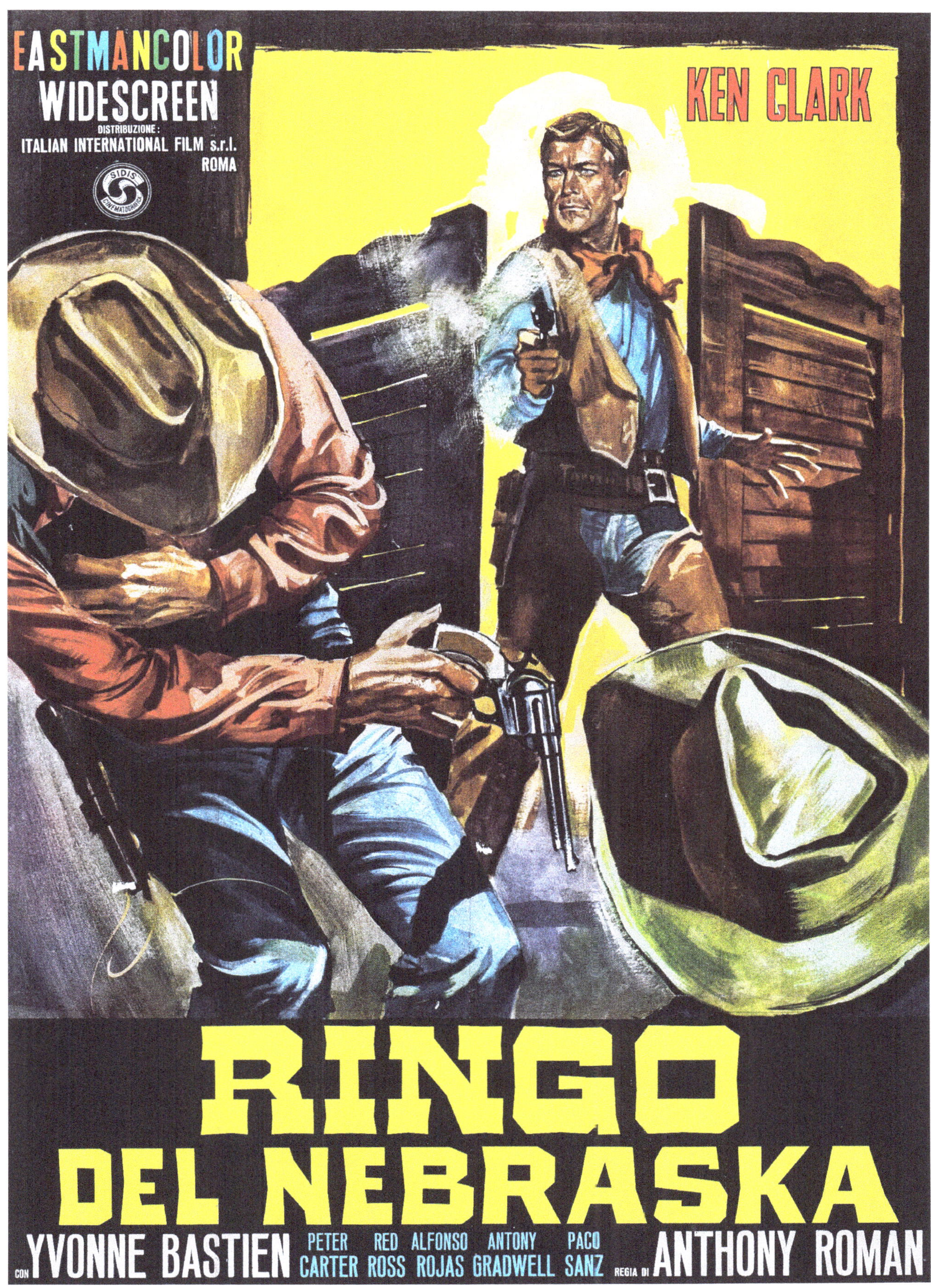

("Ringc From Nebraska", 1966, Italy/Spain). Artist: unsigned.

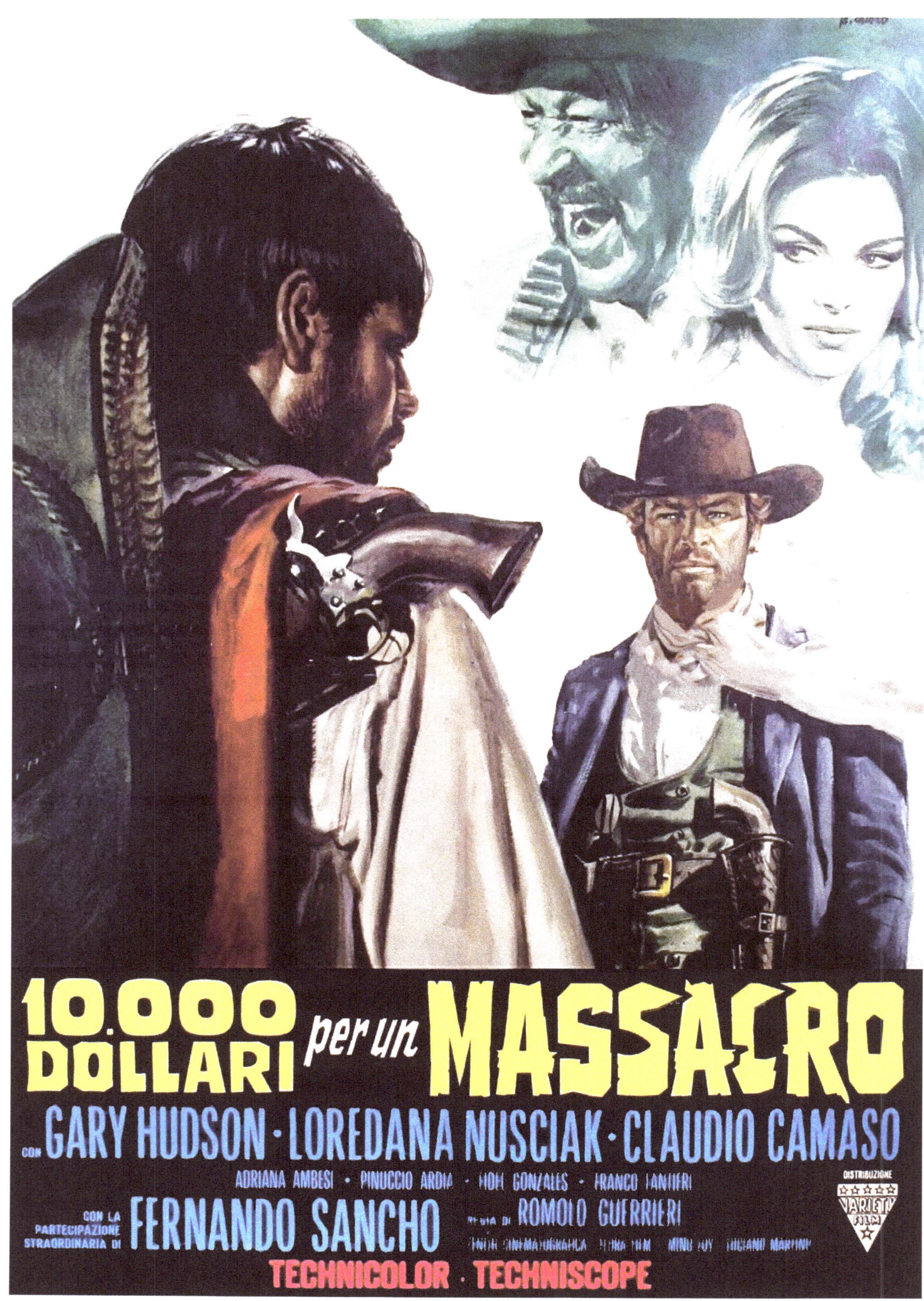

(''$10,000 For A Massacre'', 1967, Italy). Artist: Renato Casaro.

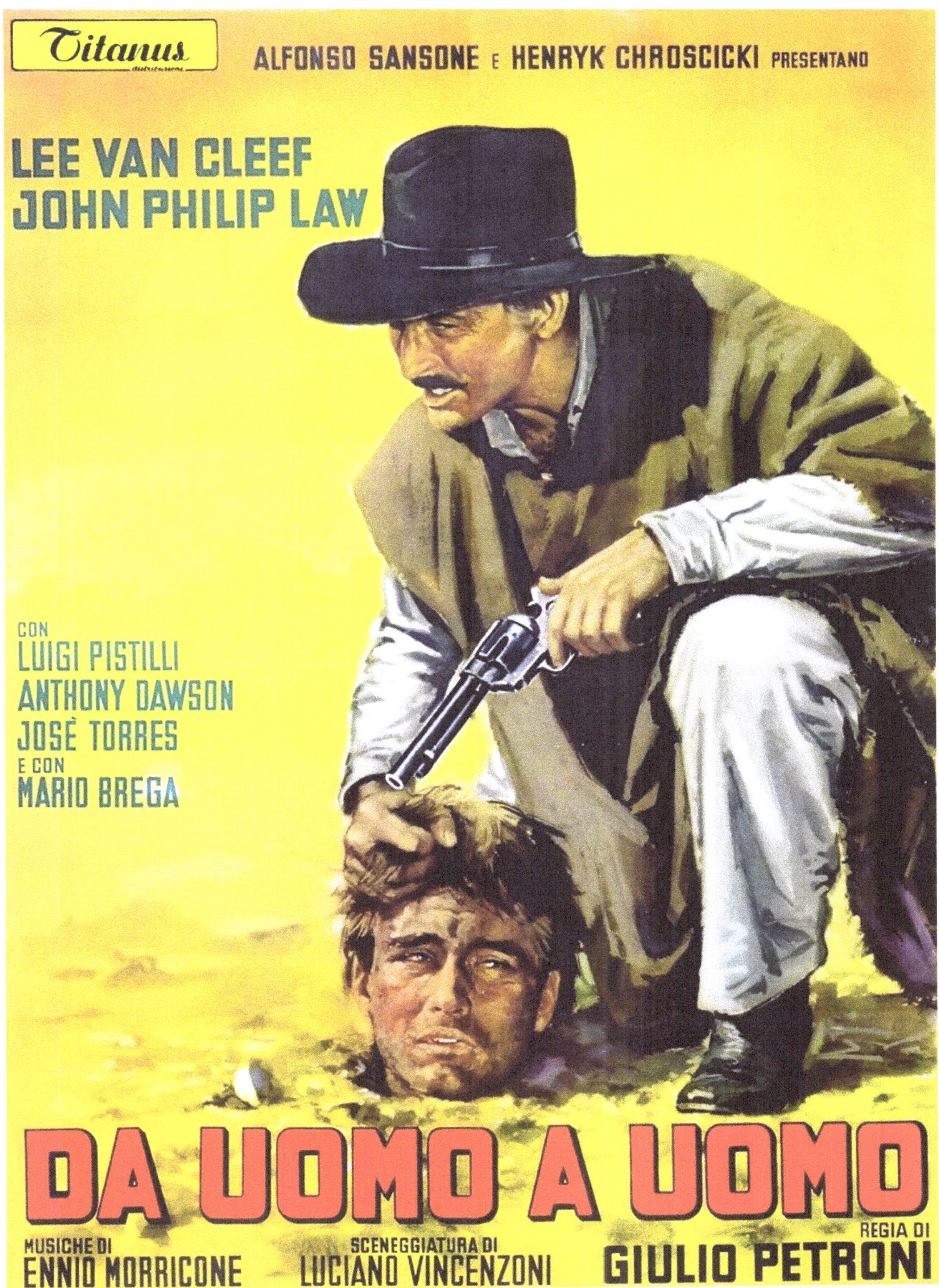

DA UOMO A UOMO

("From Man To Man", 1967, Italy). Artist: unsigned.

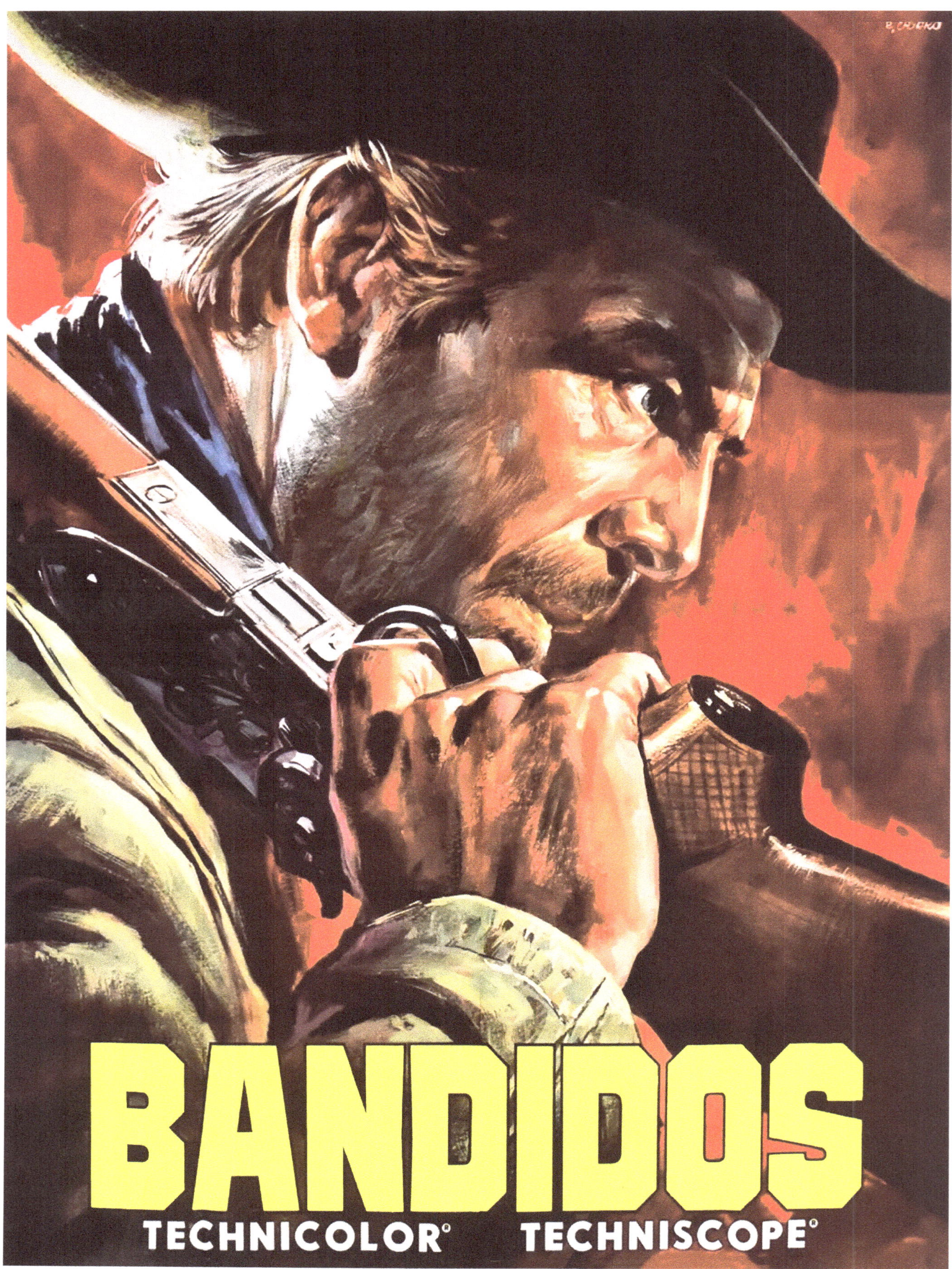

BANDIDOS

(''Bandits'', 1967, Italy/Spain). Artist: Renato Casaro.

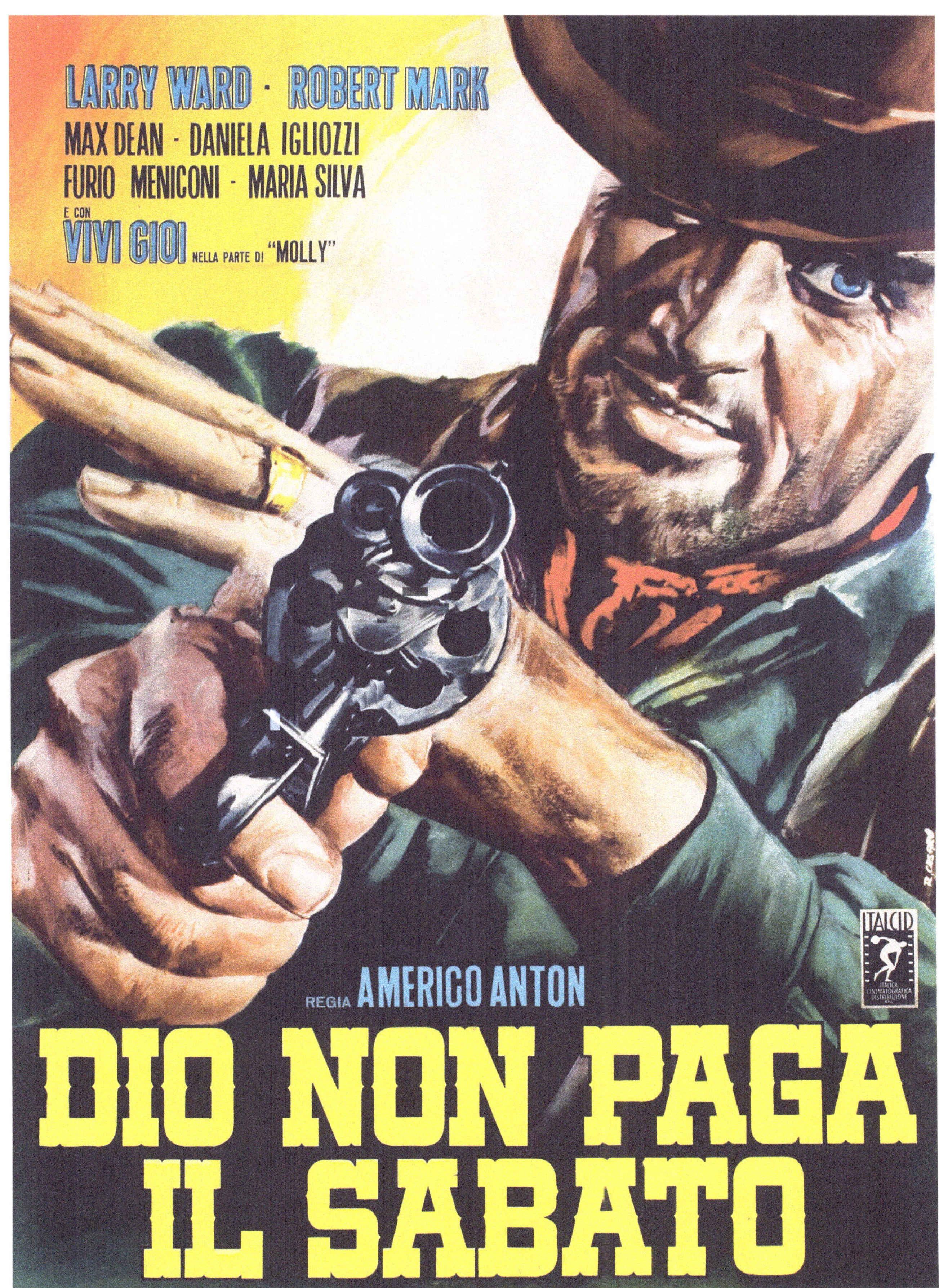

("God Never Pays On The Sabbath", 1967, Italy/Spain). Artist: Renato Casaro.

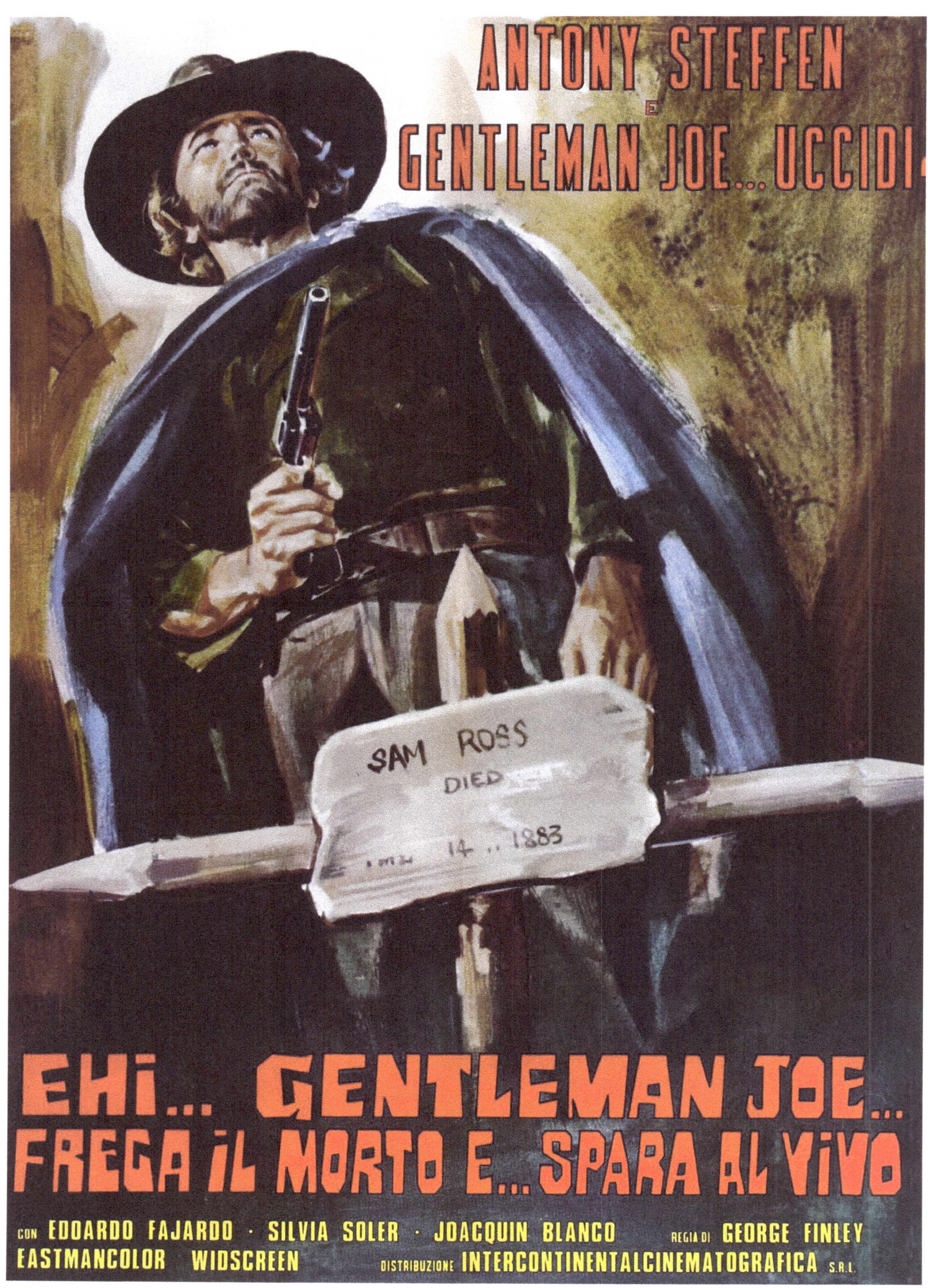

EHI... GENTLEMAN JOE... FREGA IL MORTO E... SPARA AL VIVO

(''Hey, Gentleman Joe... Tend The Dead And Shoot The Living'', 1967, Italy/Spain). Artist: Ezio Tarantelli.

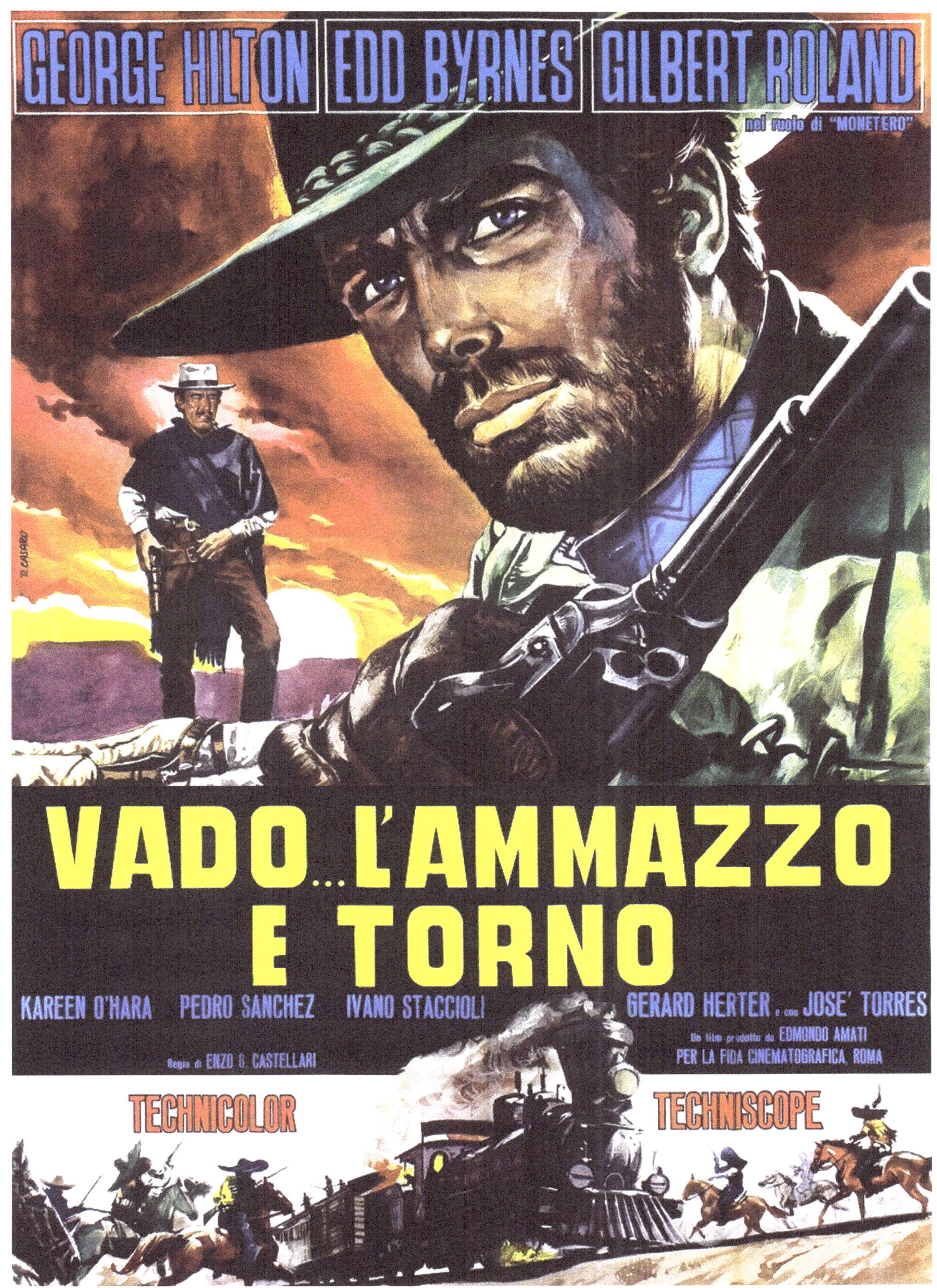

("I'll Go, Kill Him And Come Back", 1967, Italy). Artist: Renato Casaro.

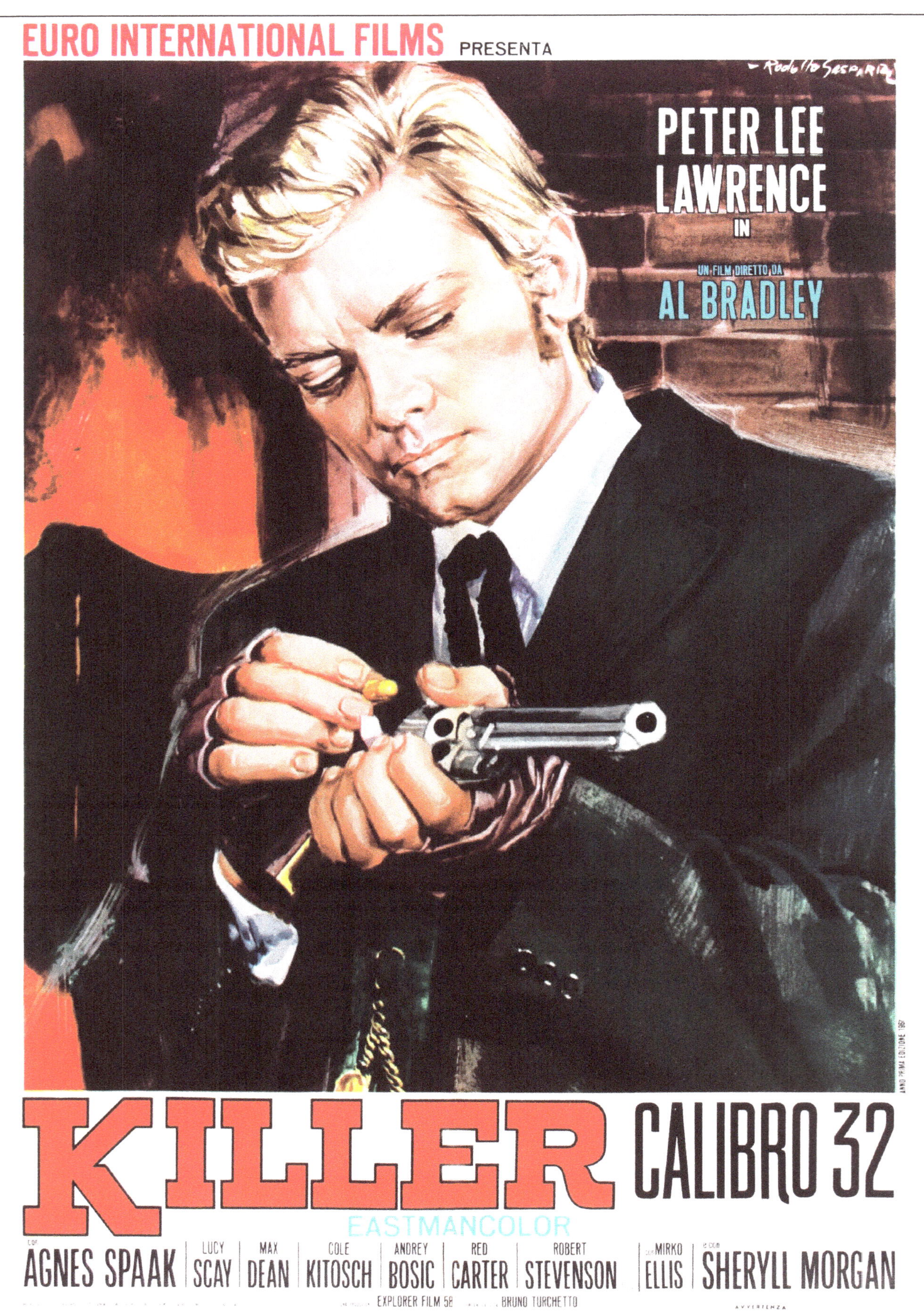

KILLER CALIBRO 32

("Killer, Calibre 32", 1967, Italy). Artist: Rodolfo Gasparri.

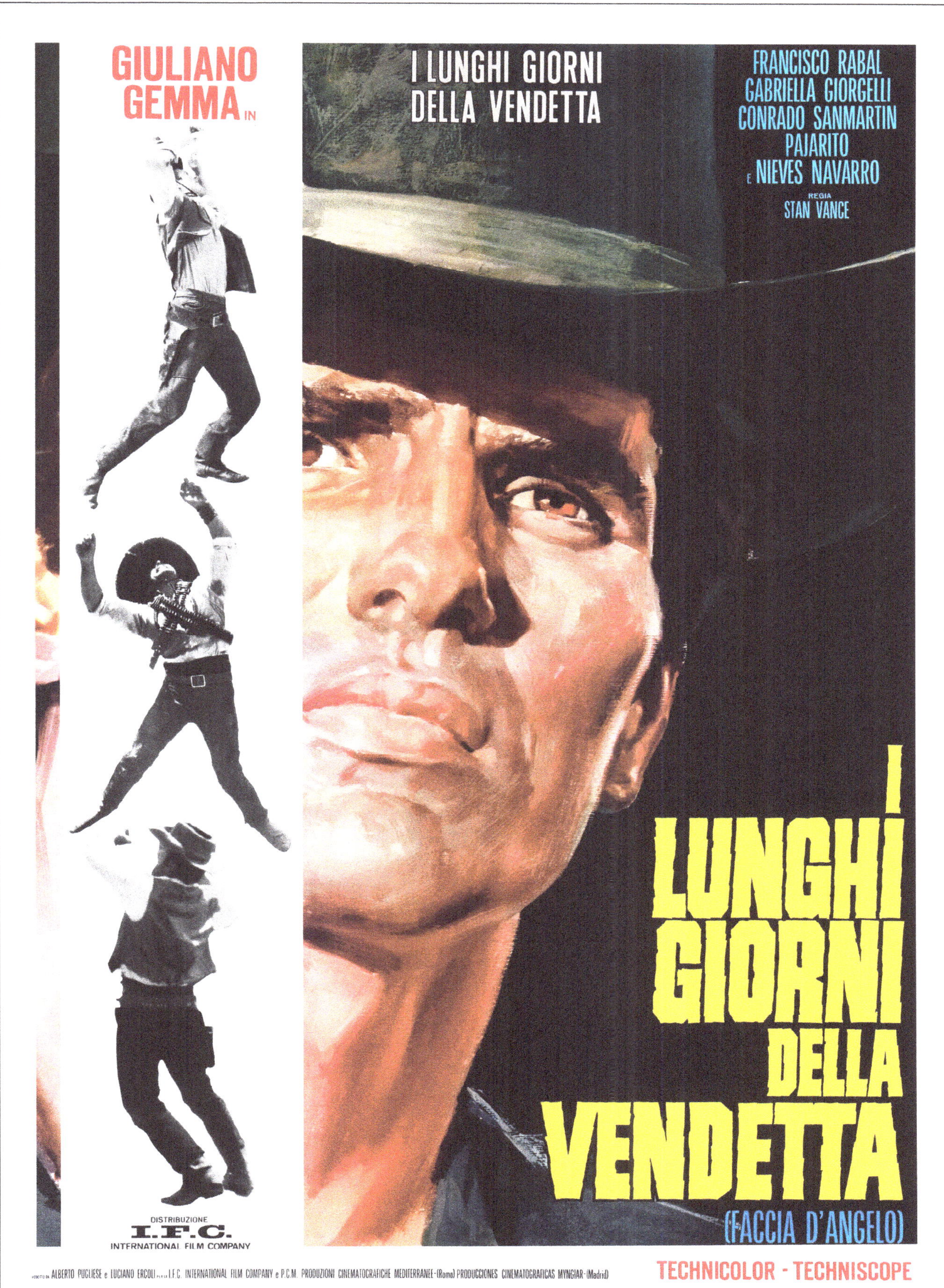

GIULIANO GEMMA IN
I LUNGHI GIORNI DELLA VENDETTA
FRANCISCO RABAL
GABRIELLA GIORGELLI
CONRADO SANMARTIN
PAJARITO
E NIEVES NAVARRO
REGIA
STAN VANCE
I LUNGHI GIORNI DELLA VENDETTA
(FACCIA D'ANGELO)
DISTRIBUZIONE
I.F.C.
INTERNATIONAL FILM COMPANY
TECHNICOLOR - TECHNISCOPE
PRODOTTO DA ALBERTO PUGLIESE e LUCIANO ERCOLI per la I.F.C. INTERNATIONAL FILM COMPANY e P.C.M. PRODUZIONI CINEMATOGRAFICHE MEDITERRANEE-(Roma) PRODUCCIONES CINEMATOGRAFICAS MYNGIAR-(Madrid)

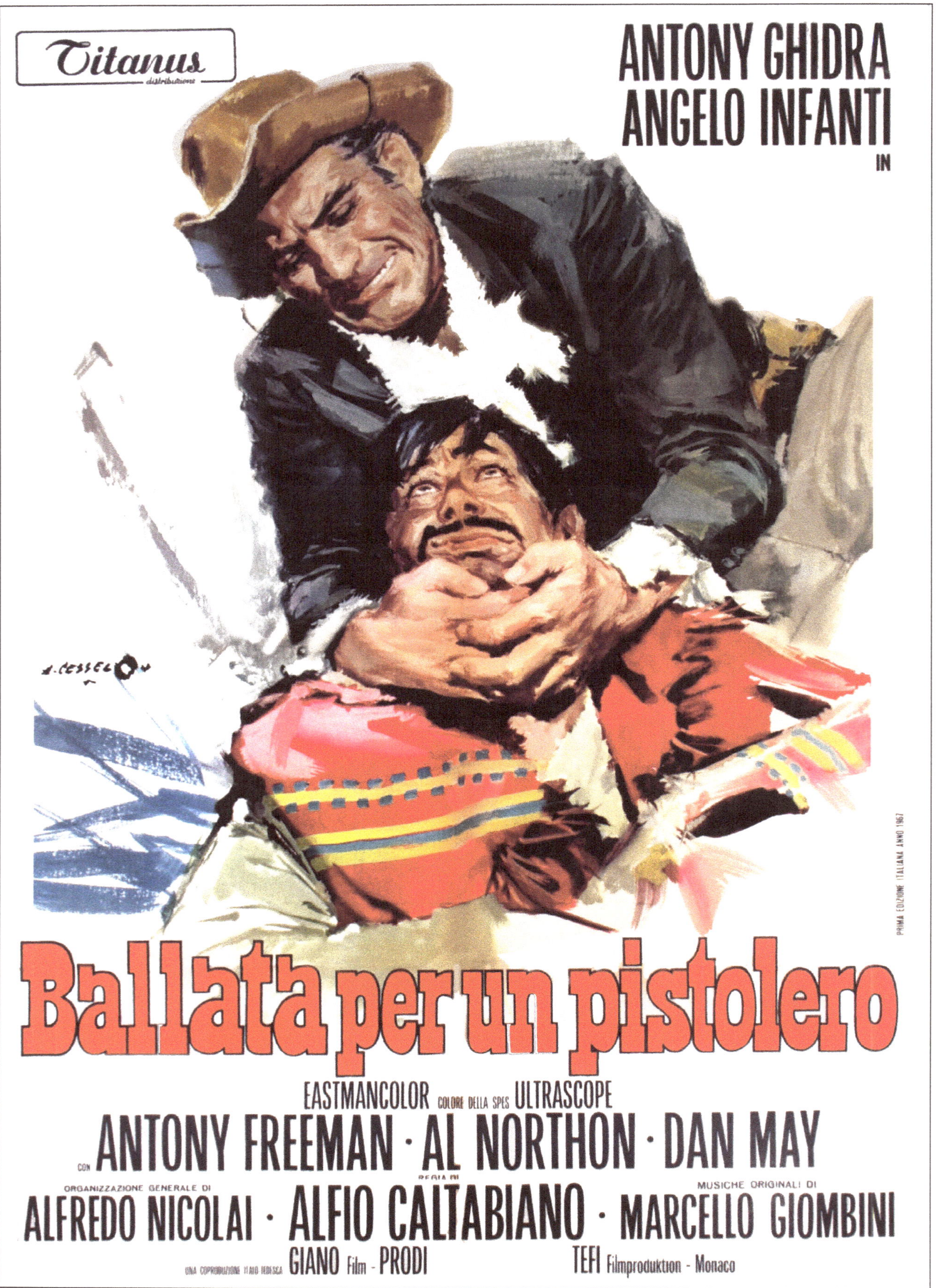

BALLATA PER UN PISTOLERO

(''Ballad Of A Gunslinger'', 1967, Italy/Germany). Artist: Angelo Cessalon.

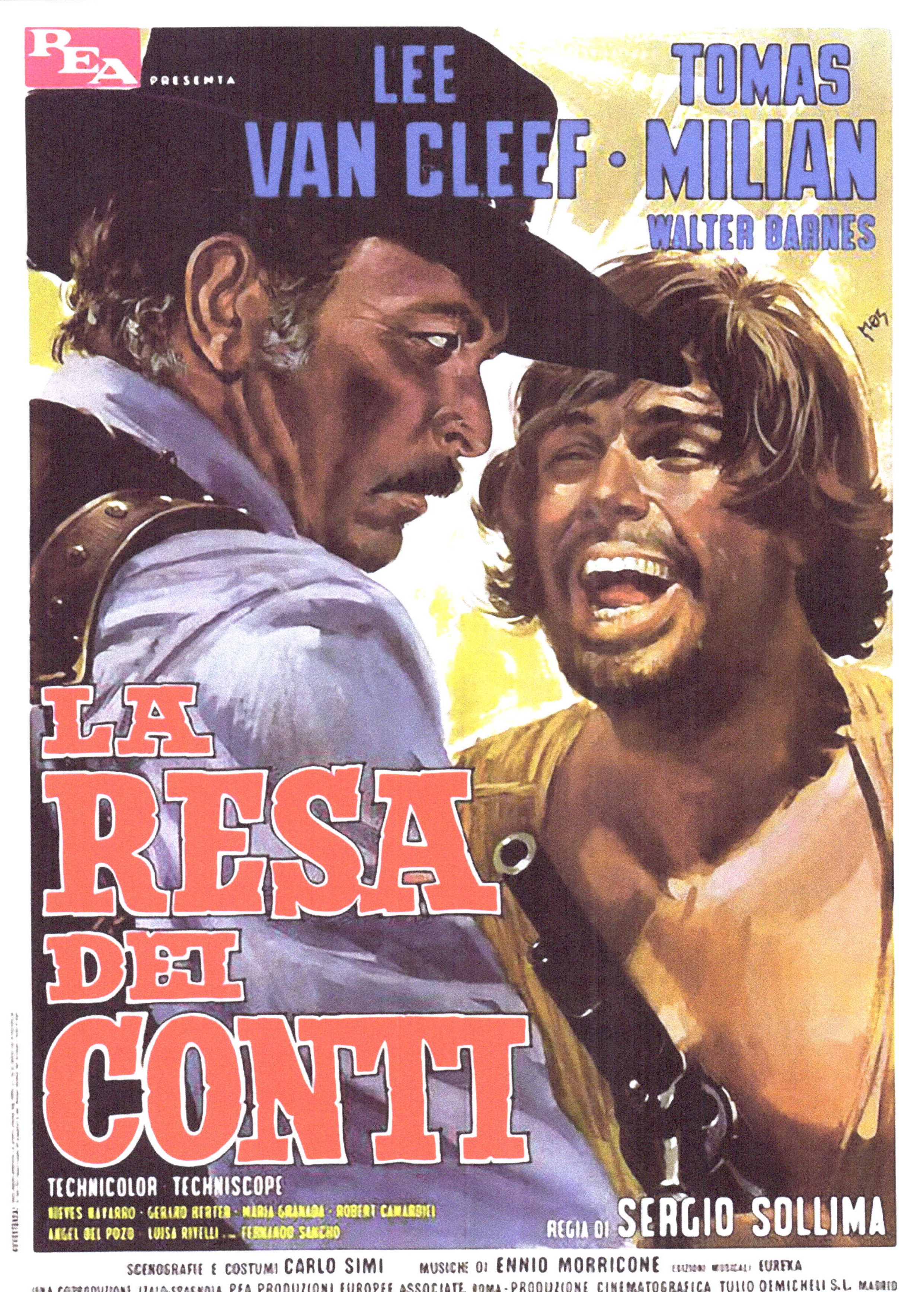

LA RESA DEI CONTI

("The Showdown", 1967, Italy/Spain). Artist: Moz.

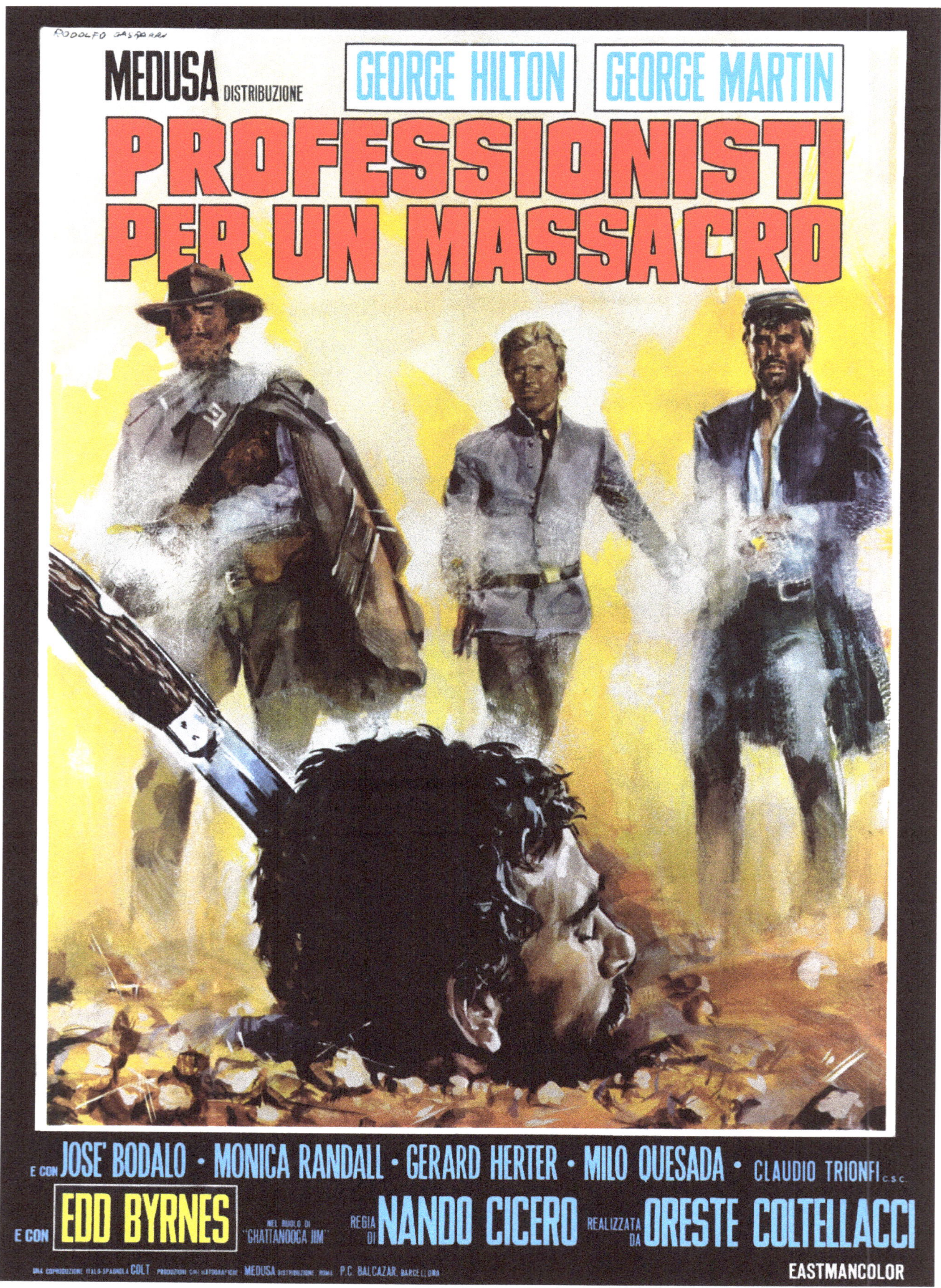

("Professionals For A Massacre", 1967, Italy/Spain). Artist: Rodolfo Gasparri.

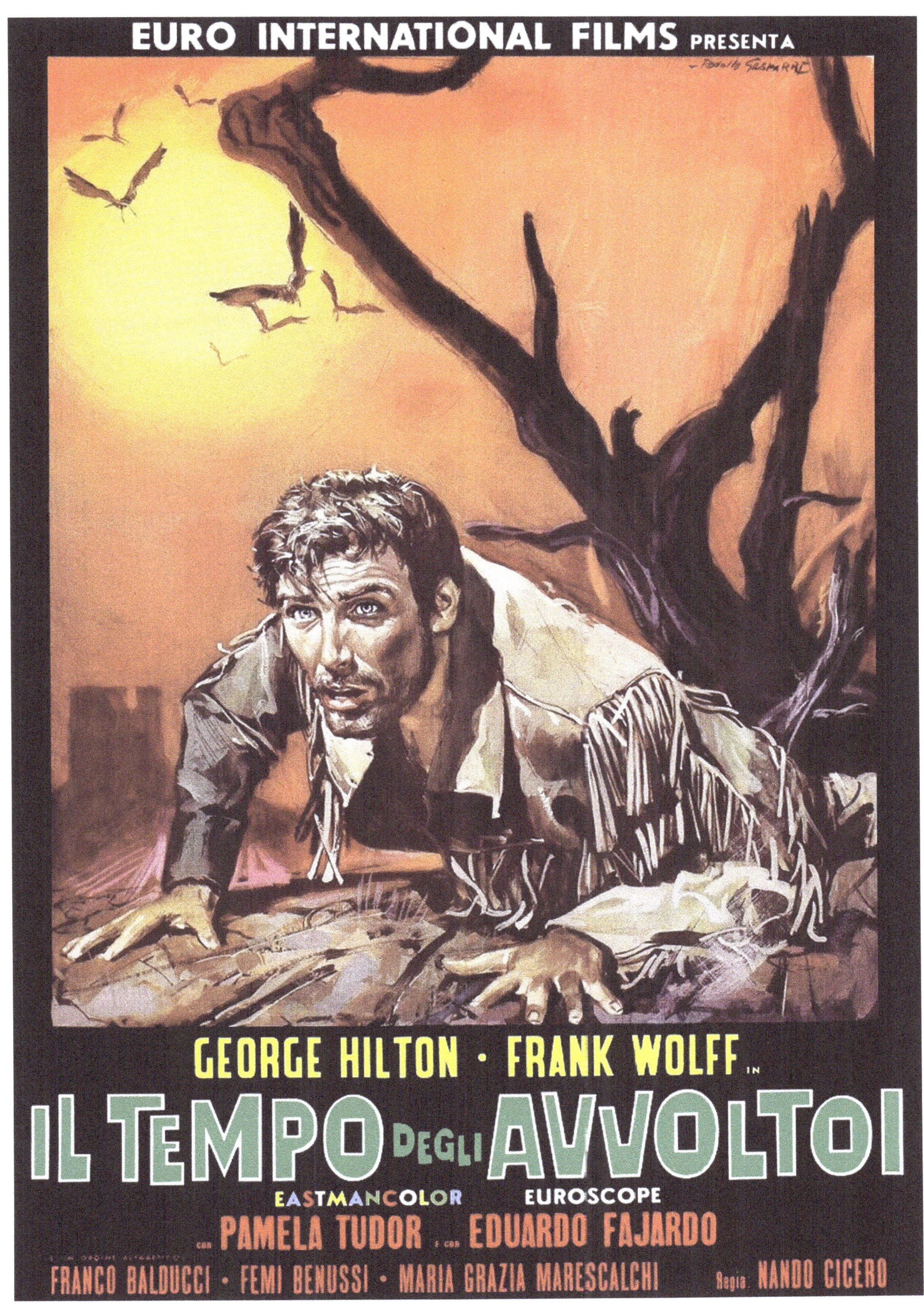

(''The Hour Of The Vulture'', 1967, Italy). Artist: Rodolfo Gasparri.

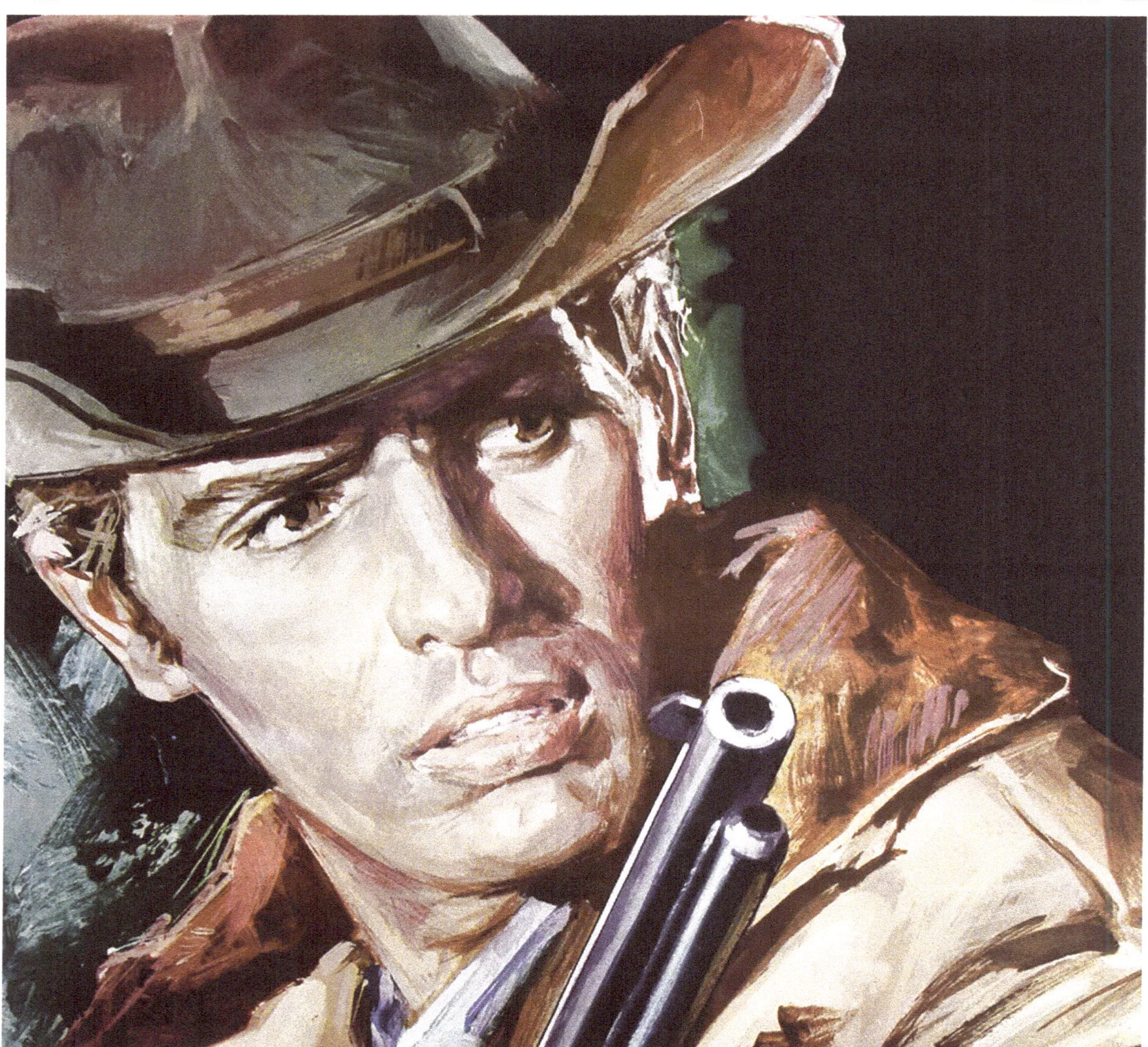

WANTED

(''Wanted'', 1967, Italy). Artist: unsigned.

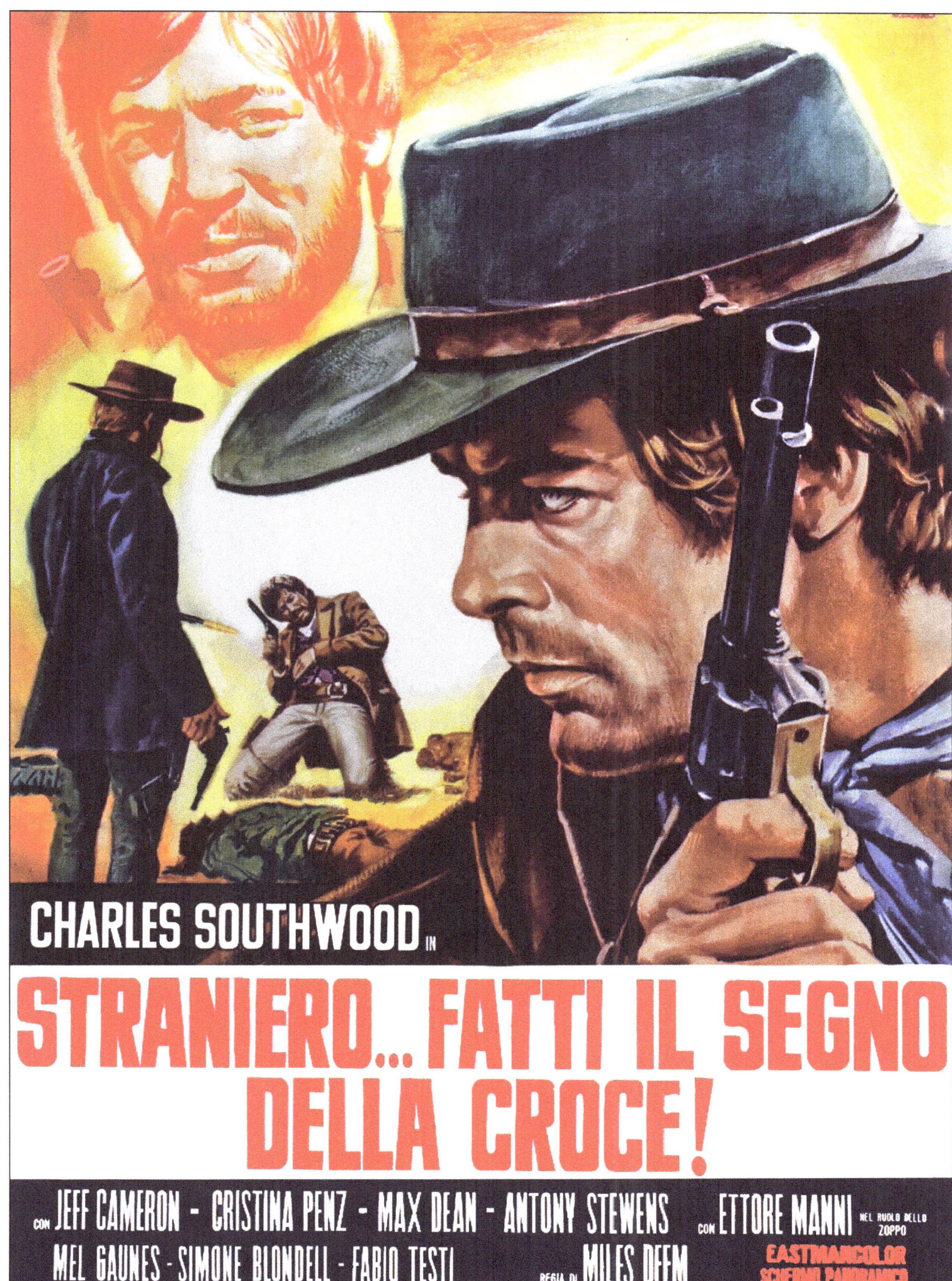

CHARLES SOUTHWOOD IN
STRANIERO... FATTI IL SEGNO DELLA CROCE!
CON JEFF CAMERON - CRISTINA PENZ - MAX DEAN - ANTONY STEWENS CON ETTORE MANNI NEL RUOLO DELLO ZOPPO
MEL GAUNES - SIMONE BLONDELL - FABIO TESTI REGIA DI MILES DEEM
EASTMANCOLOR SCHERMO PANORAMICO
DIR. PRODUZIONE MILACINEMATOGRAFICA

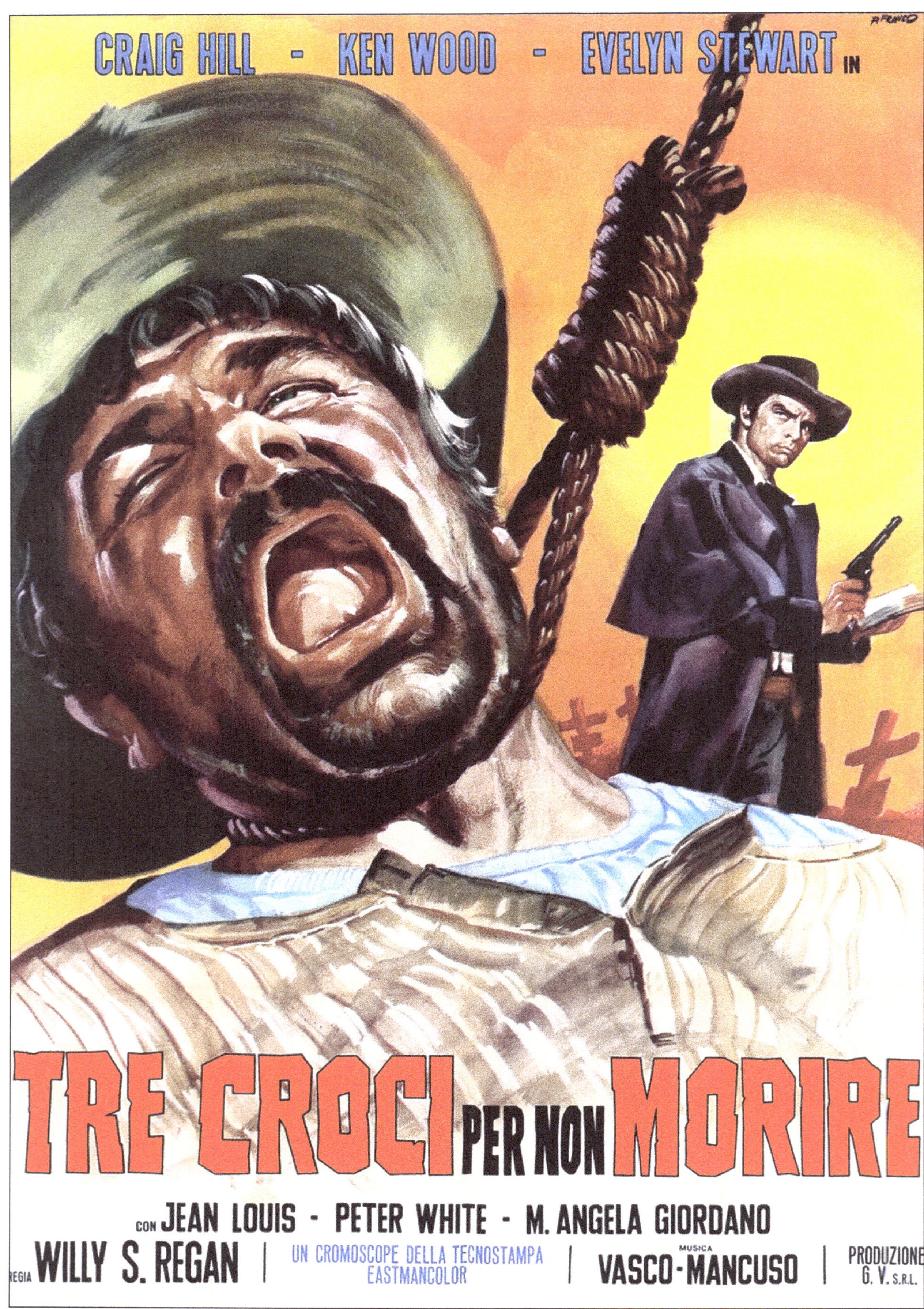

(''Three Crosses Not To Die'', 1968, Italy/Spain). Artist: P. Franco.

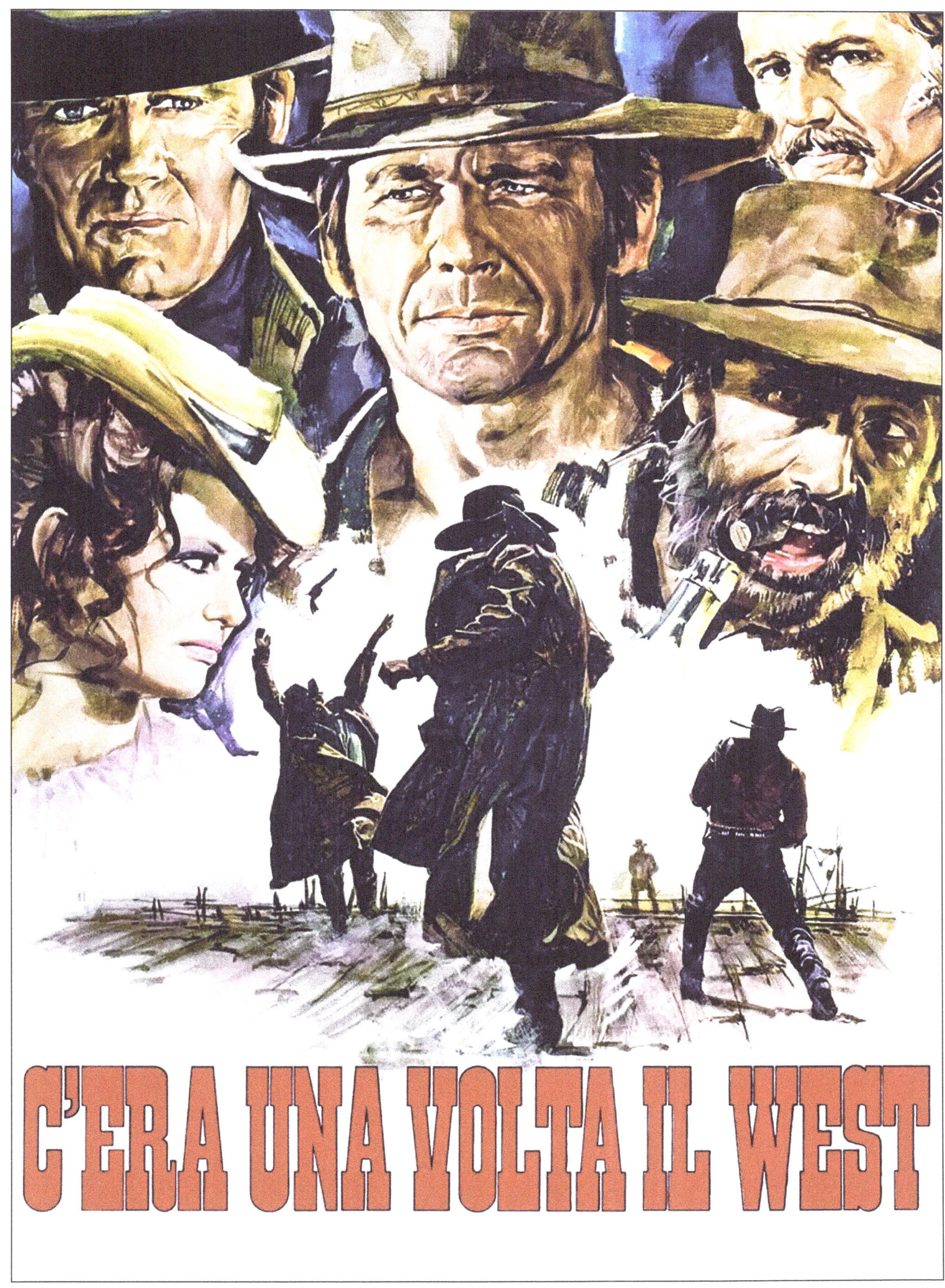

C'ERA UNA VOLTA IL WEST

(''Once Upon A Time In The West'', 1968, Italy/USA). Artist: Rodolfo Gasparri.

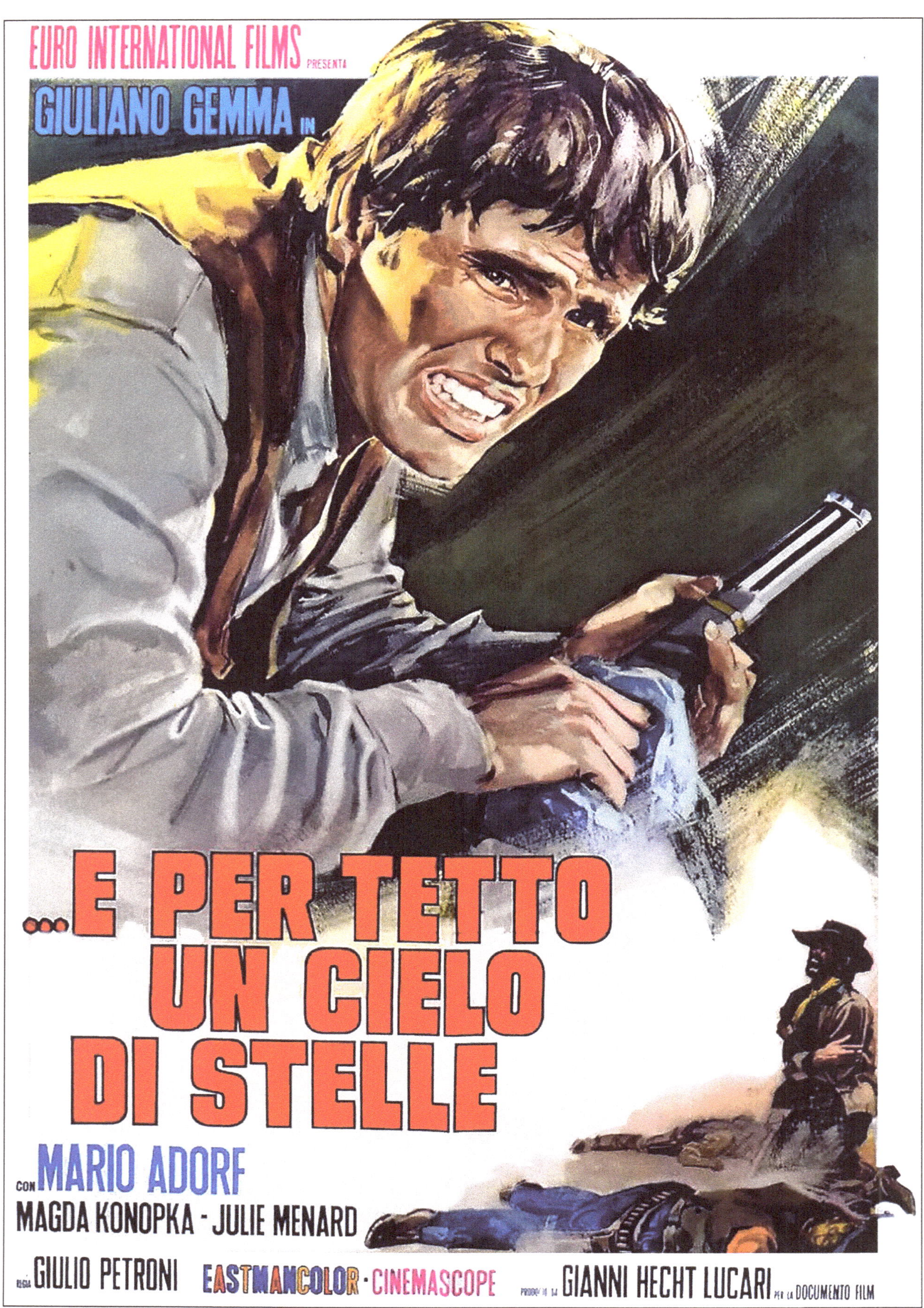

("And A Starry Sky For A Roof", 1968, Italy). Artist: Rodolfo Gasparri.

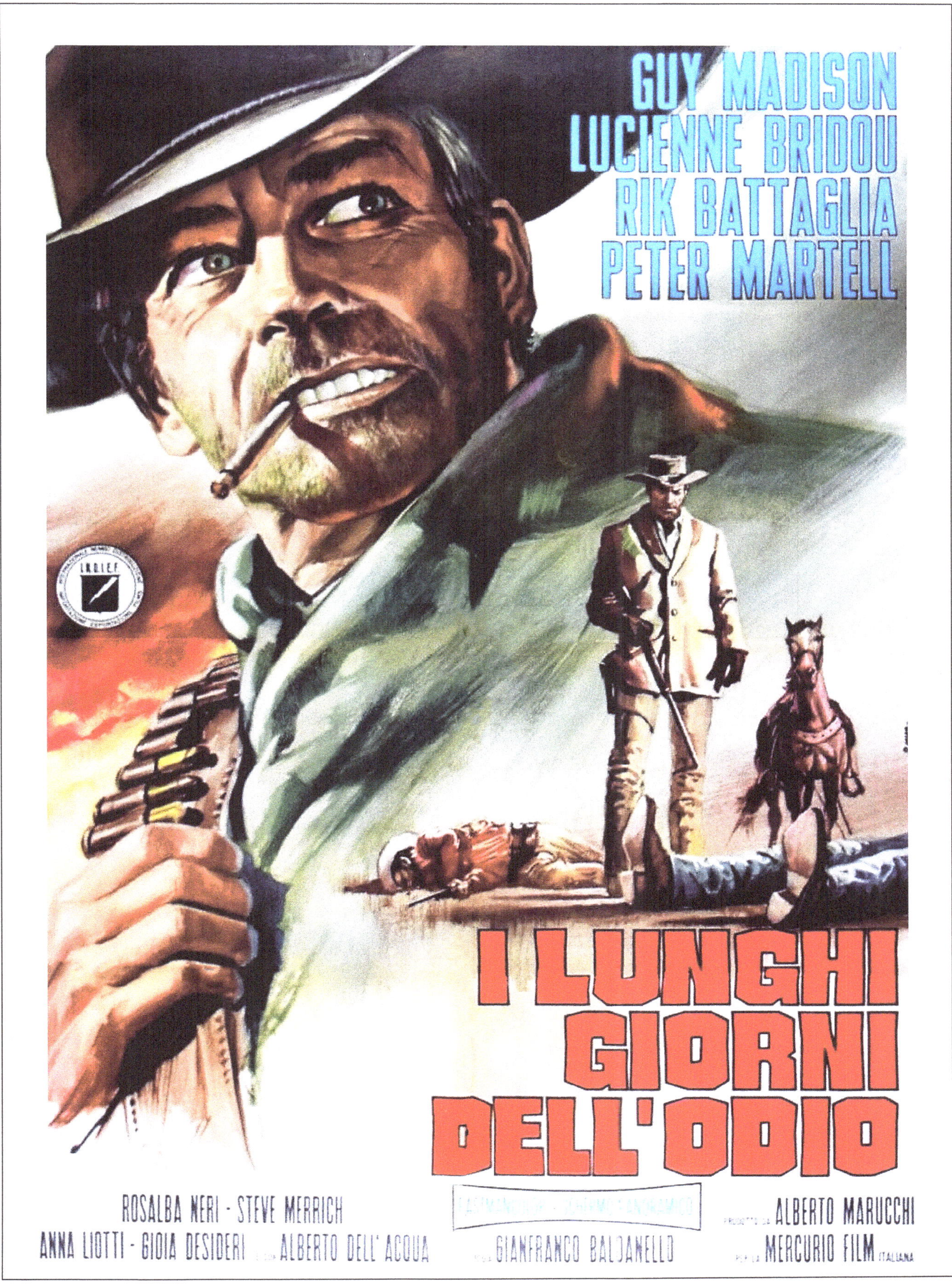

GUY MADISON
LUCIENNE BRIDOU
RIK BATTAGLIA
PETER MARTELL
I LUNGHI GIORNI DELL'ODIO
ROSALBA NERI - STEVE MERRICH
ANNA LIOTTI - GIOIA DESIDERI - ALBERTO DELL'ACQUA
GIANFRANCO BALDANELLO
ALBERTO MARUCCHI
MERCURIO FILM ITALIANA

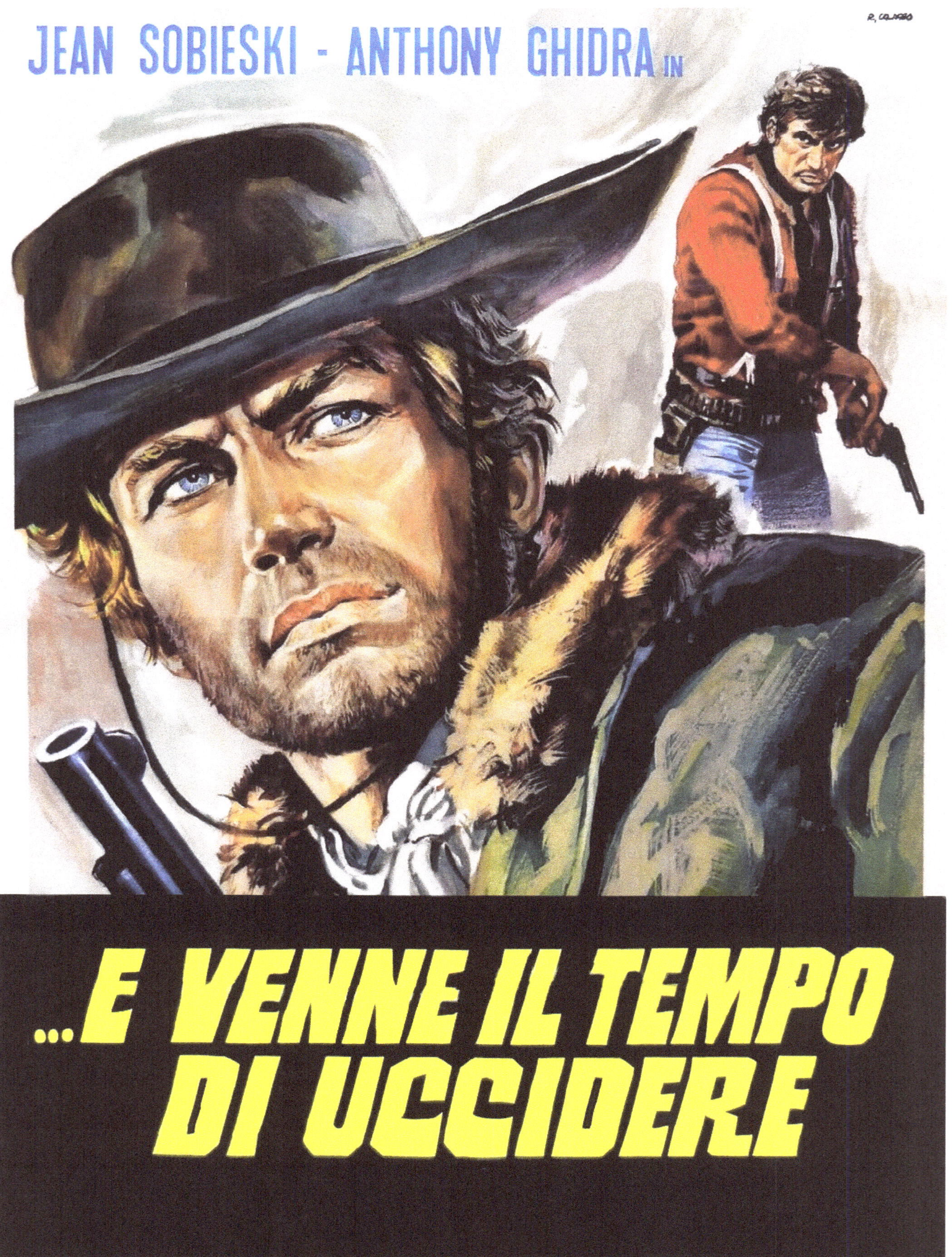

...E VENNE IL TEMPO DI UCCIDERE

(''And The Time Came To Kill'', 1968, Italy). Artist: Renato Casaro.

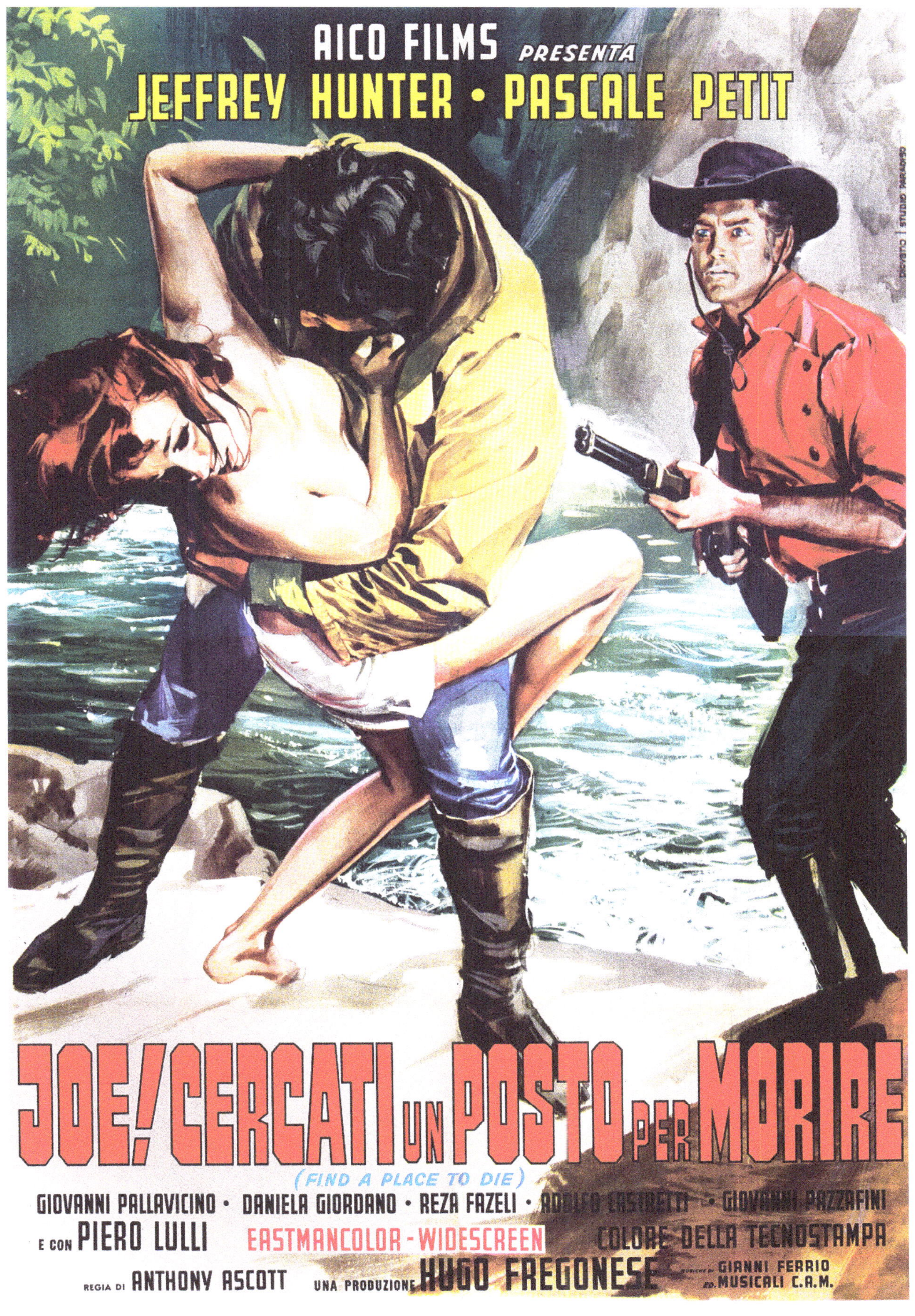

AICO FILMS presenta
JEFFREY HUNTER • PASCALE PETIT
JOE! CERCATI UN POSTO PER MORIRE
(FIND A PLACE TO DIE)
GIOVANNI PALLAVICINO • DANIELA GIORDANO • REZA FAZELI • ADOLFO LASTRETTI • GIOVANNI PAZZAFINI
E CON PIERO LULLI   EASTMANCOLOR - WIDESCREEN   COLORE DELLA TECNOSTAMPA
REGIA DI ANTHONY ASCOTT   UNA PRODUZIONE HUGO FREGONESE   MUSICHE DI GIANNI FERRIO ED. MUSICALI C.A.M.

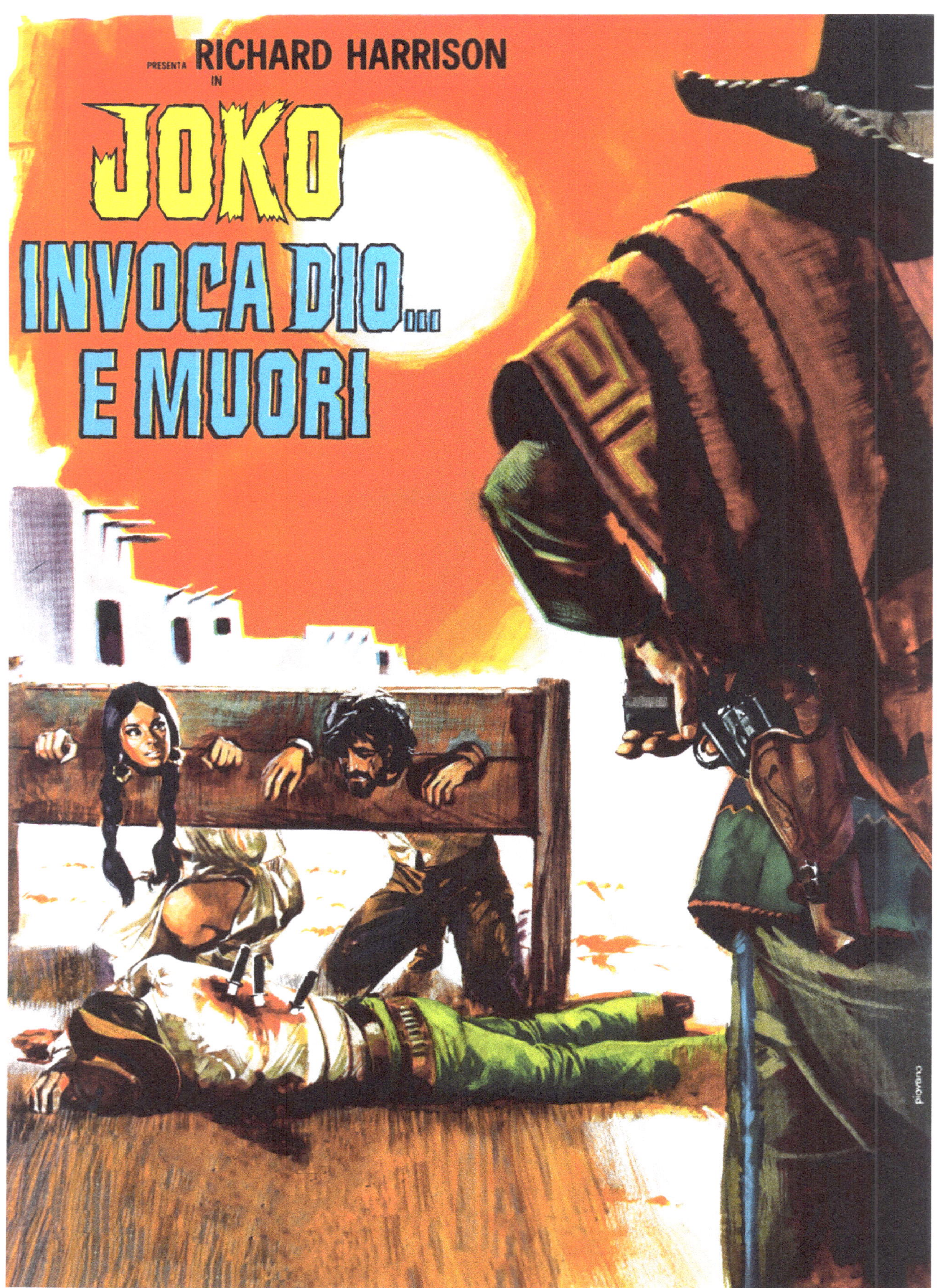

JOKO INVOCA DIO... E MUORI

("Joko: Summon God... And Die", 1968, Italy/Germany). Artist: Mario Piovano.

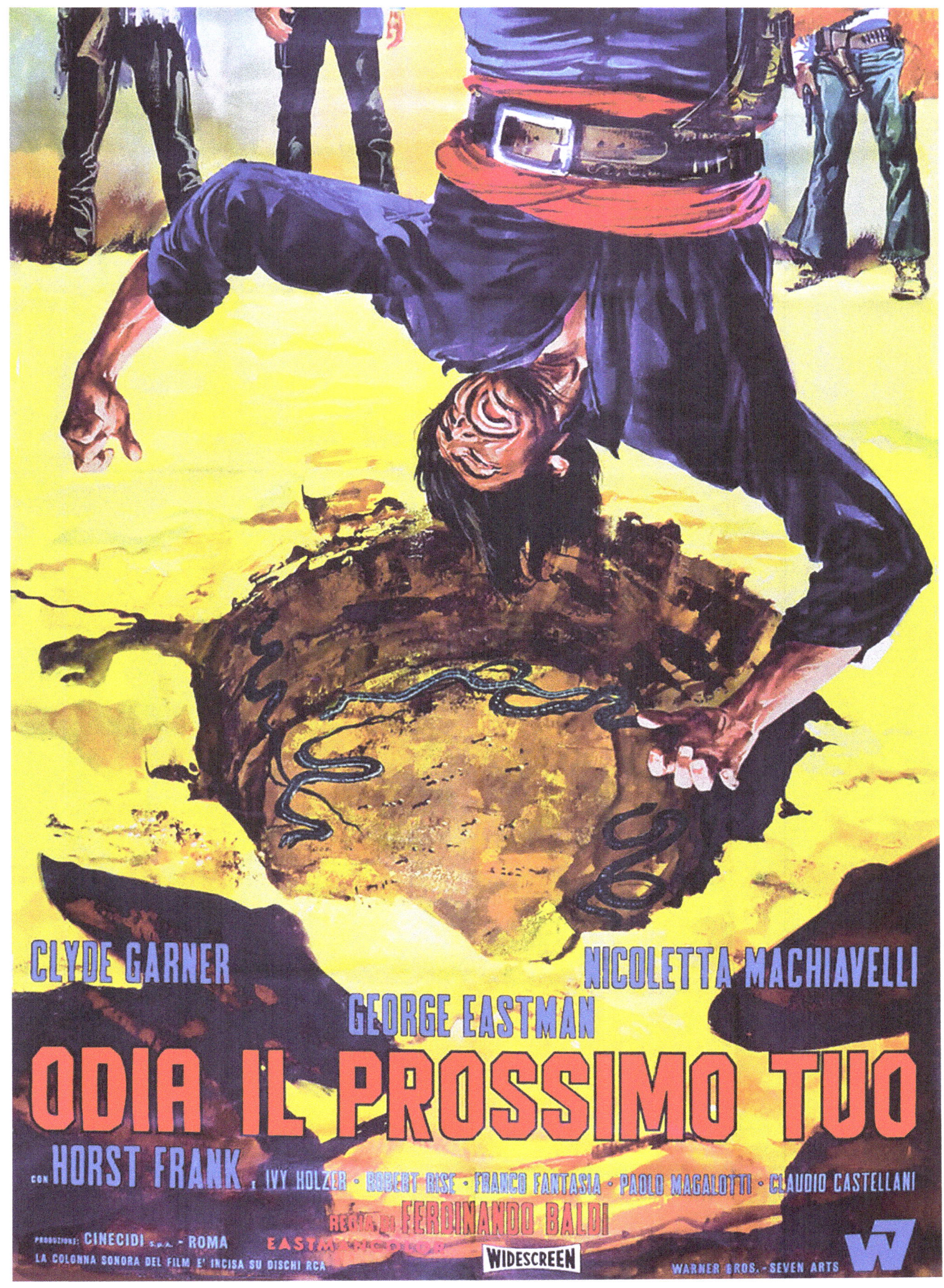

CLYDE GARNER
NICOLETTA MACHIAVELLI
GEORGE EASTMAN
ODIA IL PROSSIMO TUO
CON HORST FRANK E IVY HOLZER · ROBERT RISE · FRANCO FANTASIA · PAOLO MAGALOTTI · CLAUDIO CASTELLANI
REGIA DI FERDINANDO BALDI
PRODUZIONE: CINECIDI s.p.a. - ROMA
EASTMANCOLOR
WIDESCREEN
LA COLONNA SONORA DEL FILM E' INCISA SU DISCHI RCA
WARNER BROS. - SEVEN ARTS

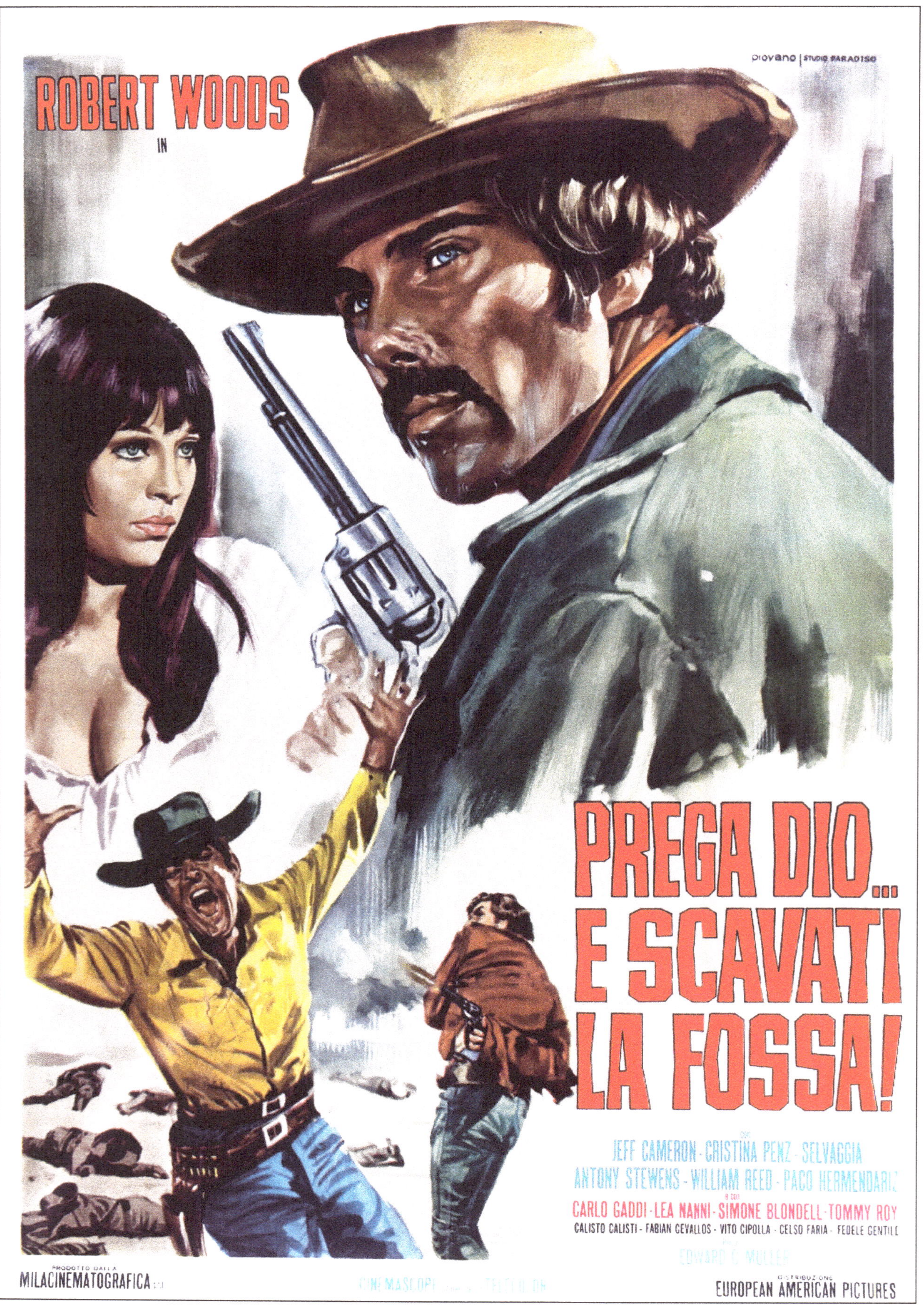

PREGA DIO... E SCAVATI LA FOSSA!

("Pray To God... And Dig Your Grave!", 1968, Italy). Artist: Mario Piovano.

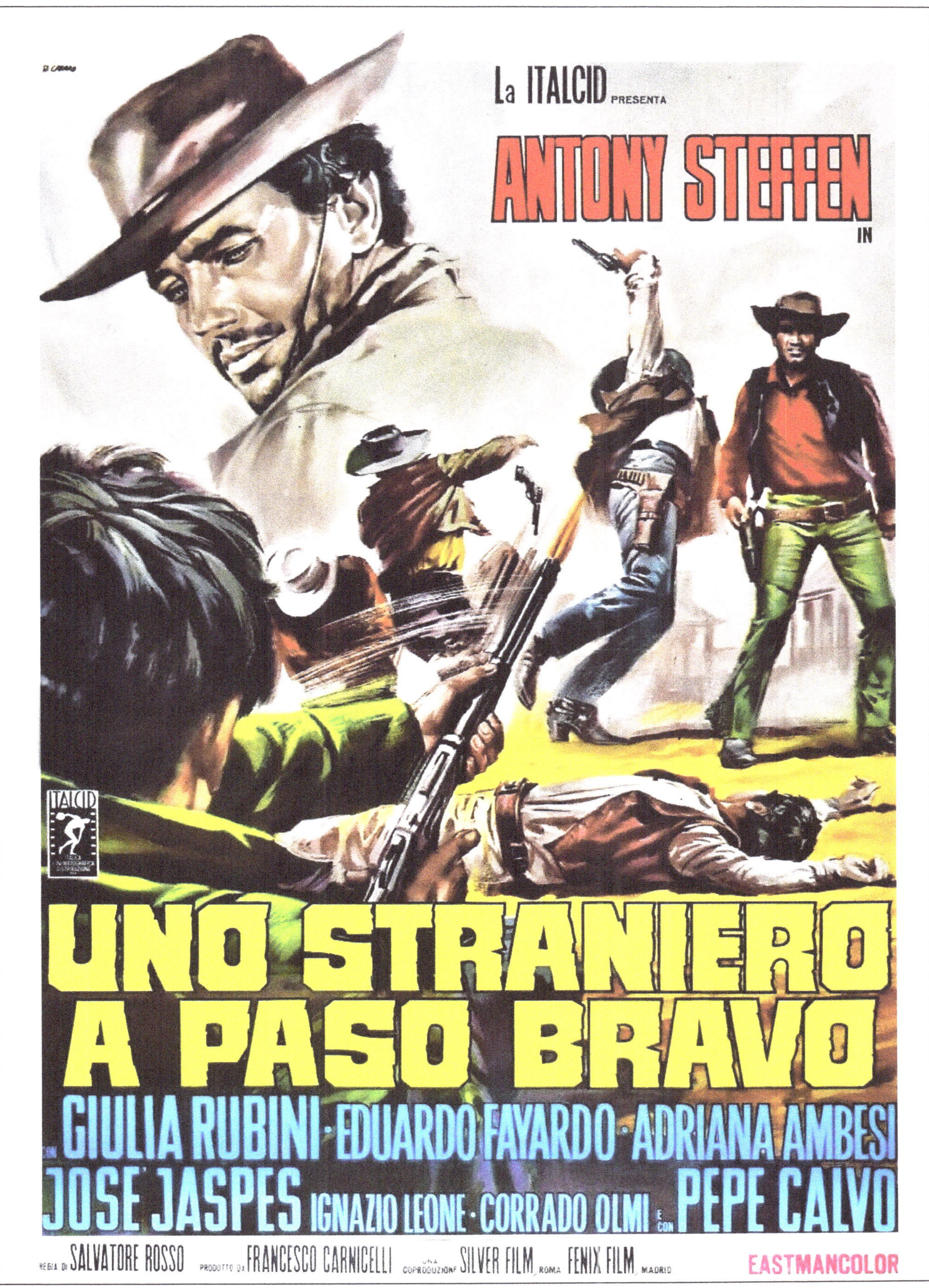

UNO STRANIERO A PASO BRAVO

("A Stranger In Paso Bravo", 1968, Italy/Spain). Artist: Renato Casaro.

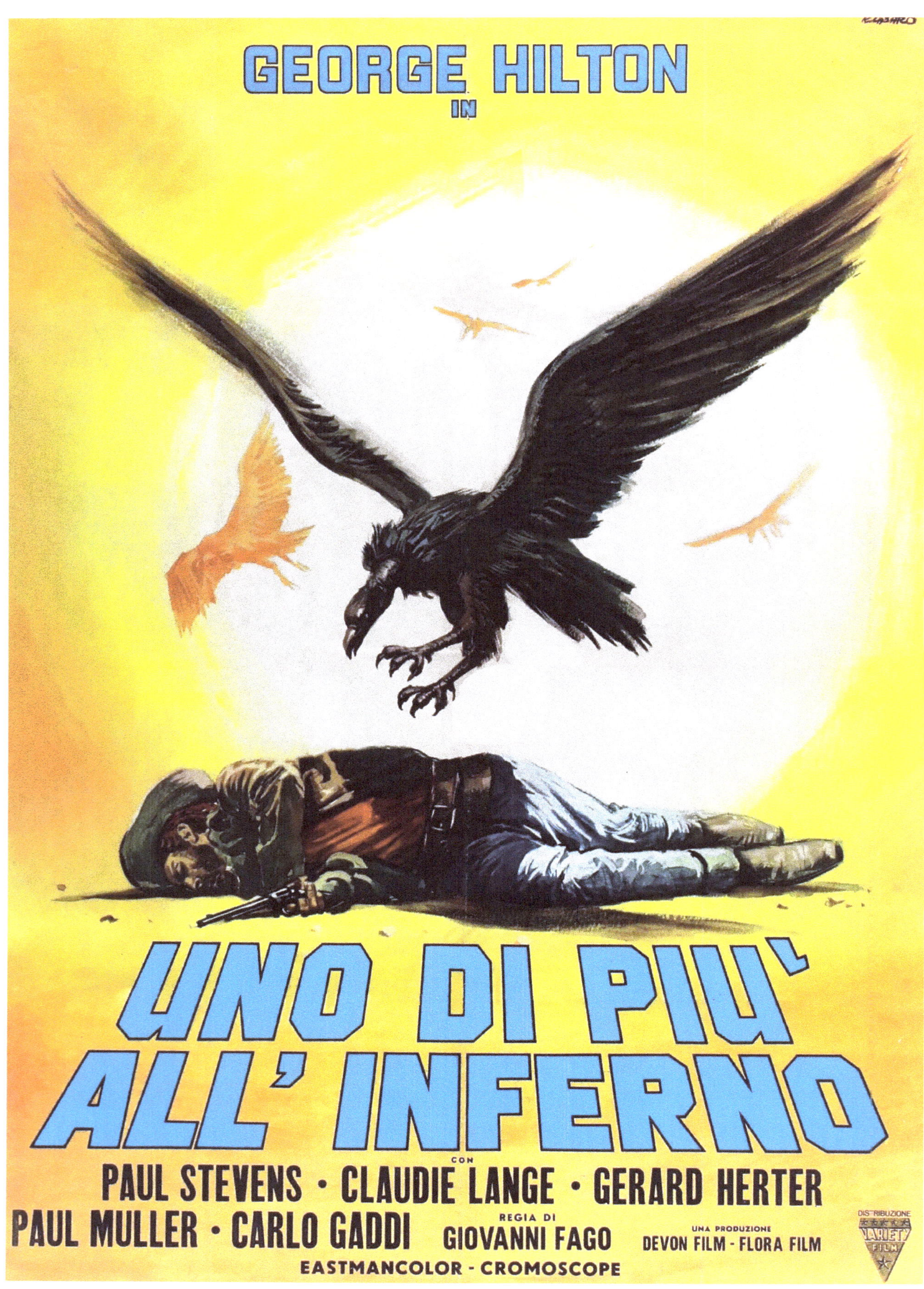

("One More In Hell", 1968, Italy). Artist: Renato Casaro.

LA DENWER FILM PRESENTA
GEORGE HILTON
SANDRA MILO
NEL RUOLO DI LIZ
JOHN JRELAND
T'AMMAZZO!...
RACCOMANDATI A DIO

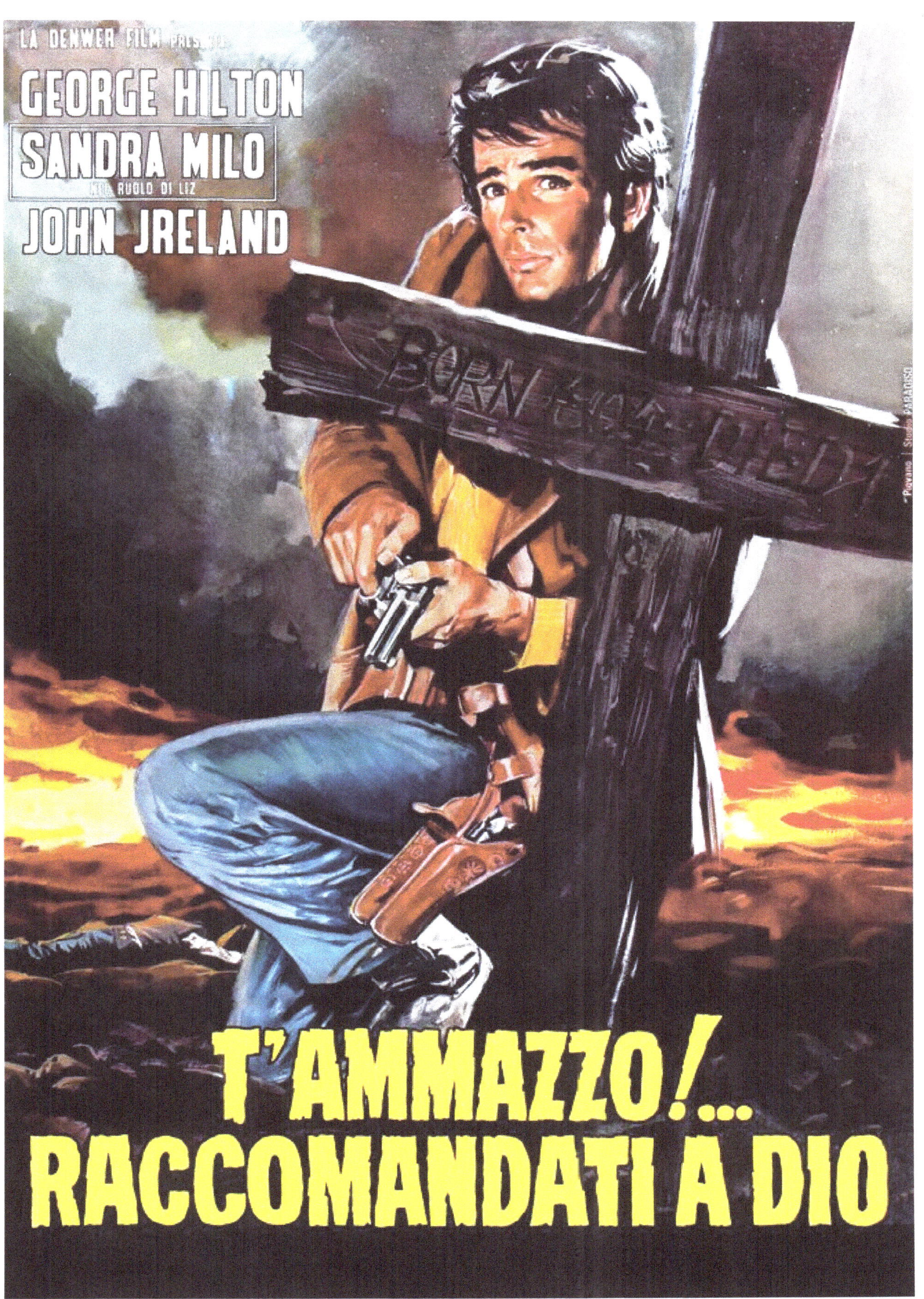

49

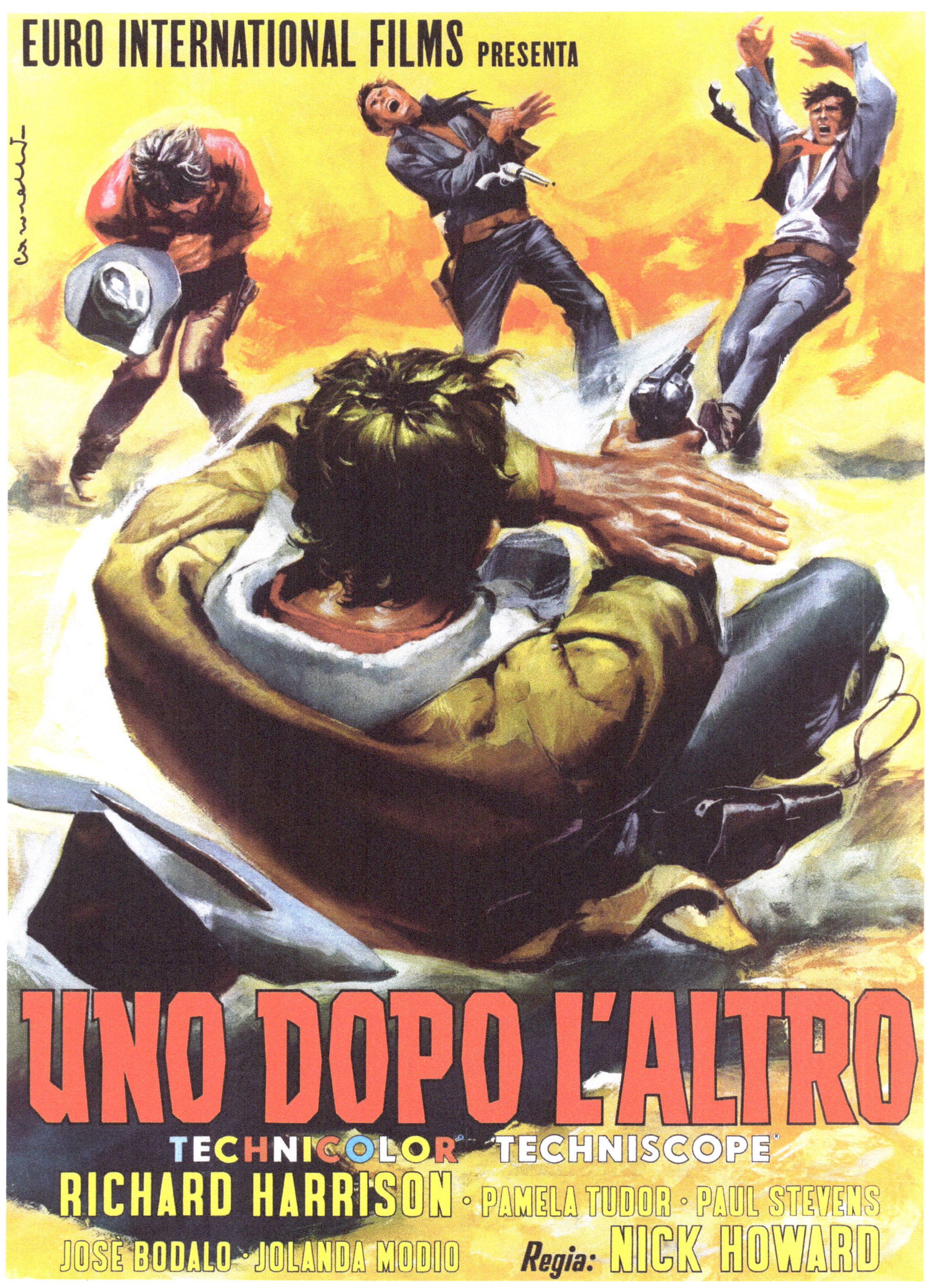

UNO DOPO L'ALTRO

(''One After The After'', 1968, Italy/Spain). Artist: Coronelli.

50

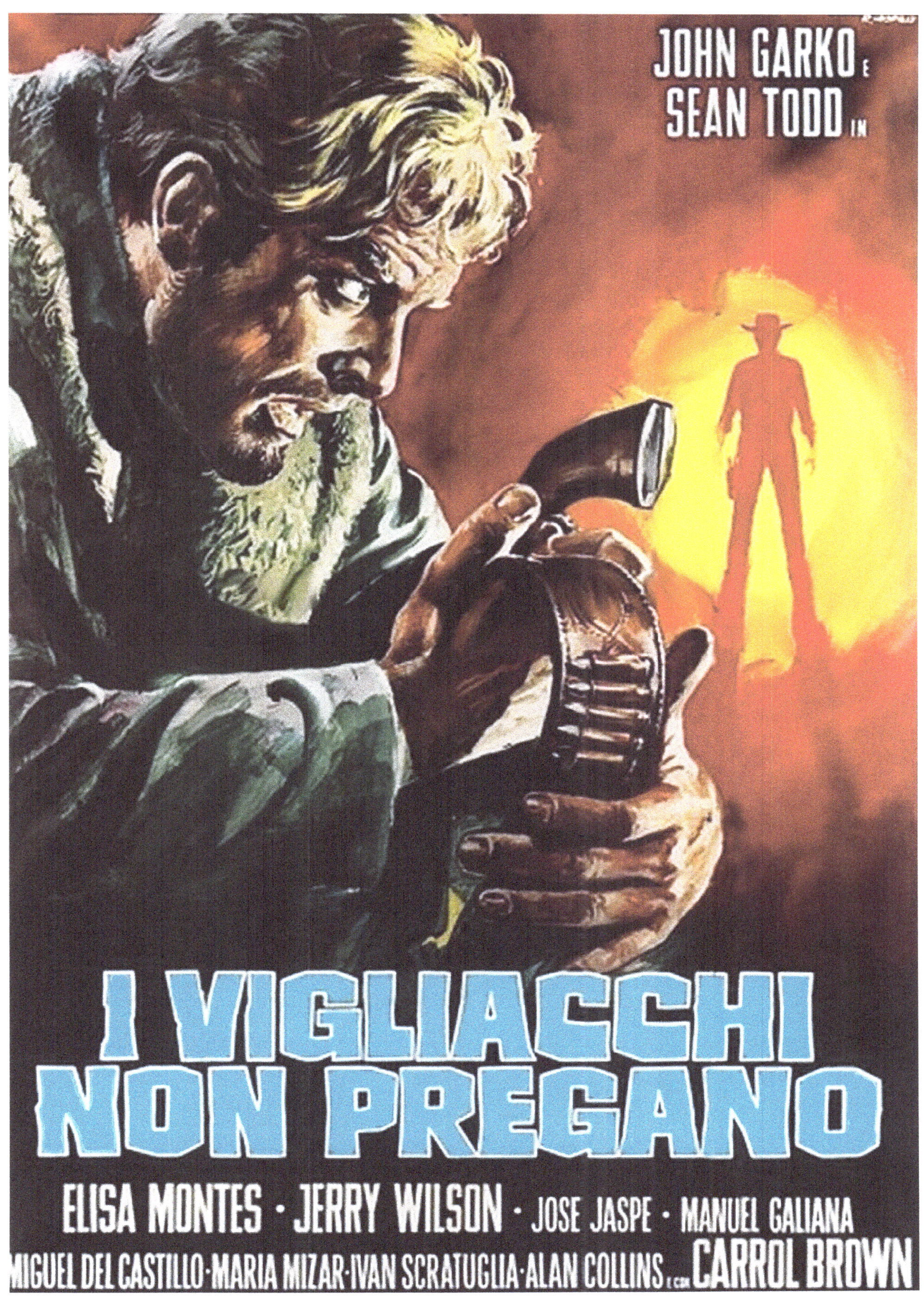

("Cowards Don't Pray", 1968, Italy/Spain). Artist: Renato Casaro.

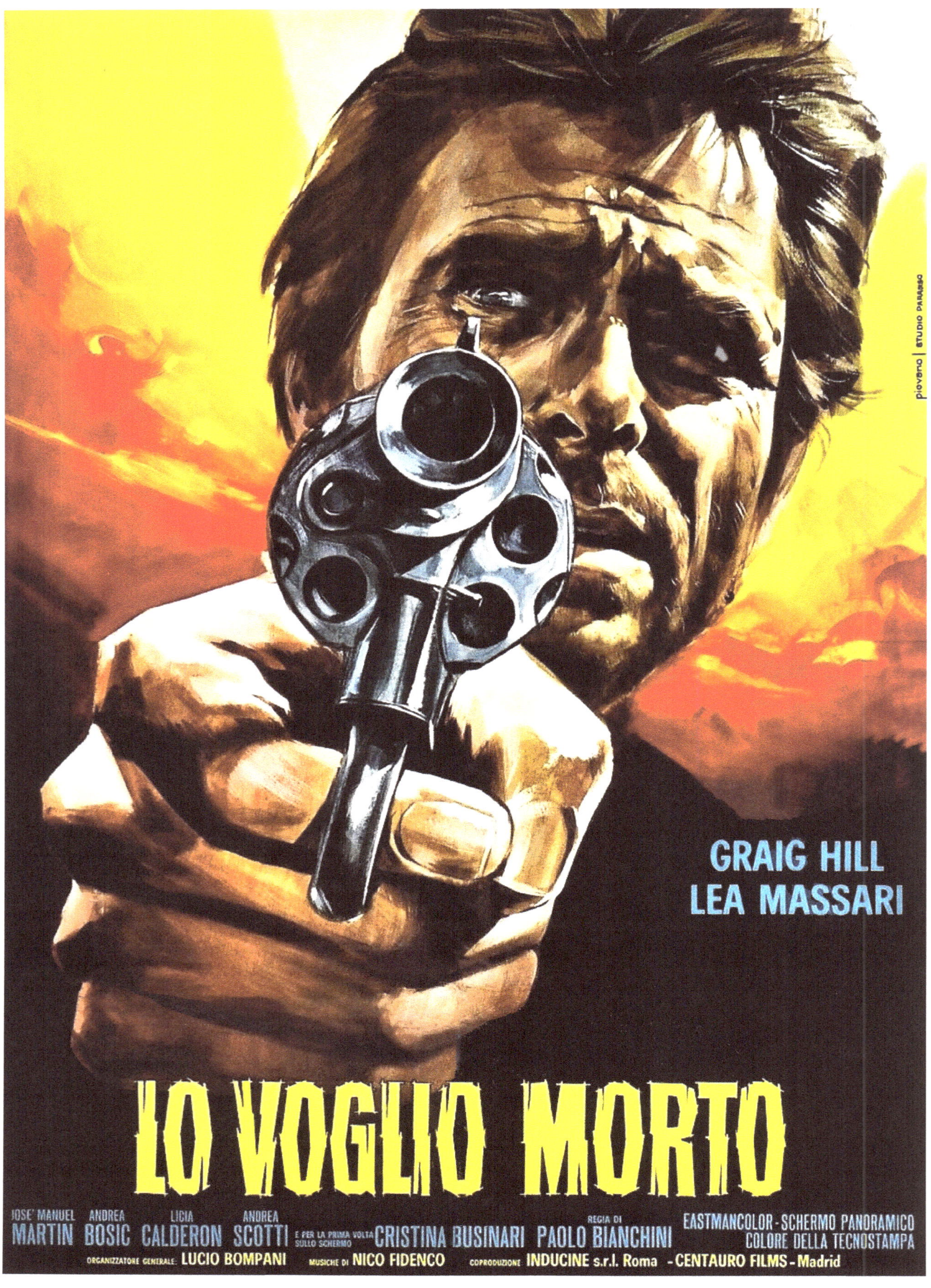

LO VOGLIO MORTO

("I Want Him Dead", 1968, Italy/Spain). Artist: Mario Piovano.

52

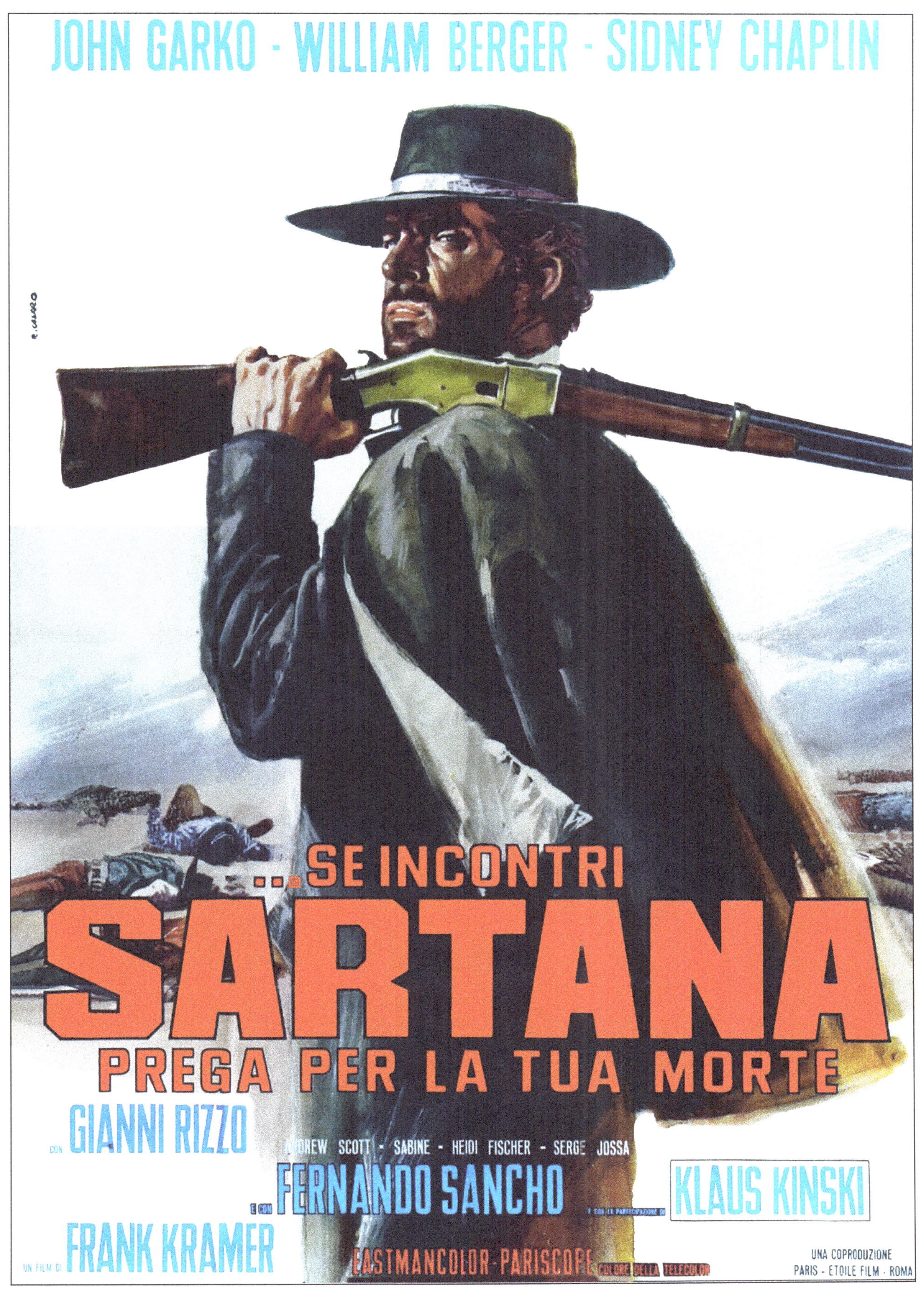

...SE INCONTRI SARTANA PREGA PER LA TUA MORTE

("...If You Meet Sartana, Pray For Death", 1968, Italy/Germany). Artist: Renato Casaro.

53

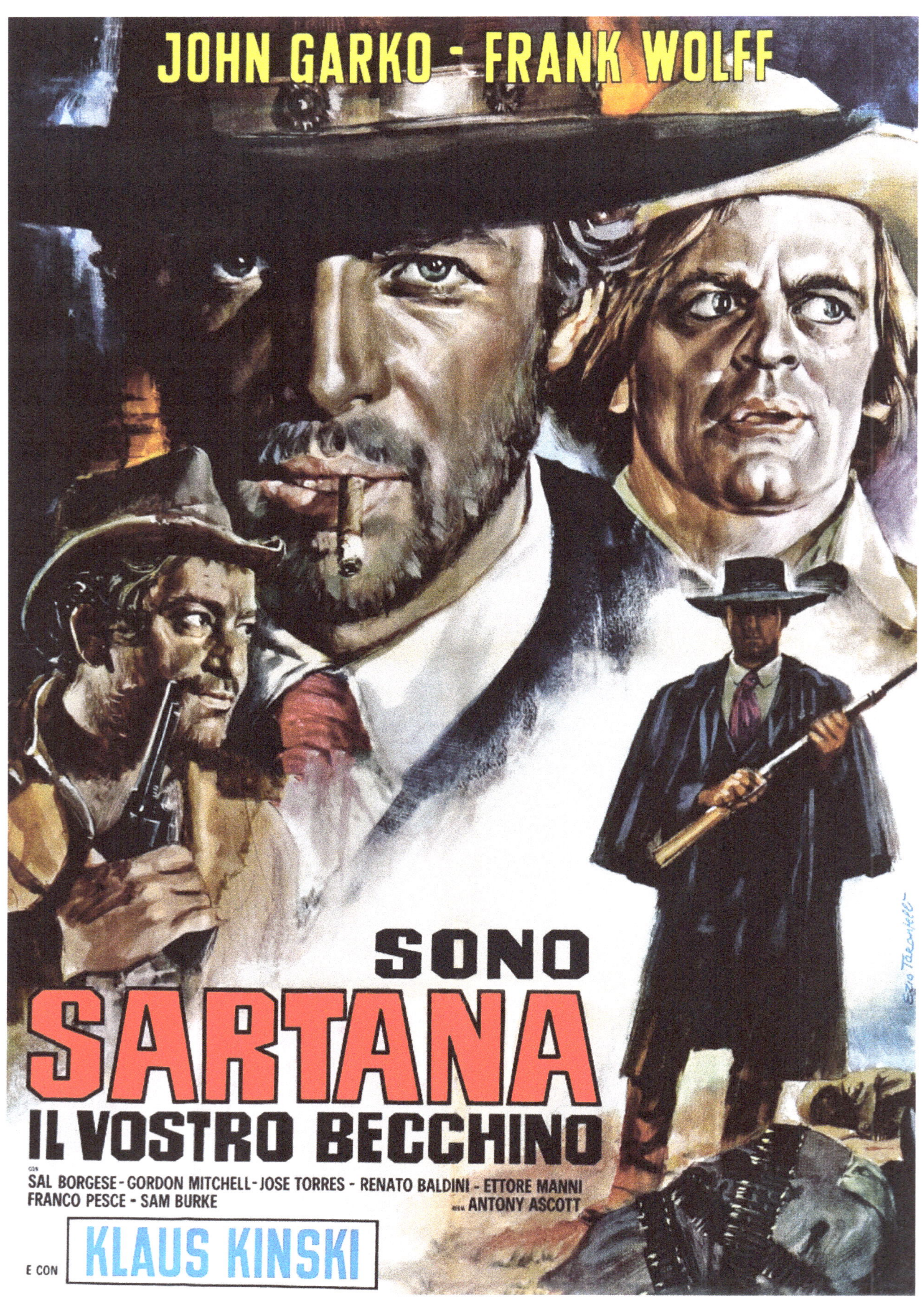

SONO SARTANA IL VOSTRO BECCHINO

(''I Am Sartana, Your Grave-Digger'', 1969, Italy). Artist: Ezio Tarantelli.

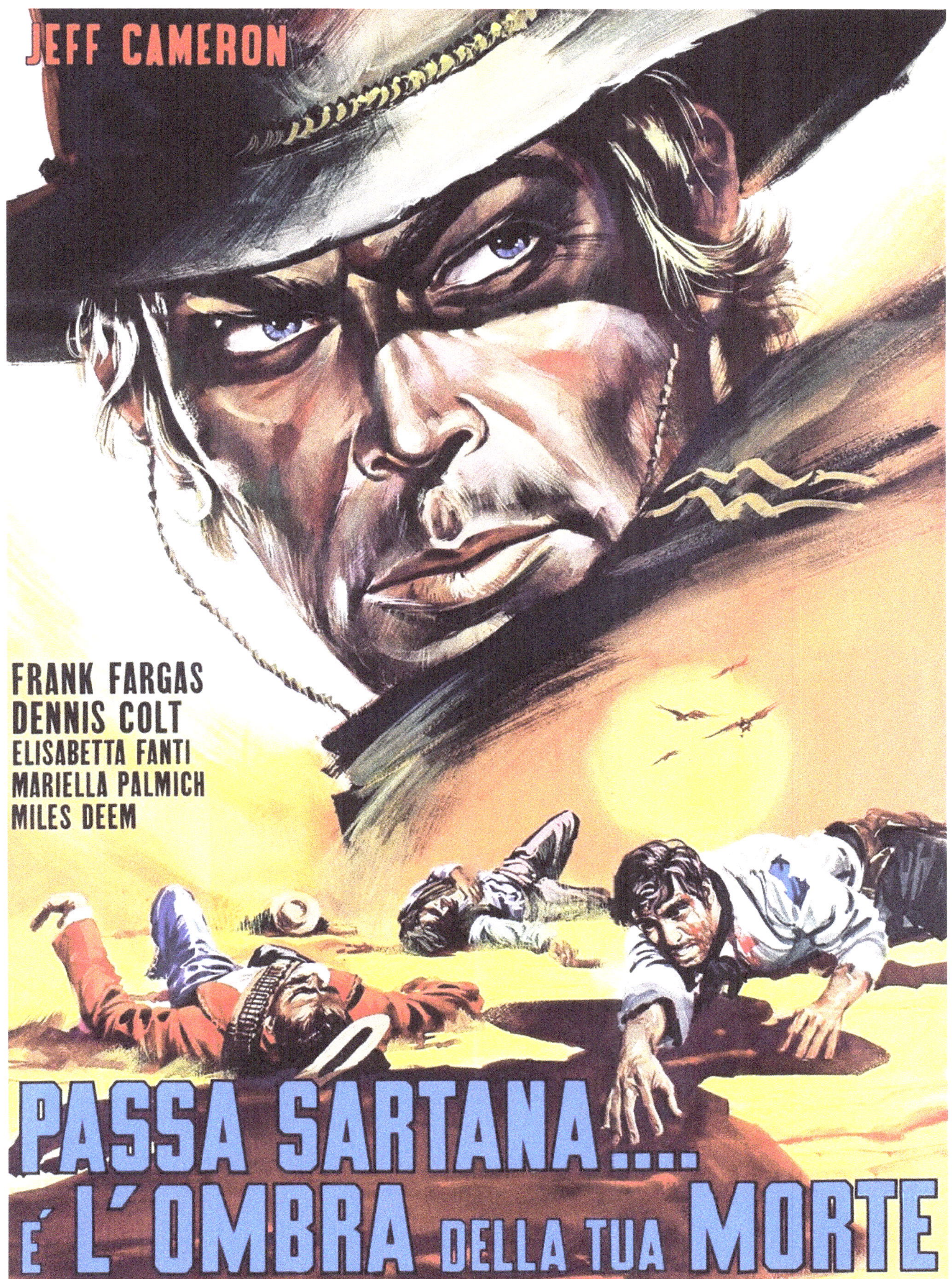

JEFF CAMERON
FRANK FARGAS
DENNIS COLT
ELISABETTA FANTI
MARIELLA PALMICH
MILES DEEM
PASSA SARTANA....
é L'OMBRA DELLA TUA MORTE

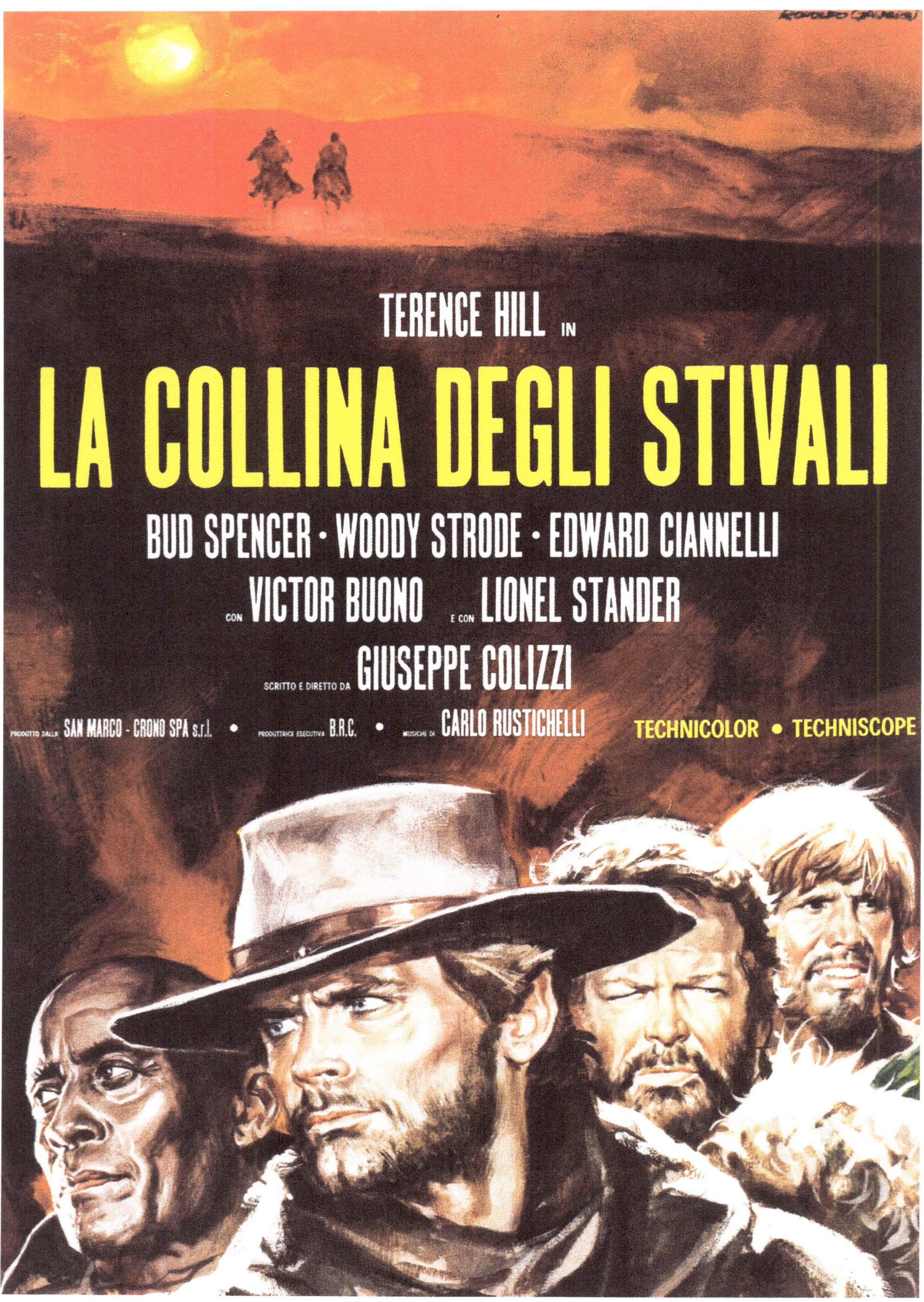

LA COLLINA DEGLI STIVALI

(''Boot Hill'', 1969, Italy). Artist: Rodolfo Gasparri.

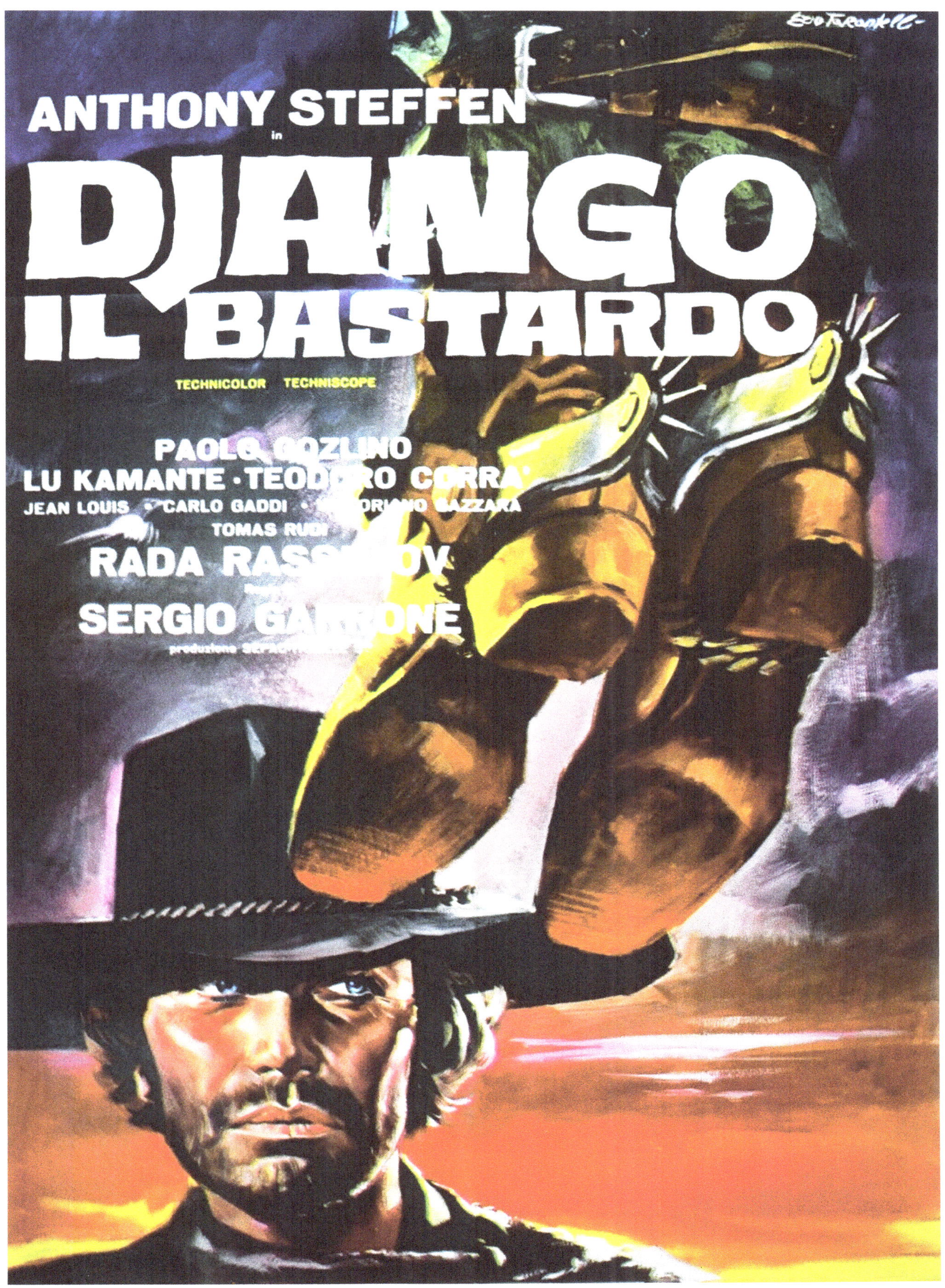

("Django The Bastard", 1969, Italy). Artist: Ezio Tarantelli.

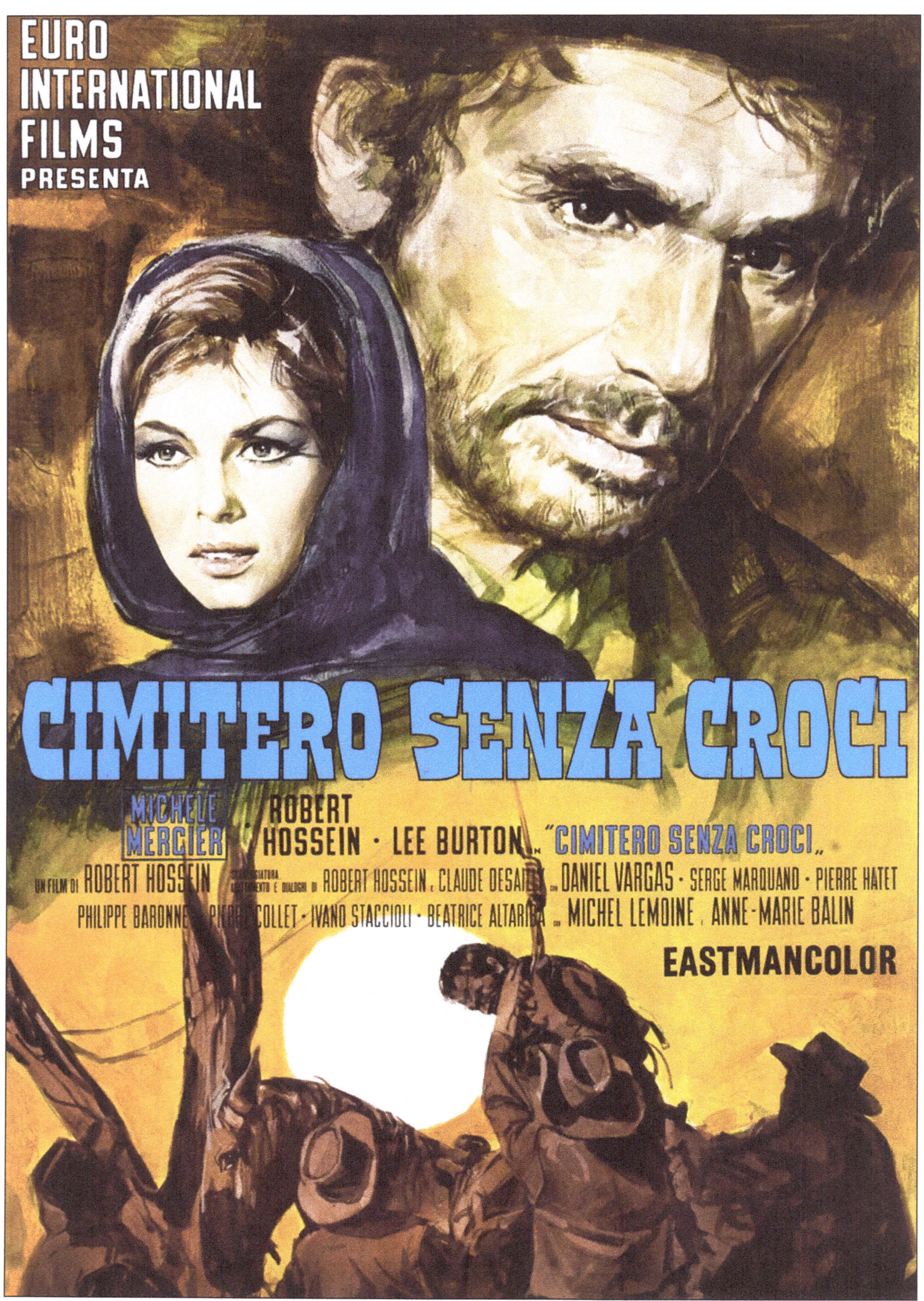

CIMITERO SENZA CROCI

(''Cemetery With No Crosses'', 1969, Italy). Artist: unsigned.

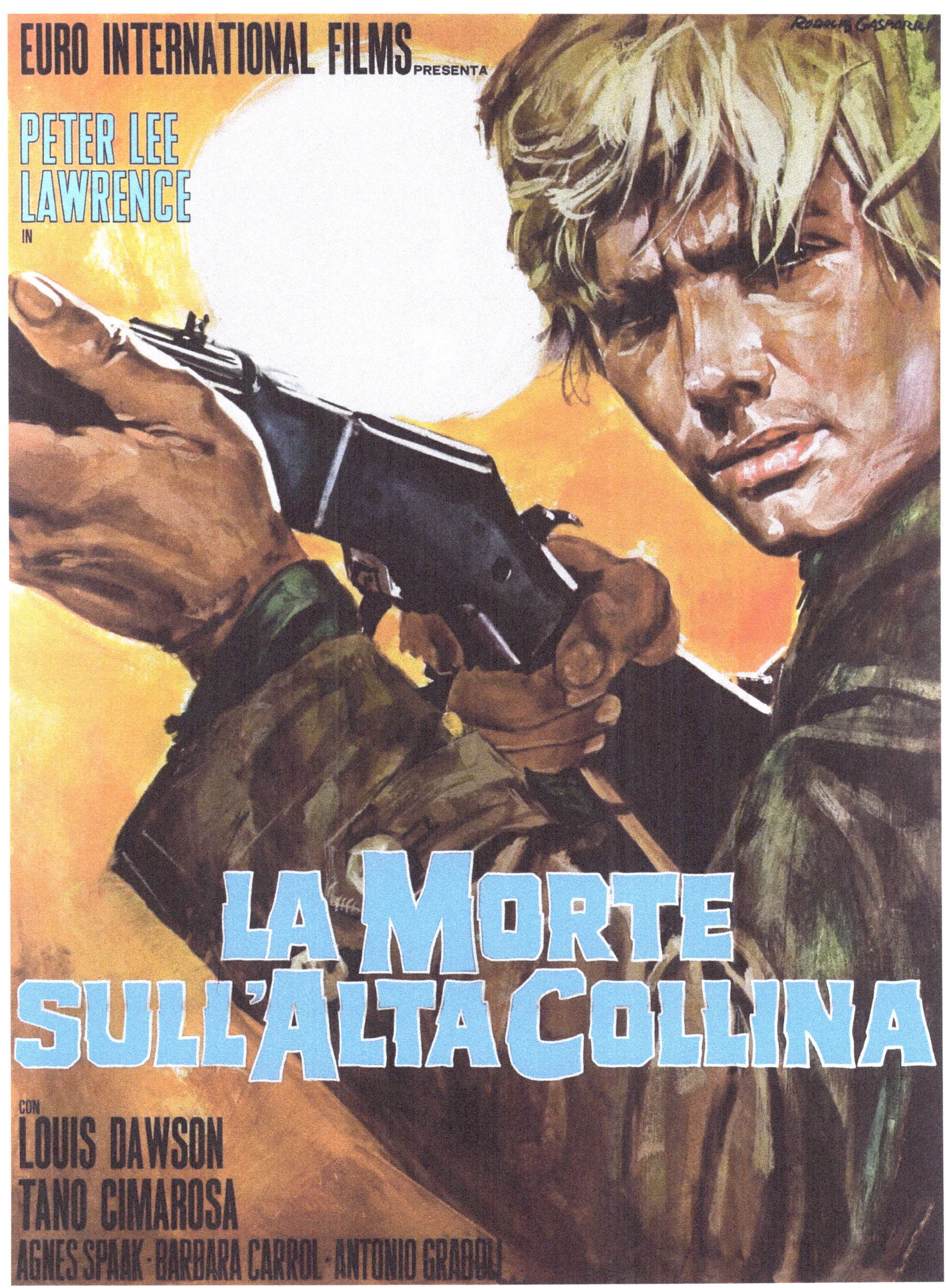

("Death On The High Hill", 1969, Italy/Spain). Artist: Rodolfo Gasparri.

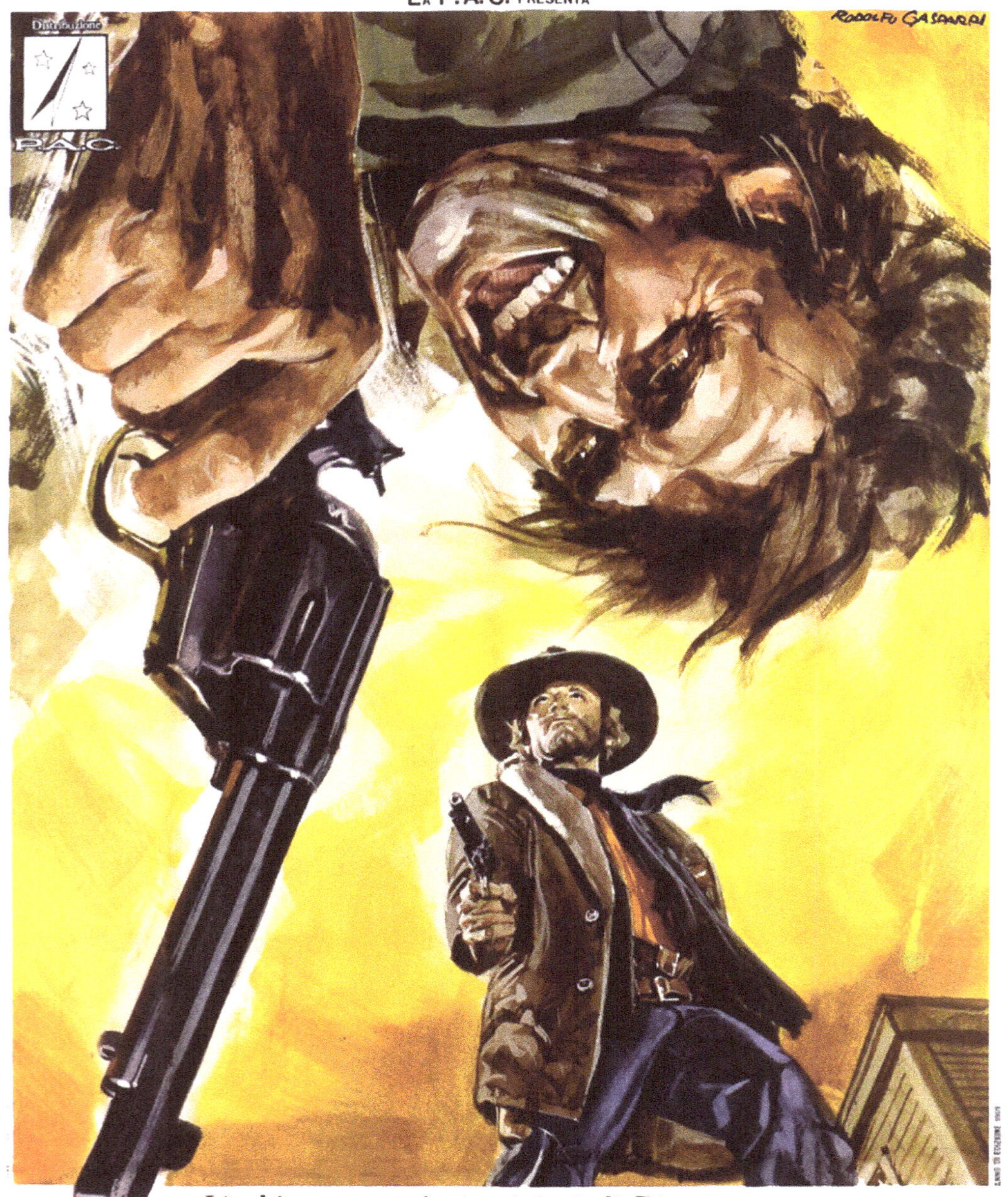

UNA LUNGA FILA DI CROCI

("A Long Row Of Crosses", 1969, Italy). Artist: Rodolfo Gasparri.

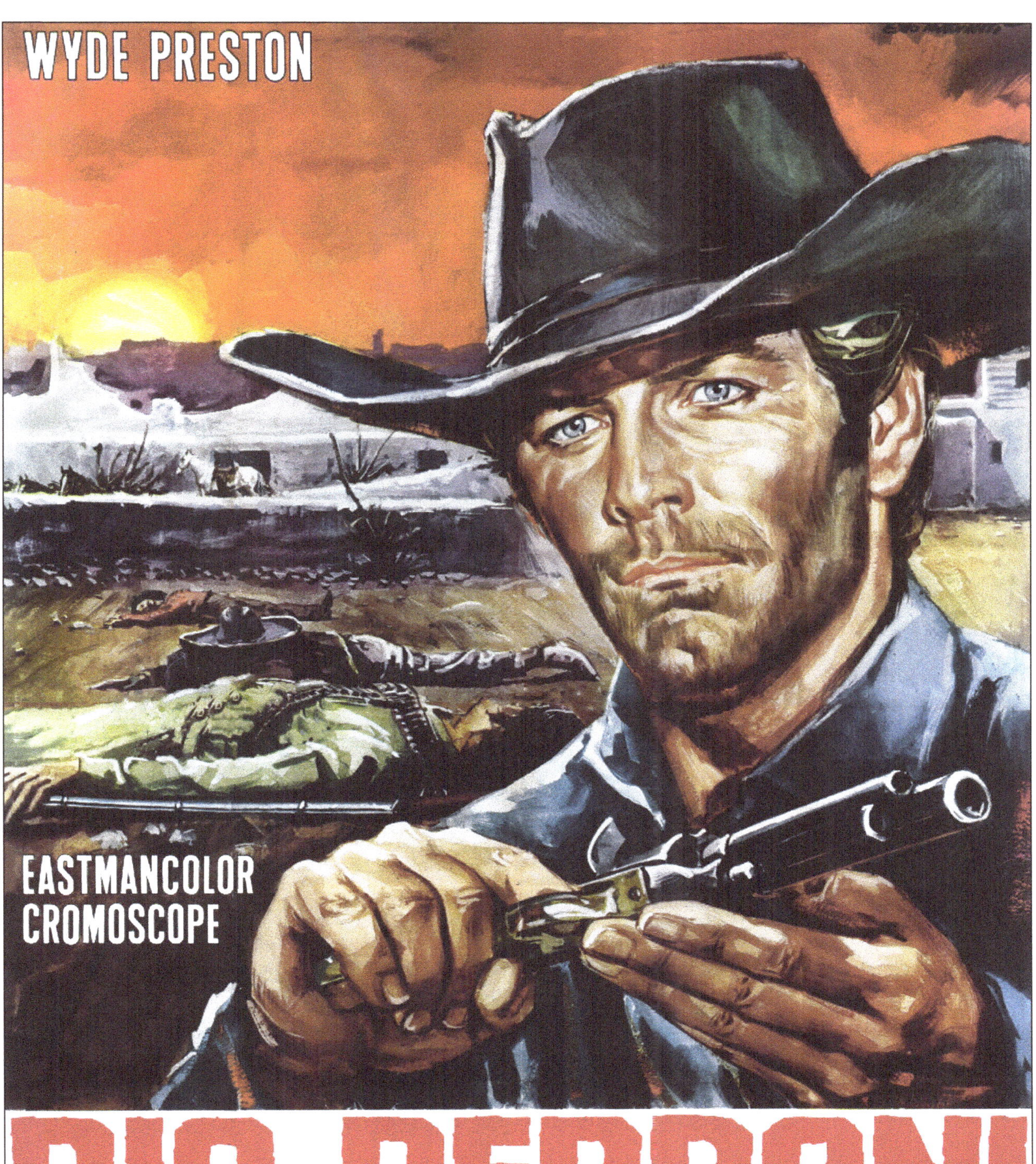

DIO PERDONI LA MIA PISTOLA

("God Forgives My Pistol", 1969, Italy). Artist: Ezio Tarantelli.

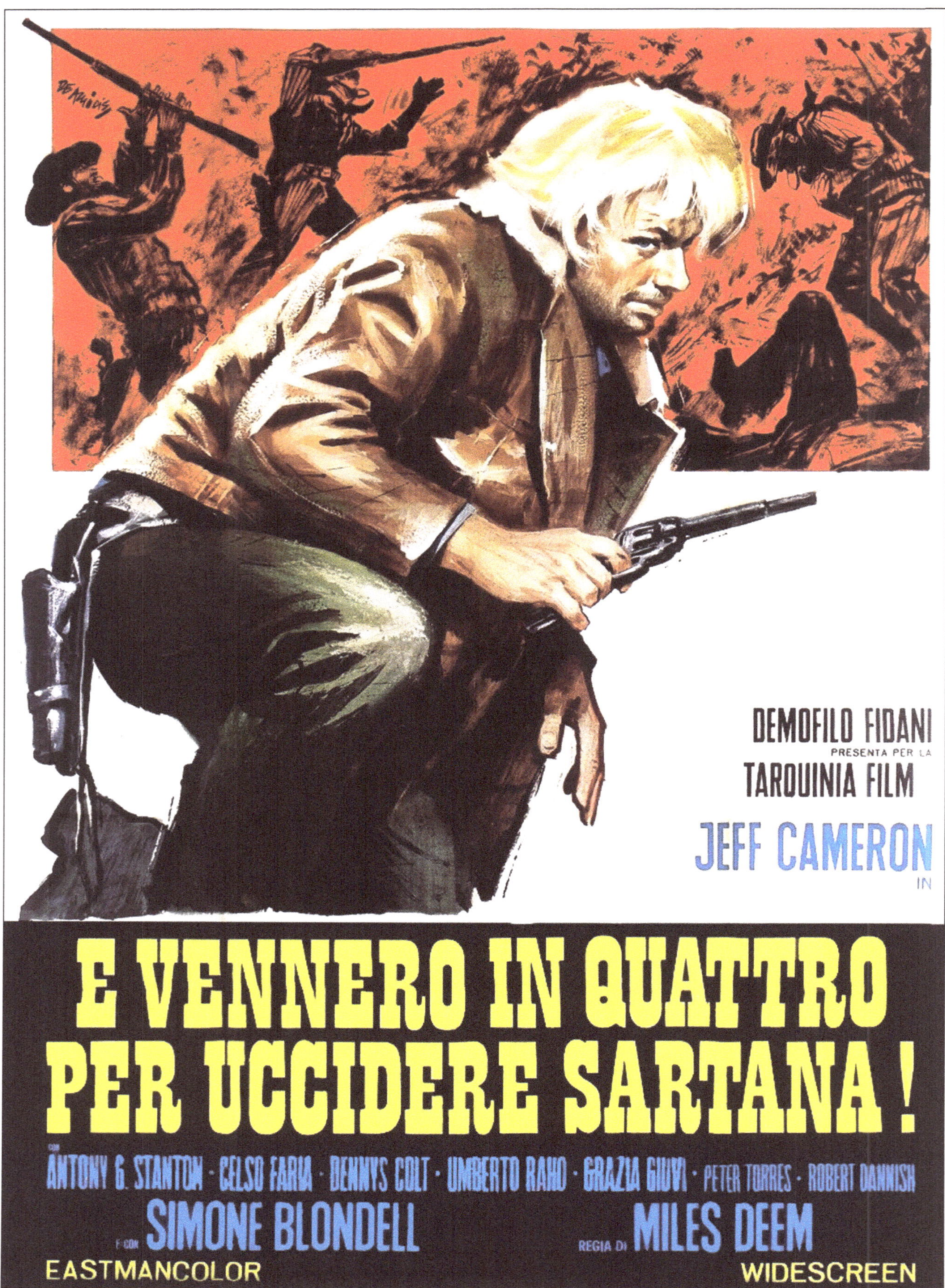

("And Four Came To KIll Sartana", 1969, Italy). Artist: De Amicis.

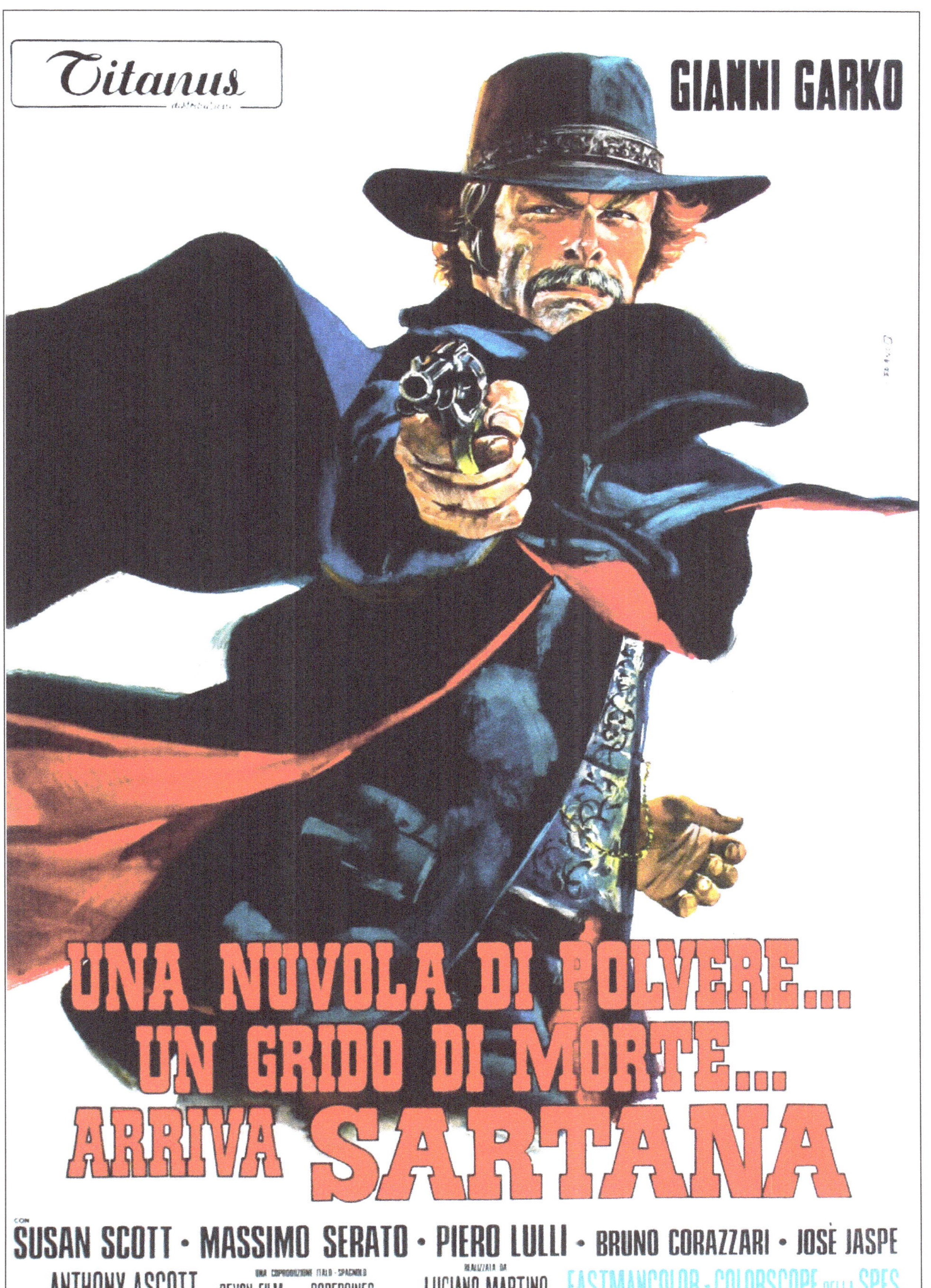

("A Cloud Of Dust... A Scream Of Death... Sartana Is Coming", 1970, Italy/Spain). Artist: P. Franco.

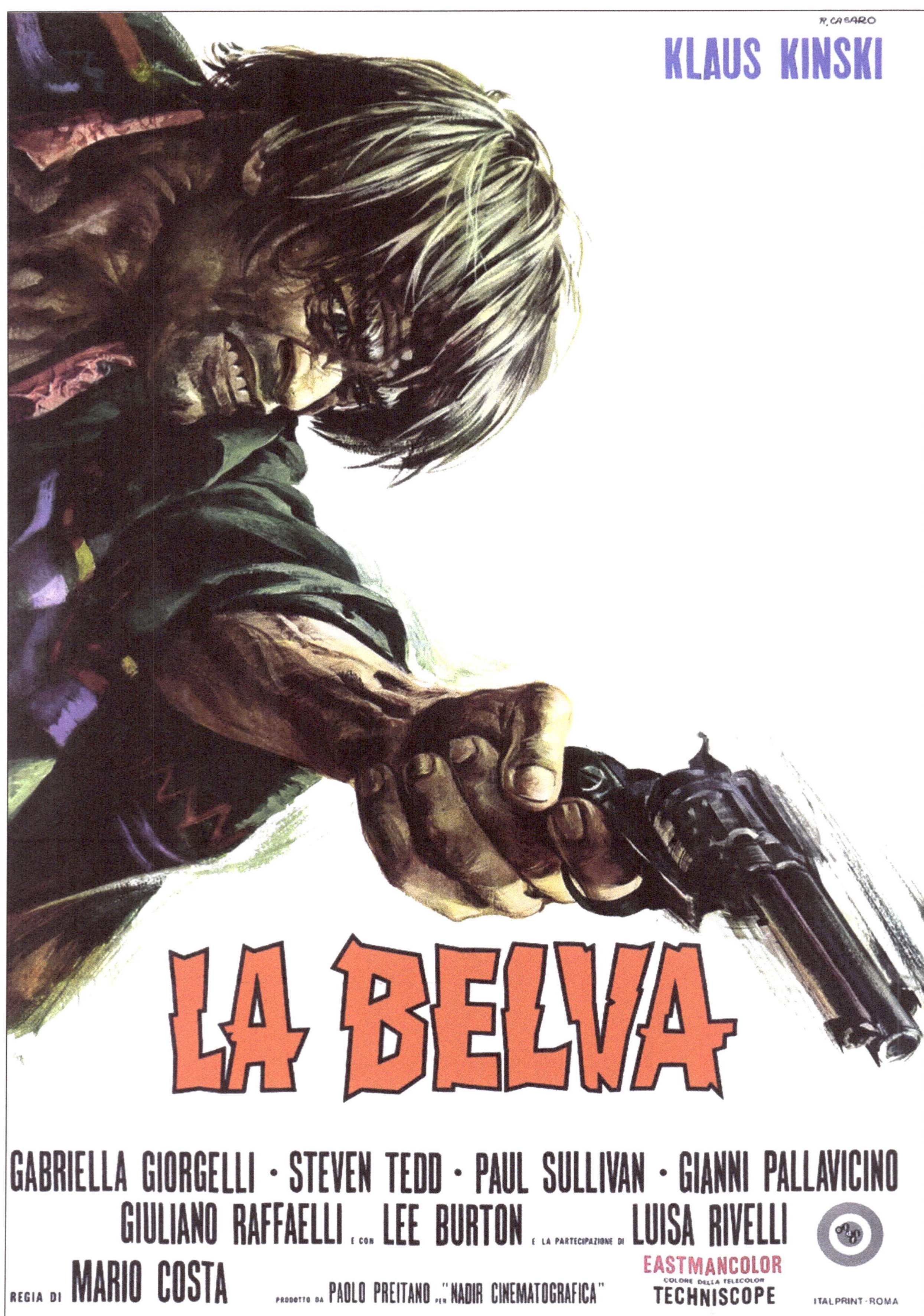

LA BELVA

("The Beast", 1970, Italy). Artist: Renato Casaro.

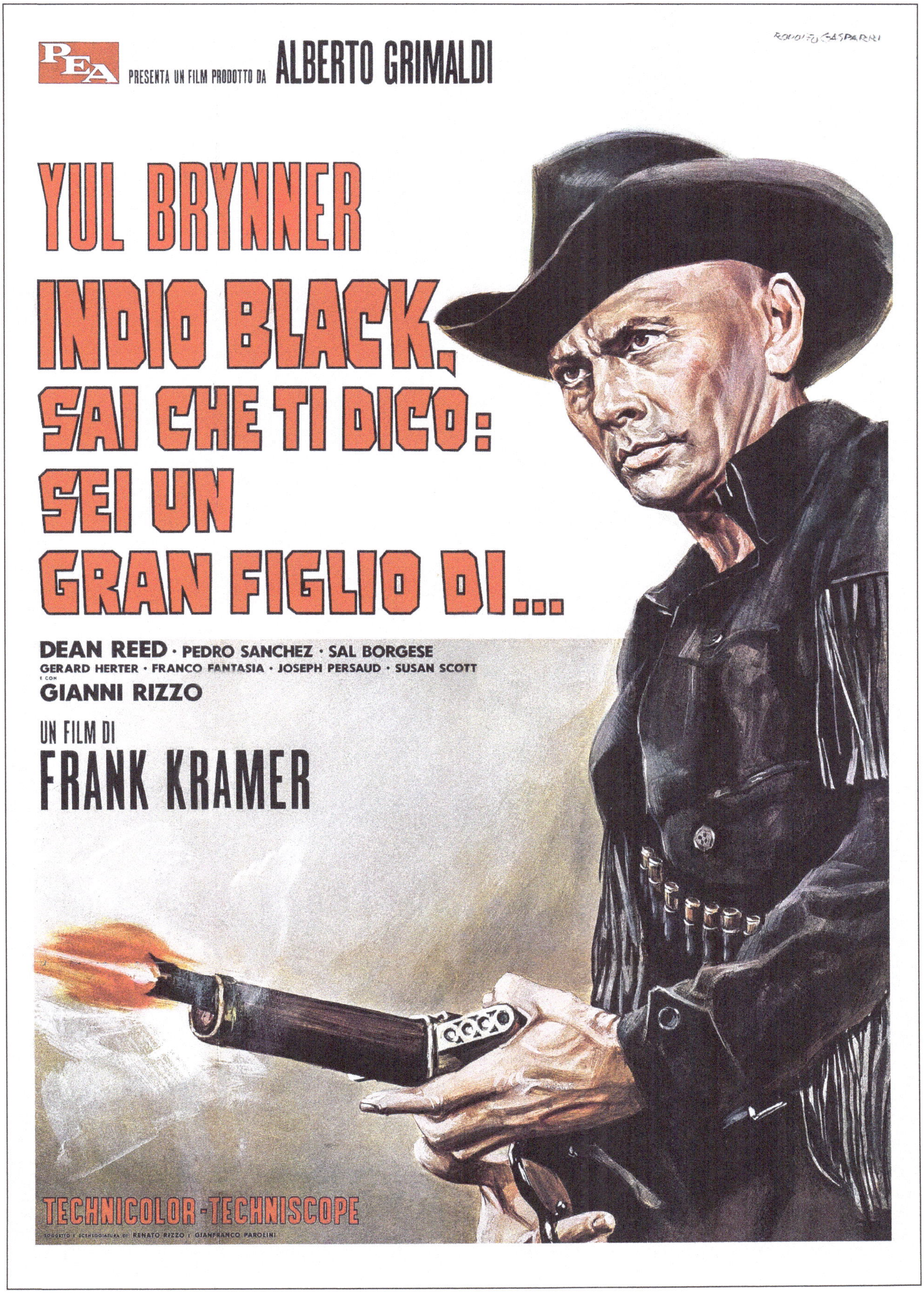

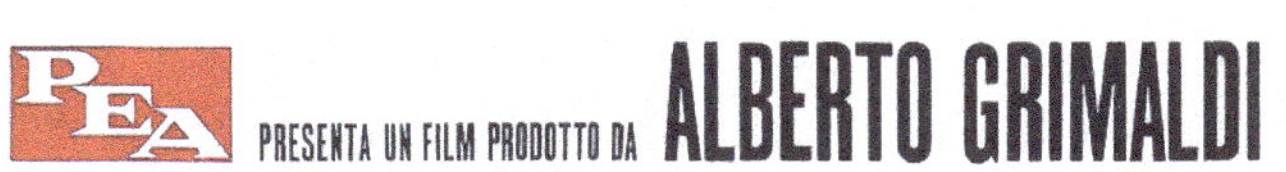

("Indio Black, Heed My Words: You're A Great Son Of...", 1970, Italy/Spain). Artist: Rodolfo Gasparri.

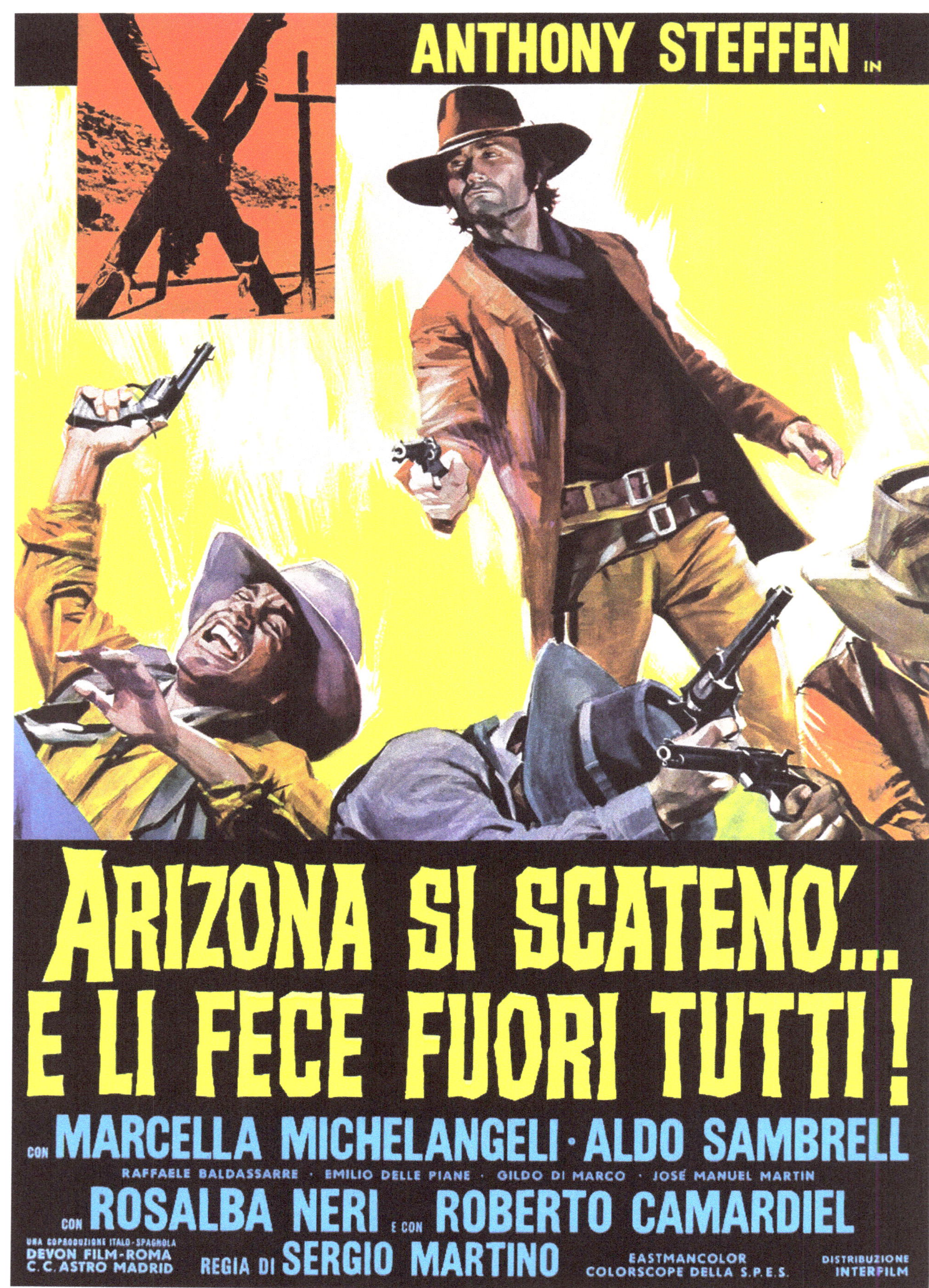

ARIZONA SI SCATENÒ... E LI FECE FUORI TUTTI!

(''Arizona Went Wild... And Killed Them All!'', 1970, Italy/Spain). Artist: unsigned.

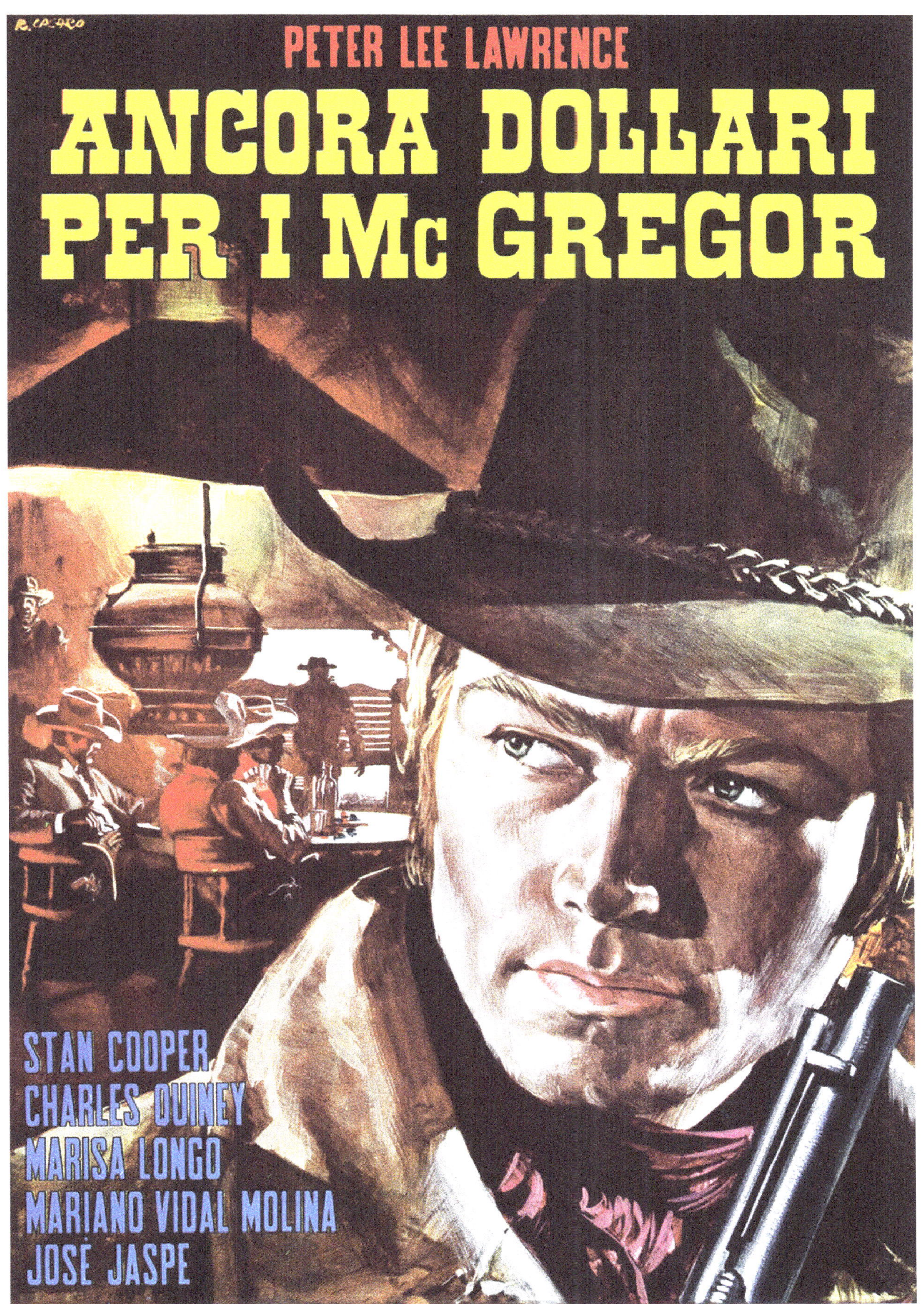

("More Dollars For The McGregors", 1970, Italy/Spain). Artist: Renato Casaro.

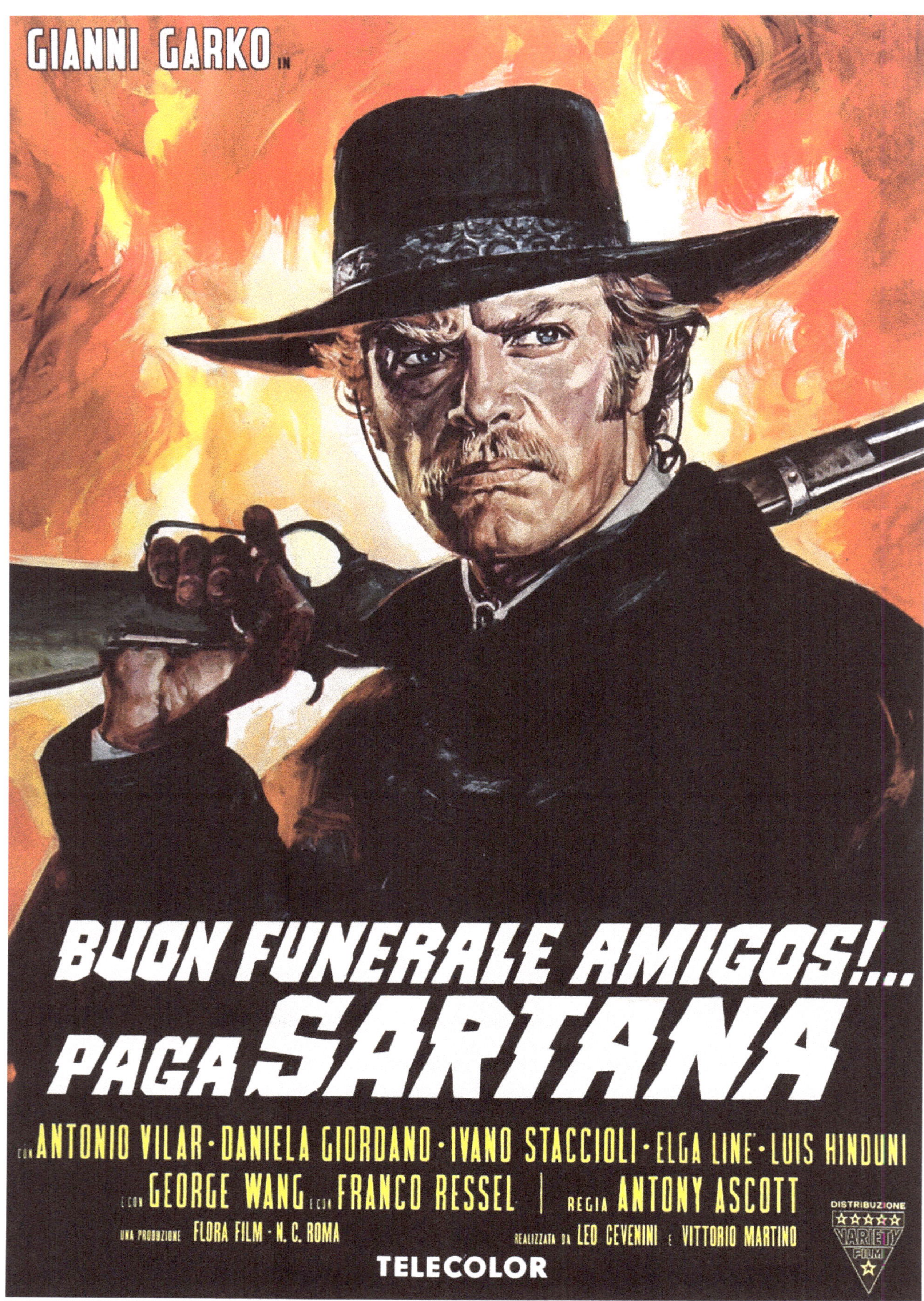

BUON FUNERALE AMIGOS!... PAGA SARTANA

(''Have A Good Funeral, Friends...Sartana Is Paying'', 1970, Italy/Spain). Artist: Renato Casaro.

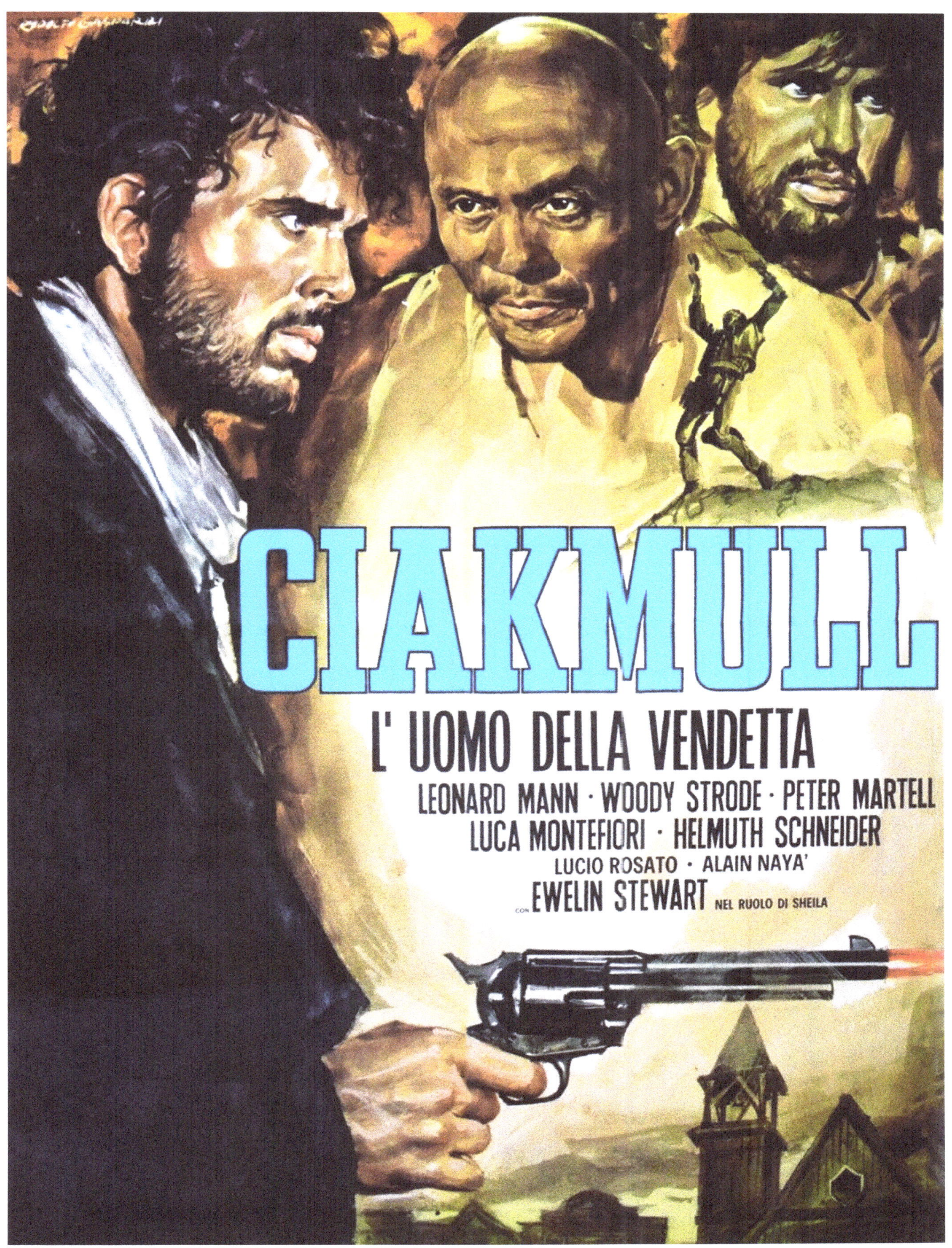

("Ciakmul , The Avenger", 1970, Italy). Artist: Rodolfo Gasparri.

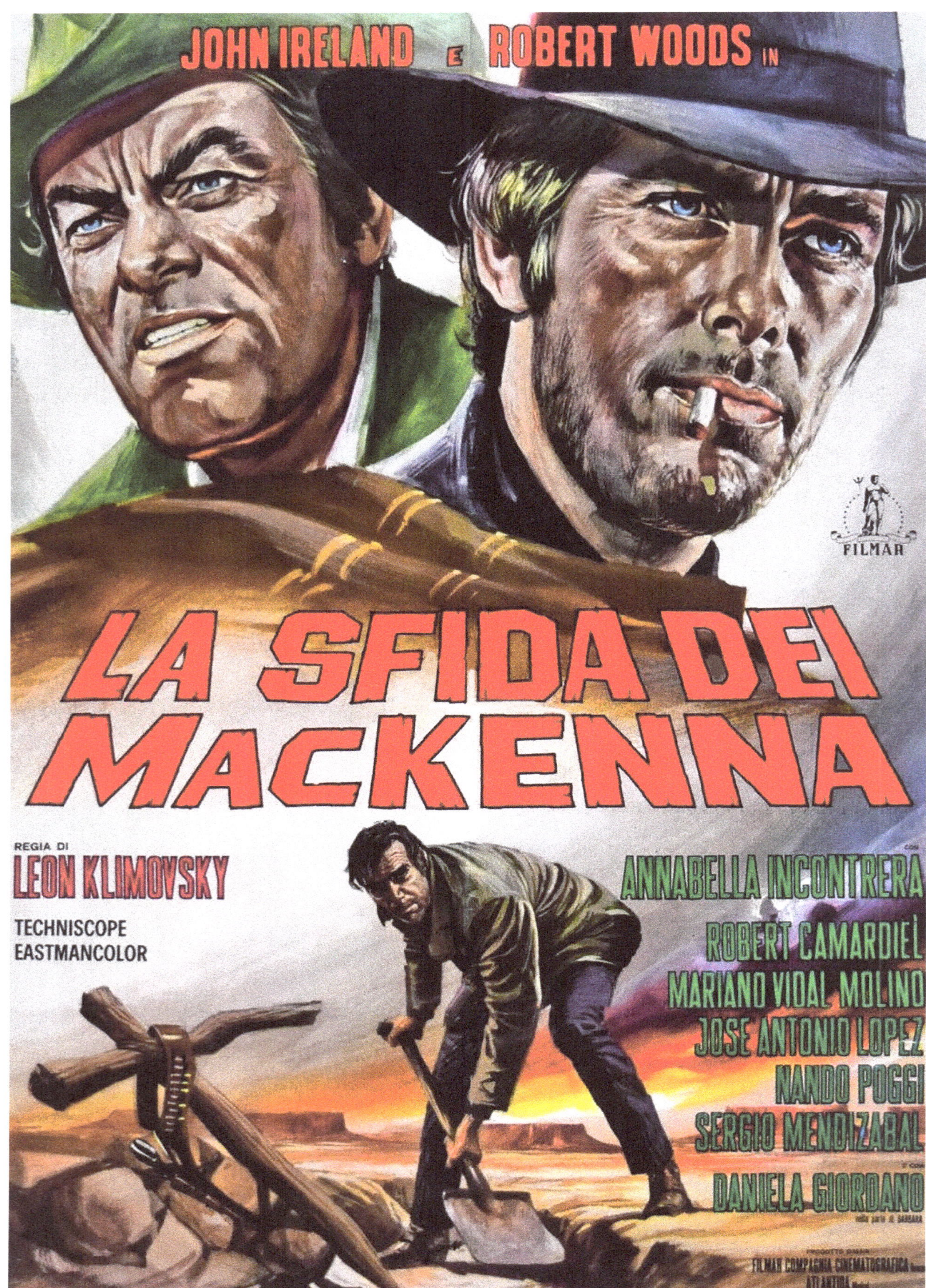

JOHN IRELAND E ROBERT WOODS in
FILMAR
LA SFIDA DEI MACKENNA
REGIA DI
LEON KLIMOVSKY
TECHNISCOPE
EASTMANCOLOR
ANNABELLA INCONTRERA
ROBERT CAMARDIEL
MARIANO VIDAL MOLINO
JOSE ANTONIO LOPEZ
NANDO POGGI
SERGIO MENDIZABAL
DANIELA GIORDANO
FILMAR COMPAGNIA CINEMATOGRAFICA
ATLANTIDA

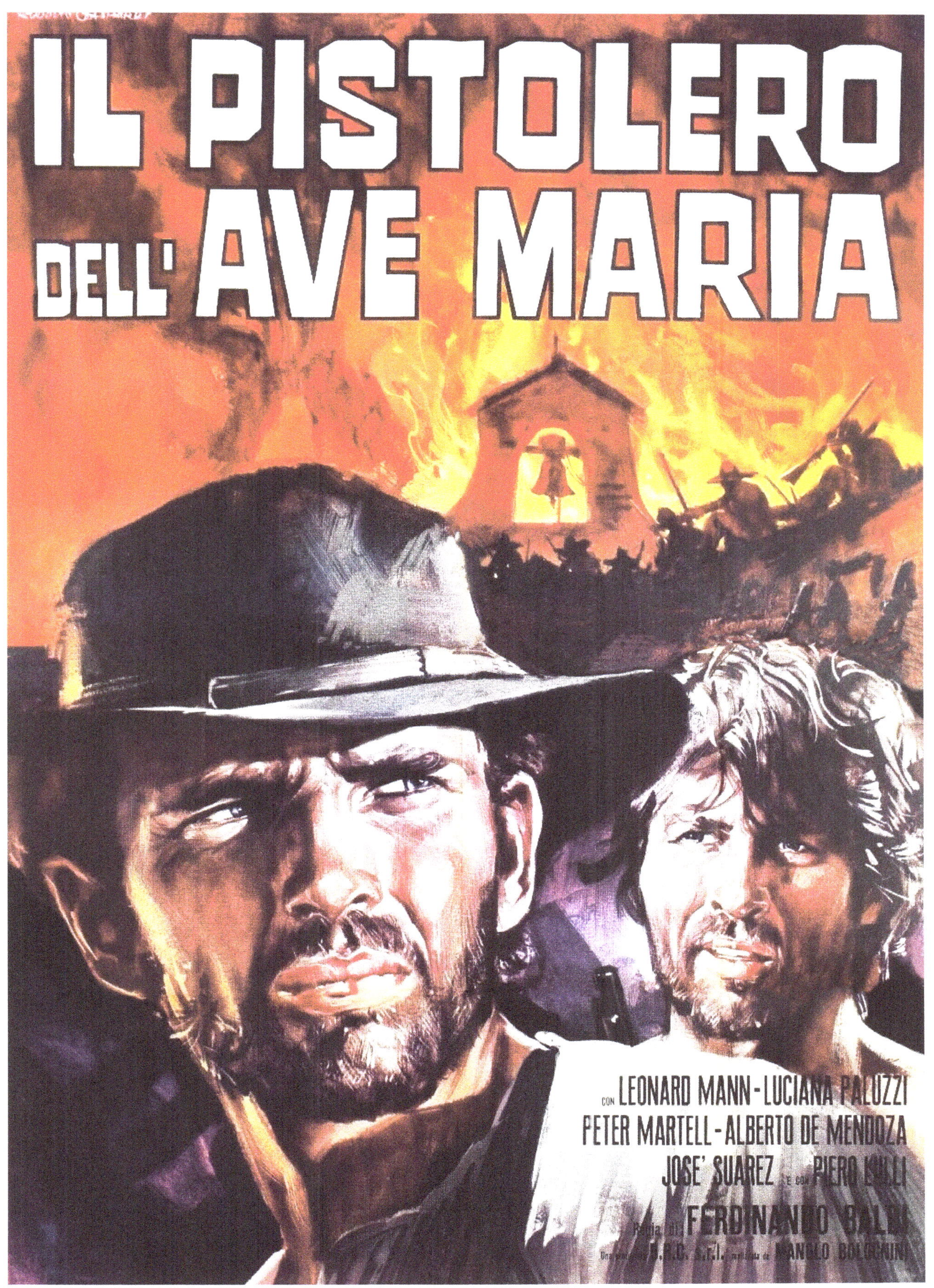

IL PISTOLERO DELL'AVE MARIA

("The Gunslinger Of Ave Maria", 1969, Italy/Spain). Artist: Rodolfo Gasparri.

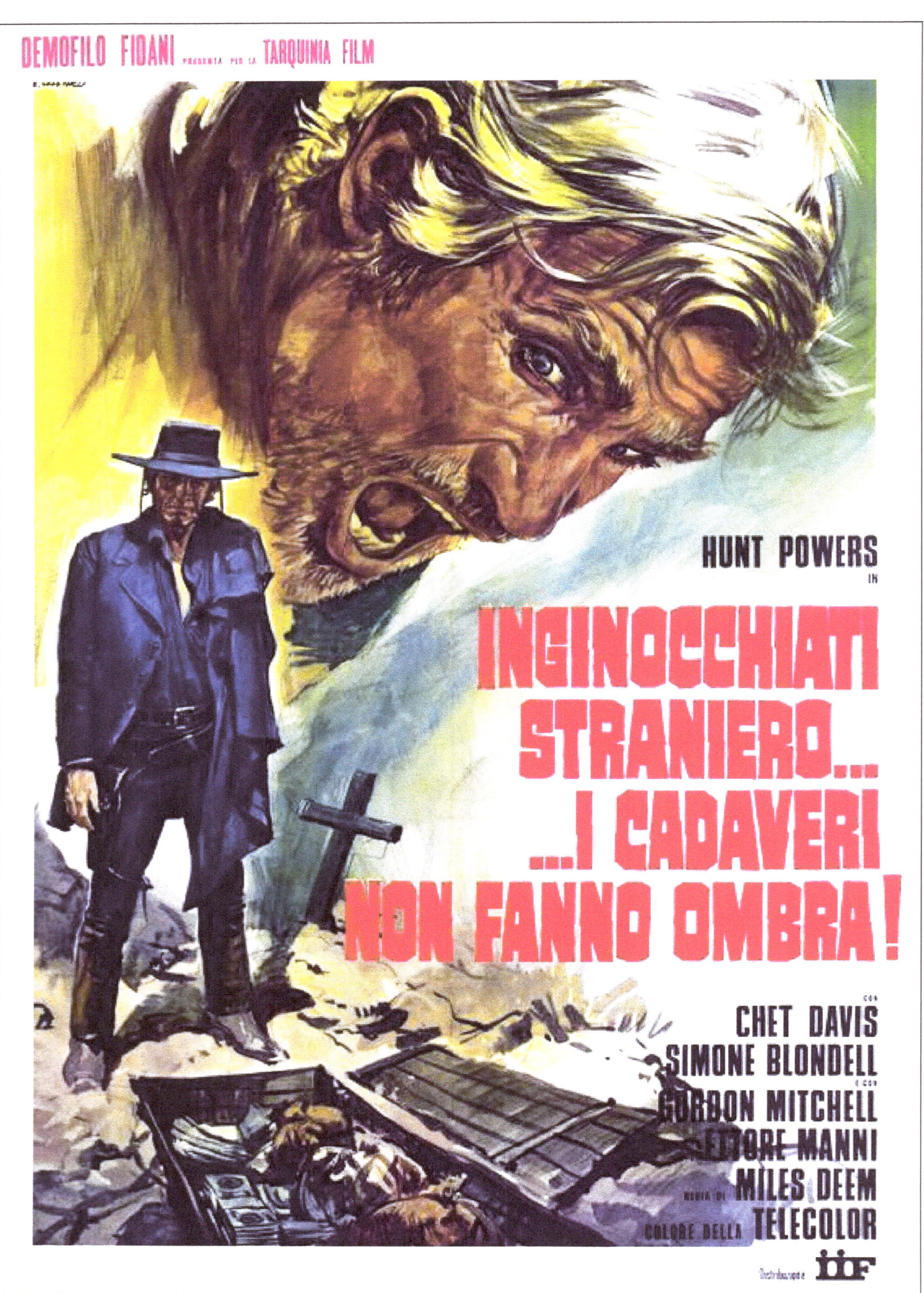

INGINOCCHIATI STRANIERO... I CADAVERI NON FANNO OMBRA!

(''On Your Knees, Stranger... Corpses Cast No Shadow!'', 1970, Italy). Artist: Renato Casaro.

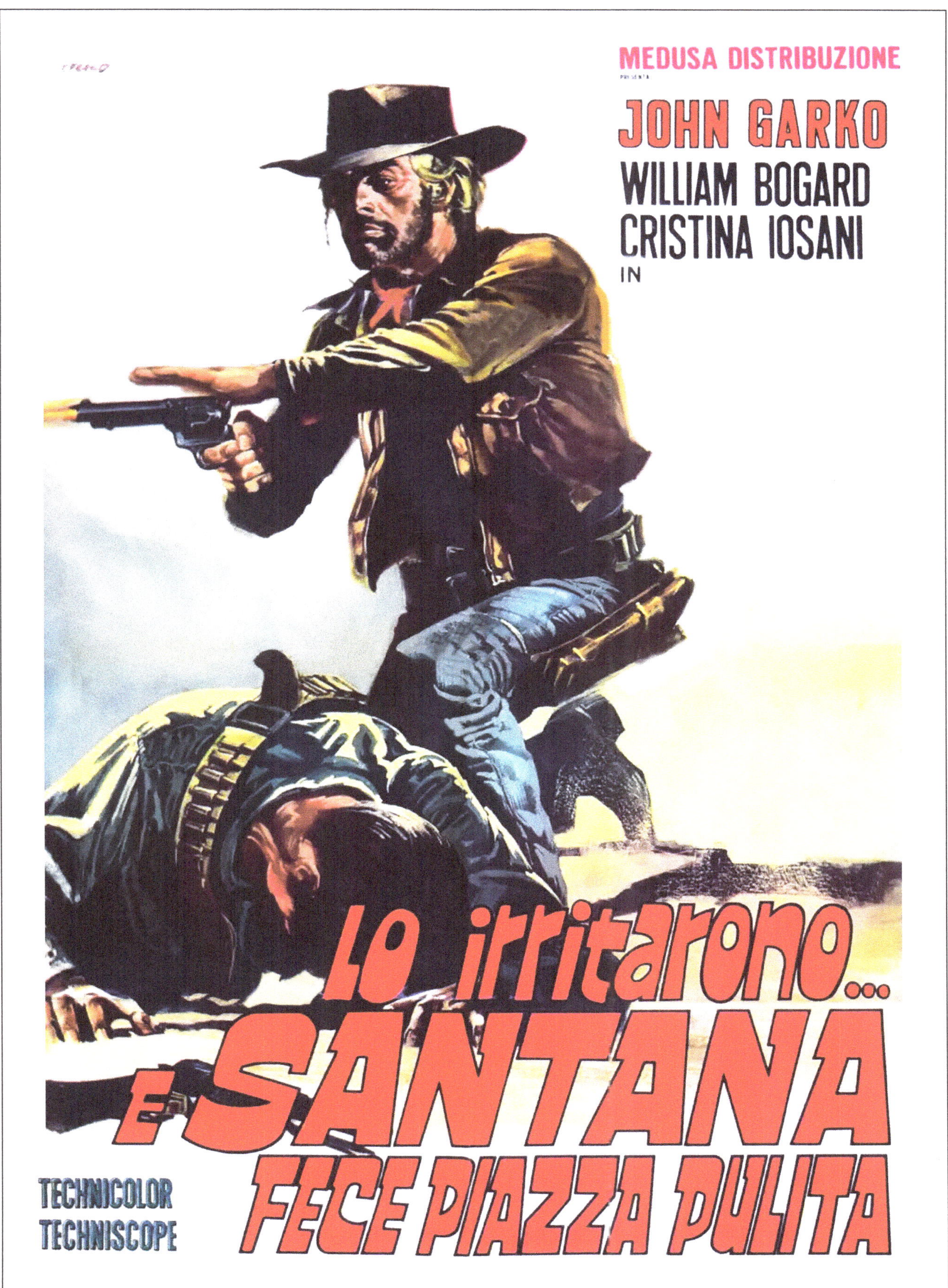

LO IRRITARONO... E SANTANA FECE PIAZZA PULITA

("They Annoyed Him... And Santana Wiped Them Out", 1970, Italy/Spain). Artist: P. Franco.

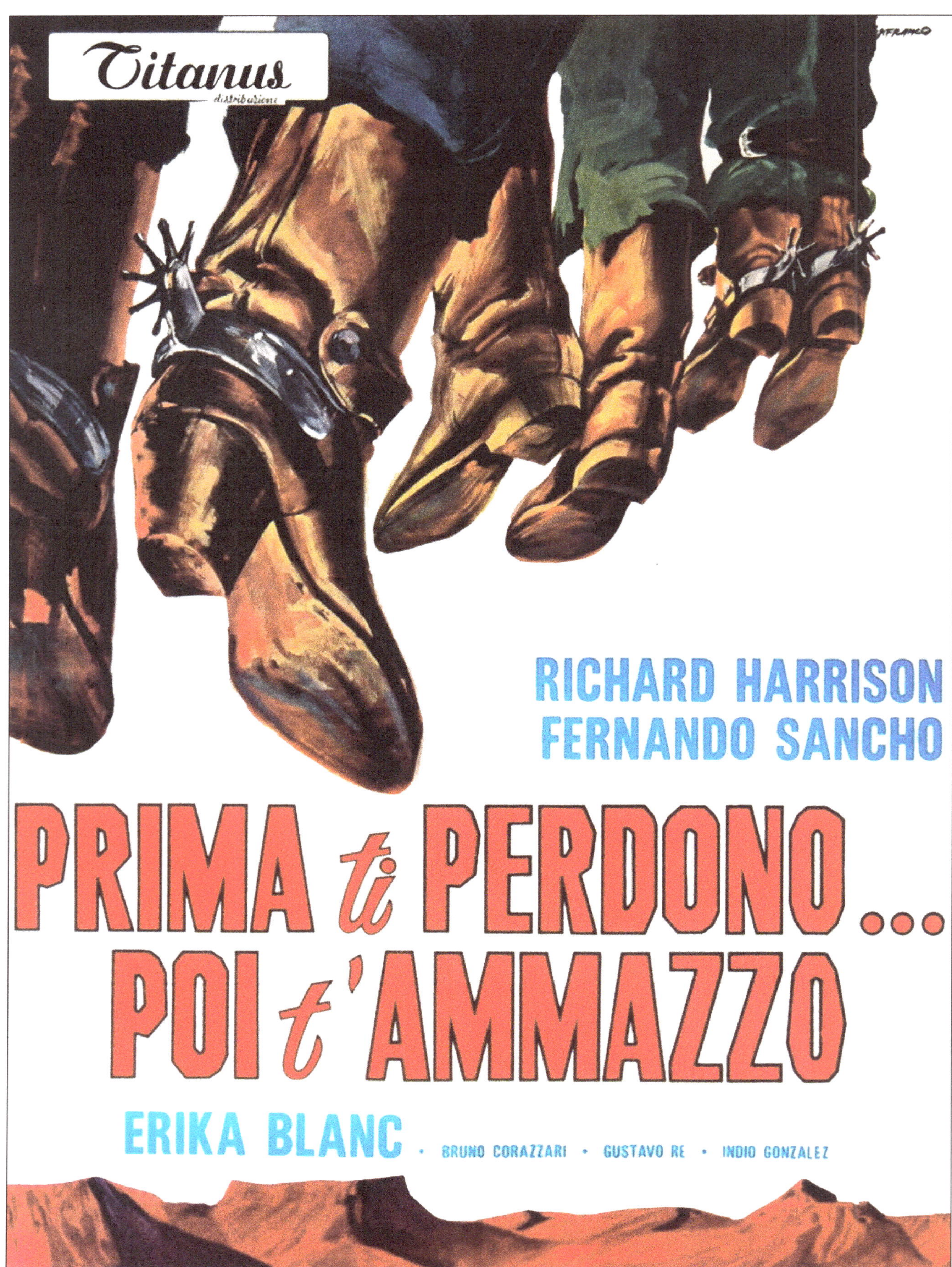

PRIMA TI PERDONO... POI T'AMMAZZO

("First I Forgive You... Then I Kill You", 1970, Italy/Spain). Artist: P. Franco.

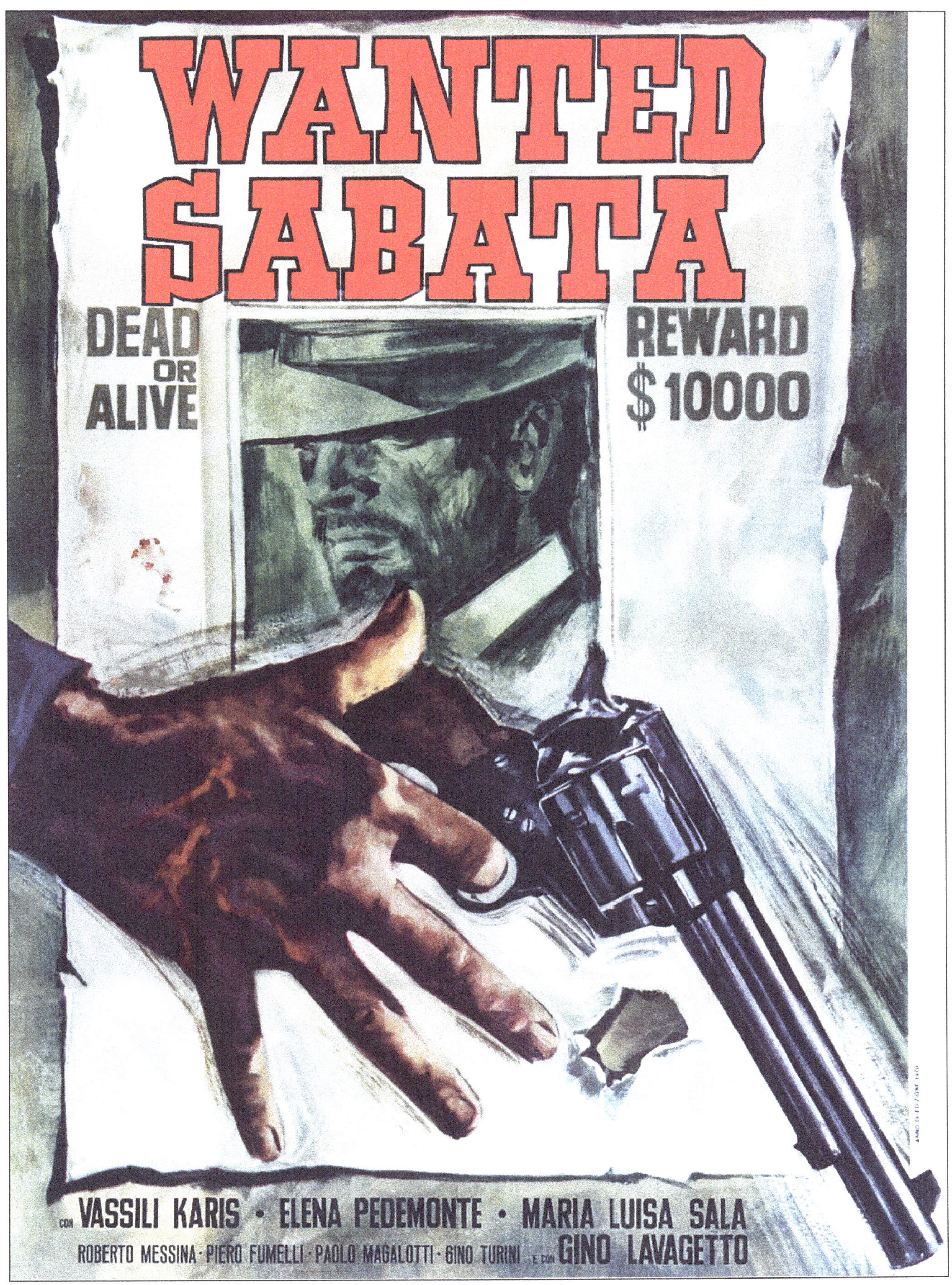

("Wanted: Sabata", 1970, Italy). Artist: unsigned.

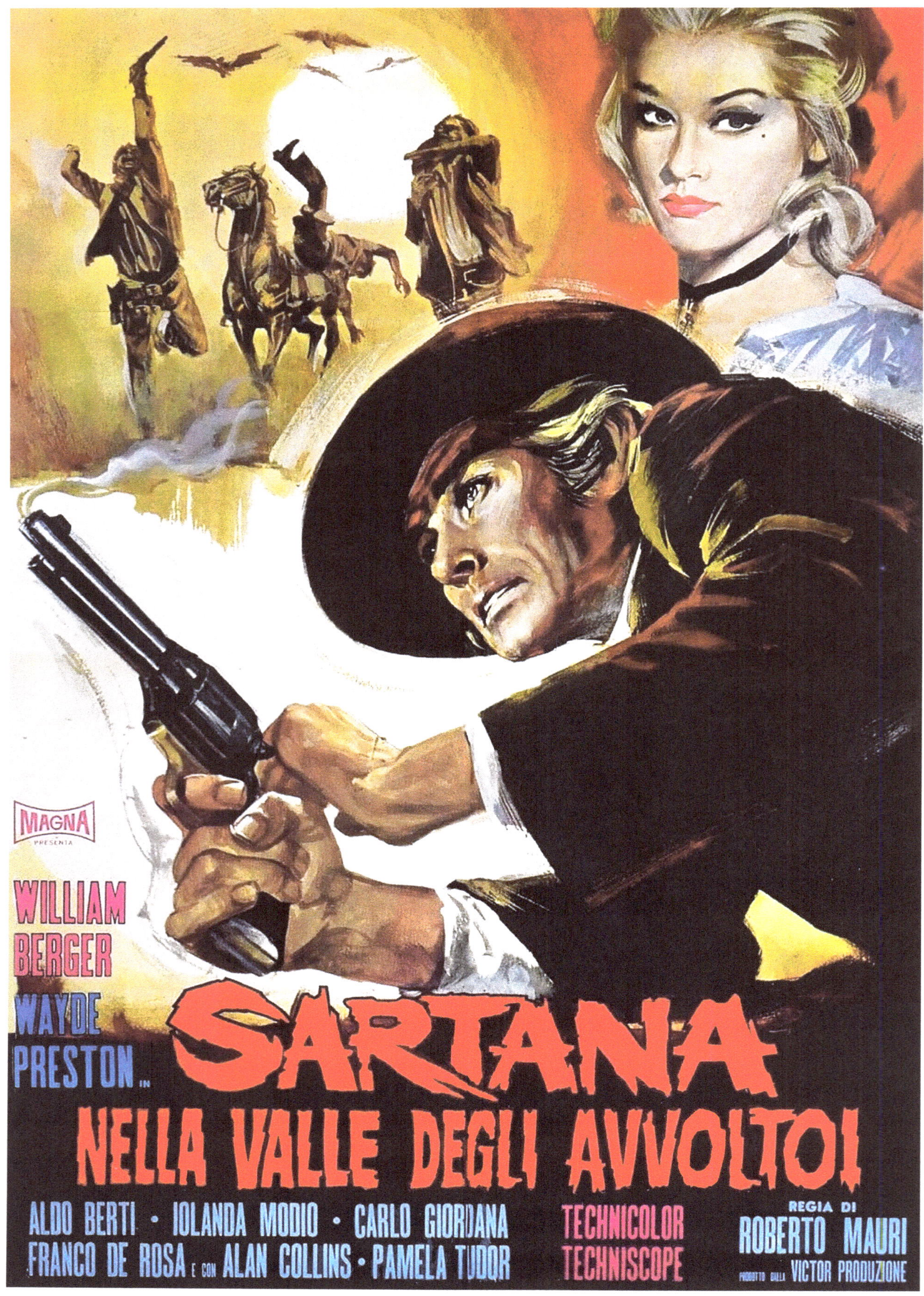

SARTANA NELLA VALLE DEGLI AVVOLTOI

("Sartana In The Valley Of Vultures", 1970, Italy). Artist: unsigned.

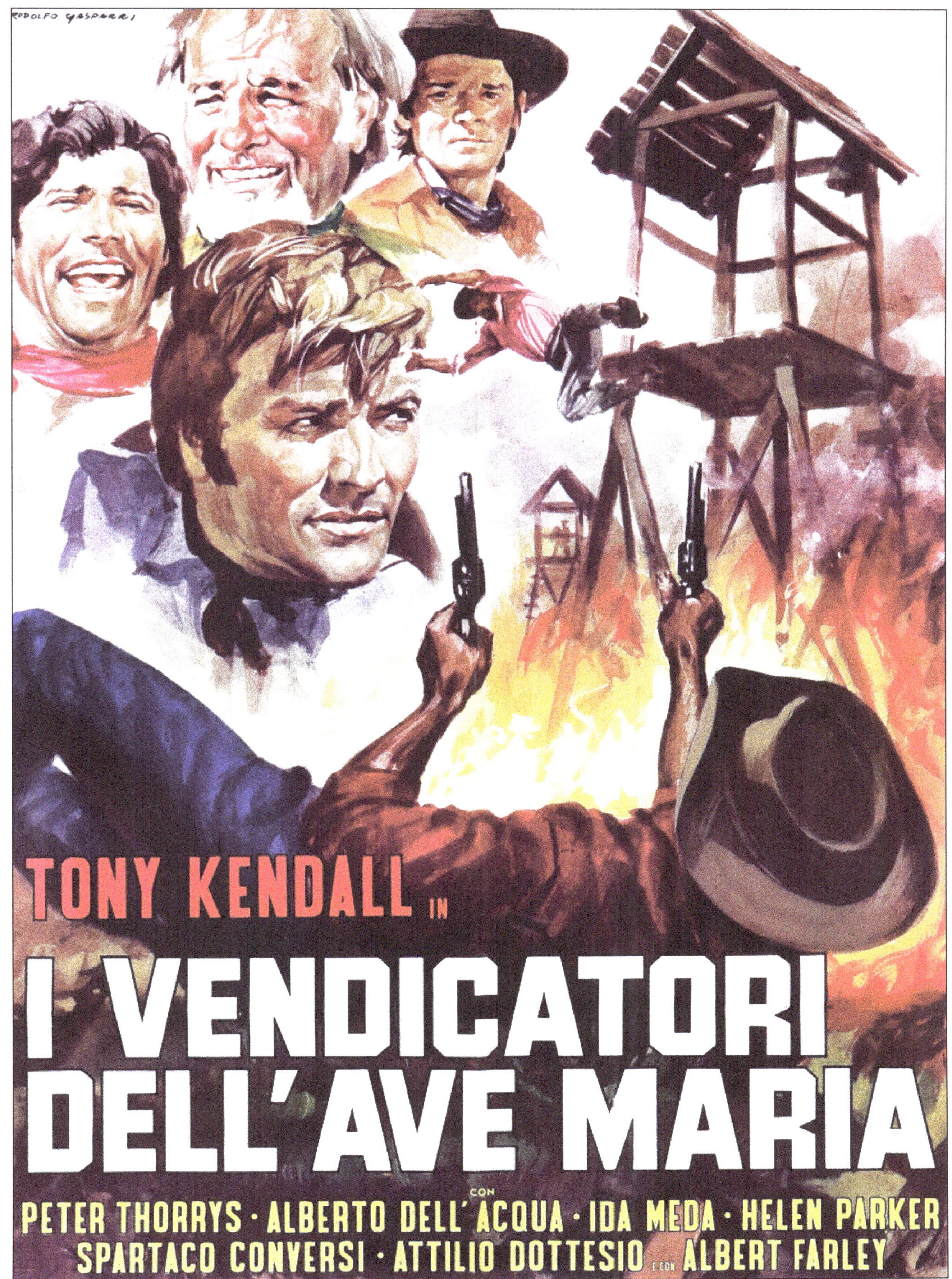

("The Avengers Of Ave Maria", 1970, Italy). Artist: Rodolfo Gasparri.

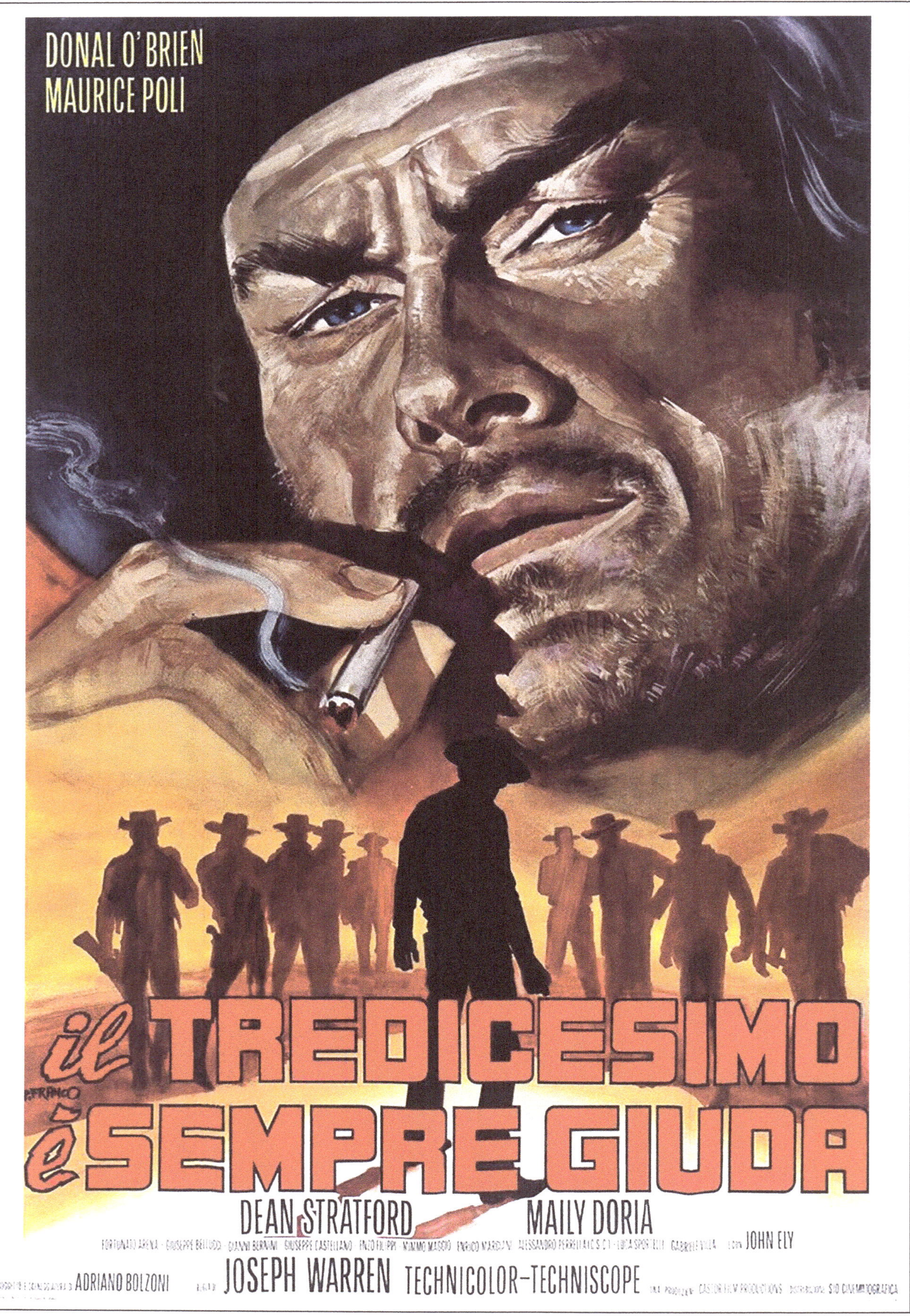

("The Thirteenth Is Always Judas", 1971, Italy). Artist: P. Franco.

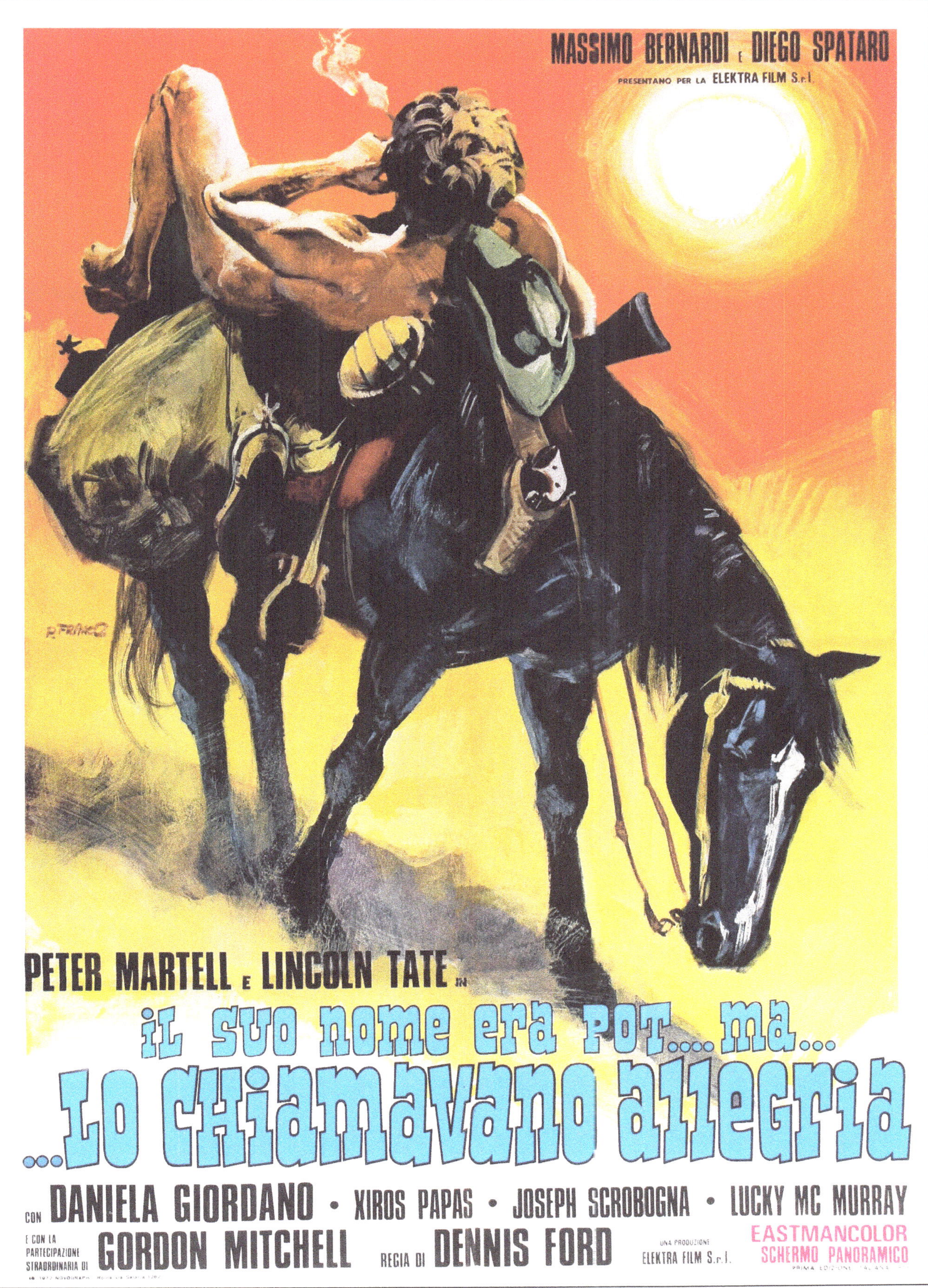

("His Name Was Pot... But They Called Him Allegria", 1971, Italy). Artist: P. Franco.

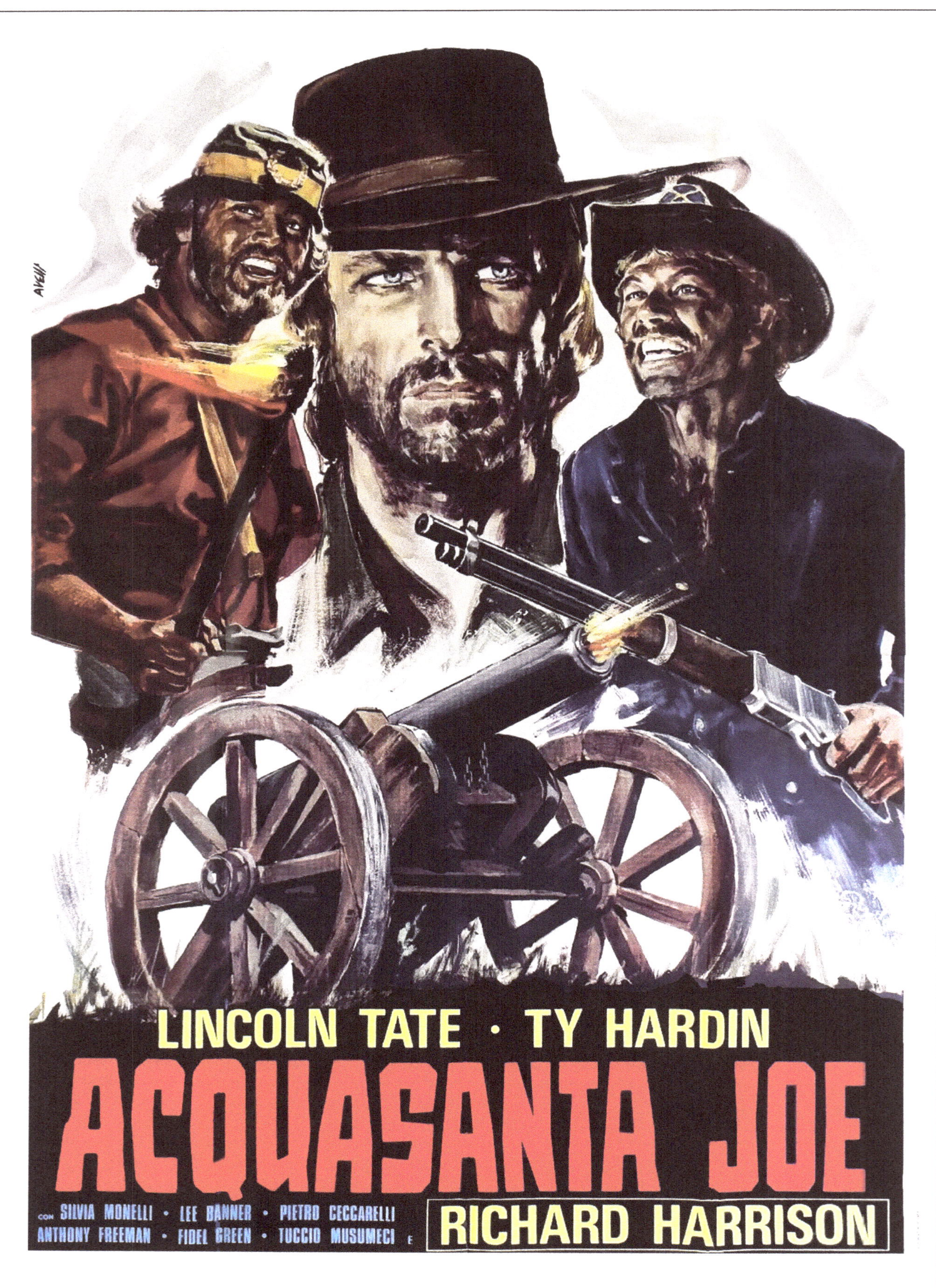

(''Holy Water Joe'', 1971, Italy). Artist: Tino Avelli.

80

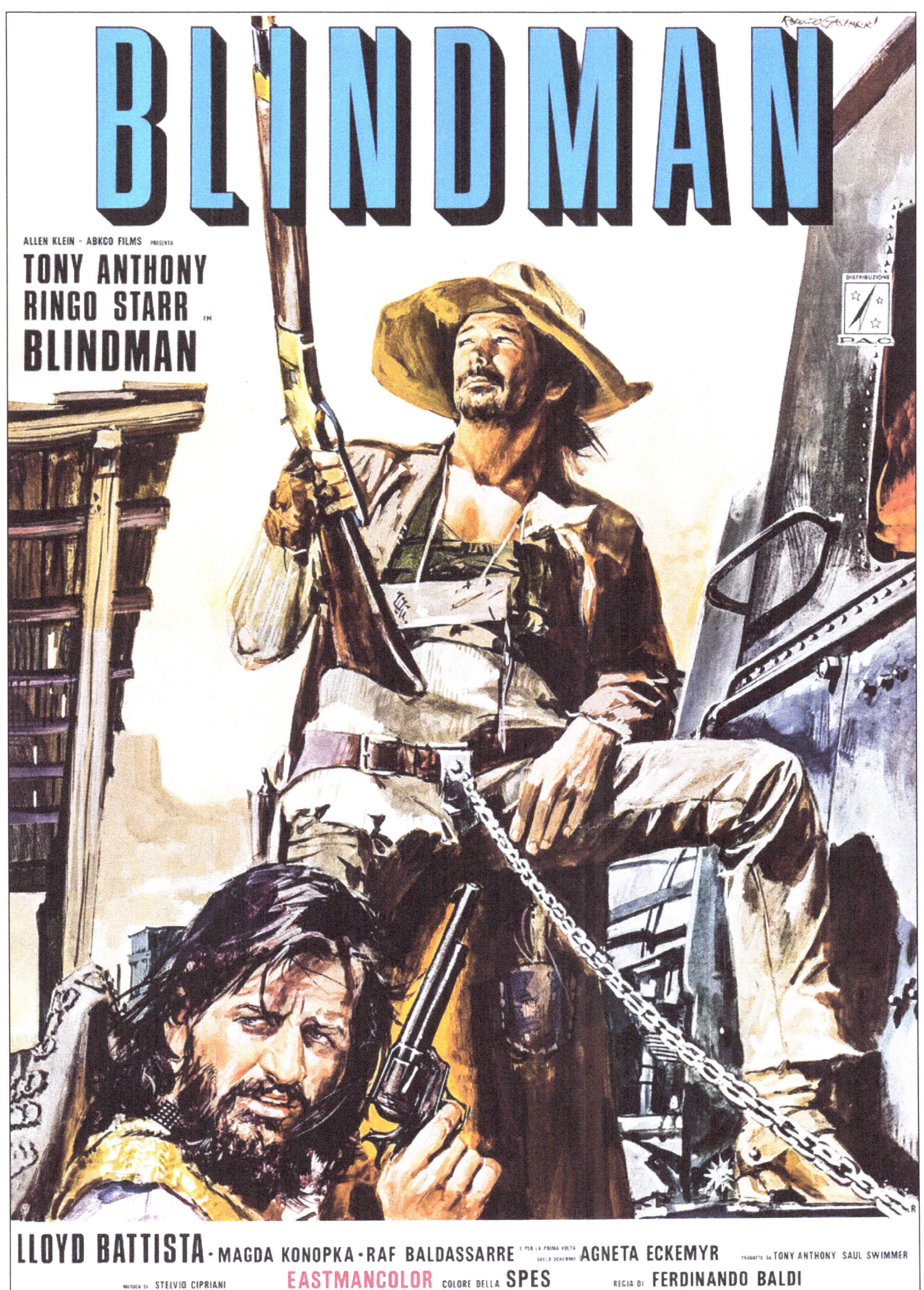

("Blindman", 1971, Italy/USA). Artist: Rodolfo Gasparri.

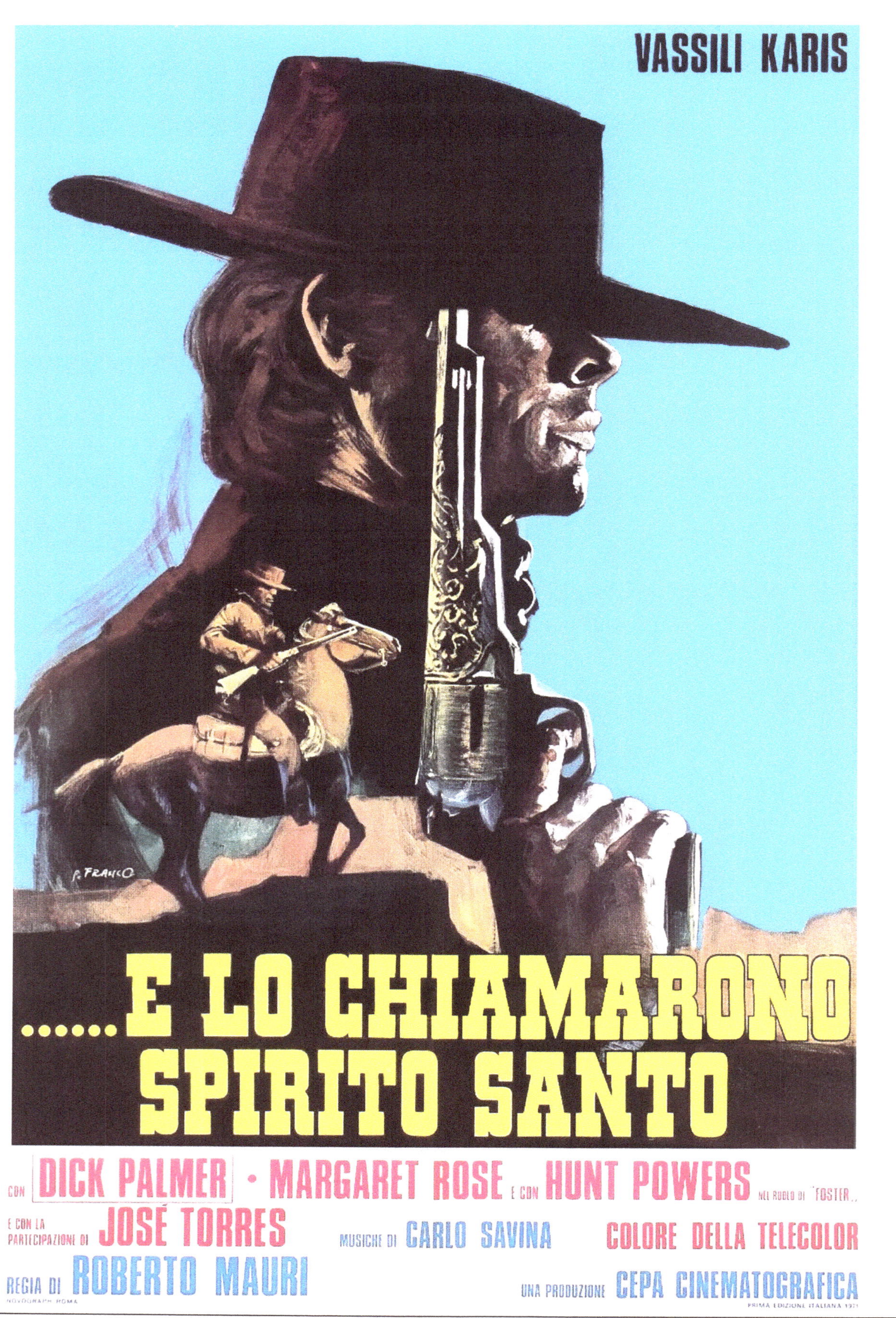

("... And They Called Him Holy Ghost", 1971, Italy). Artist: P. Franco.

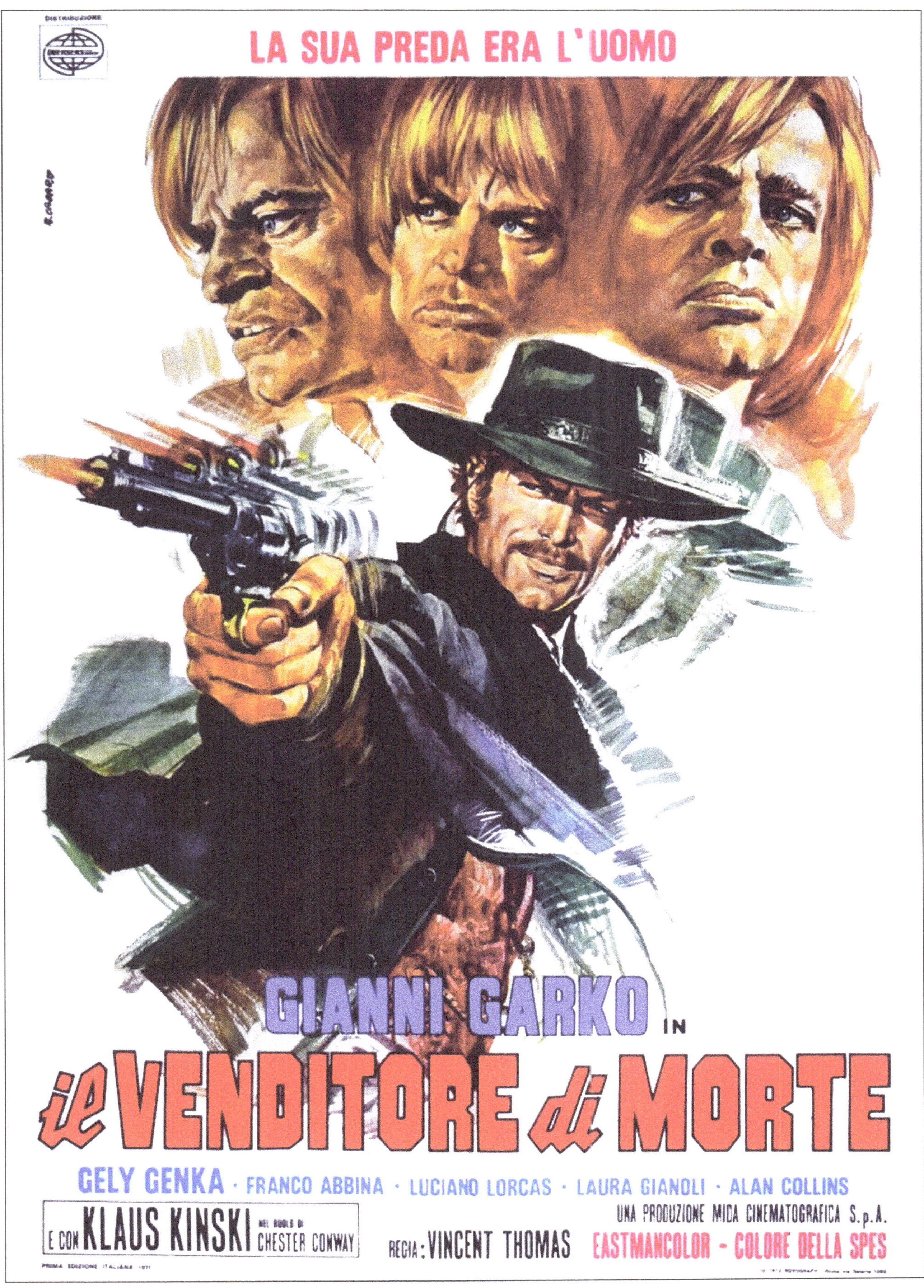

("The Merchant Of Death", 1971, Italy). Artist: Renato Casaro.

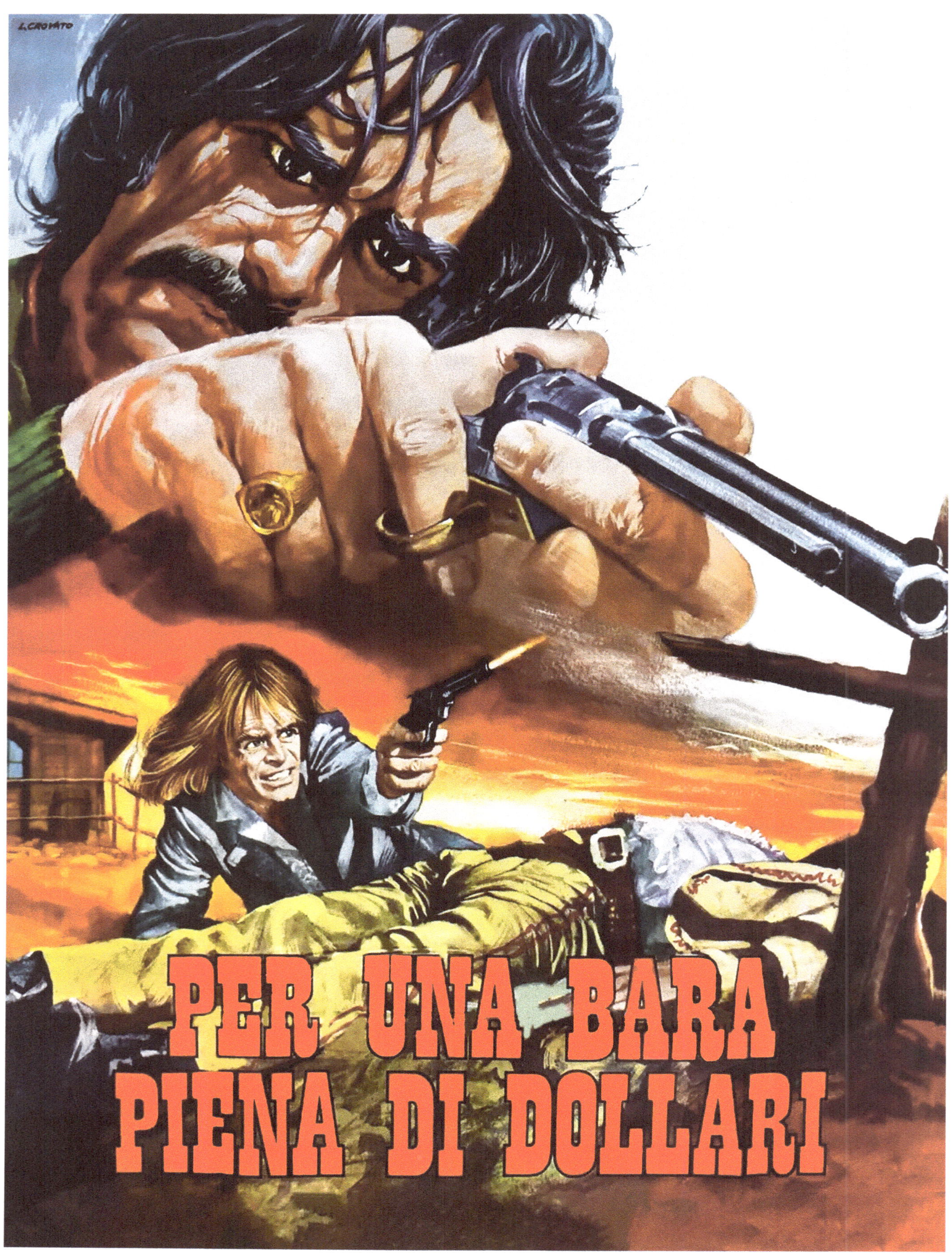

PER UNA BARA PIENA DI DOLLARI

(''For A Coffinful Of Dollars'', 1971, Italy). Artist: Luca Crovato.

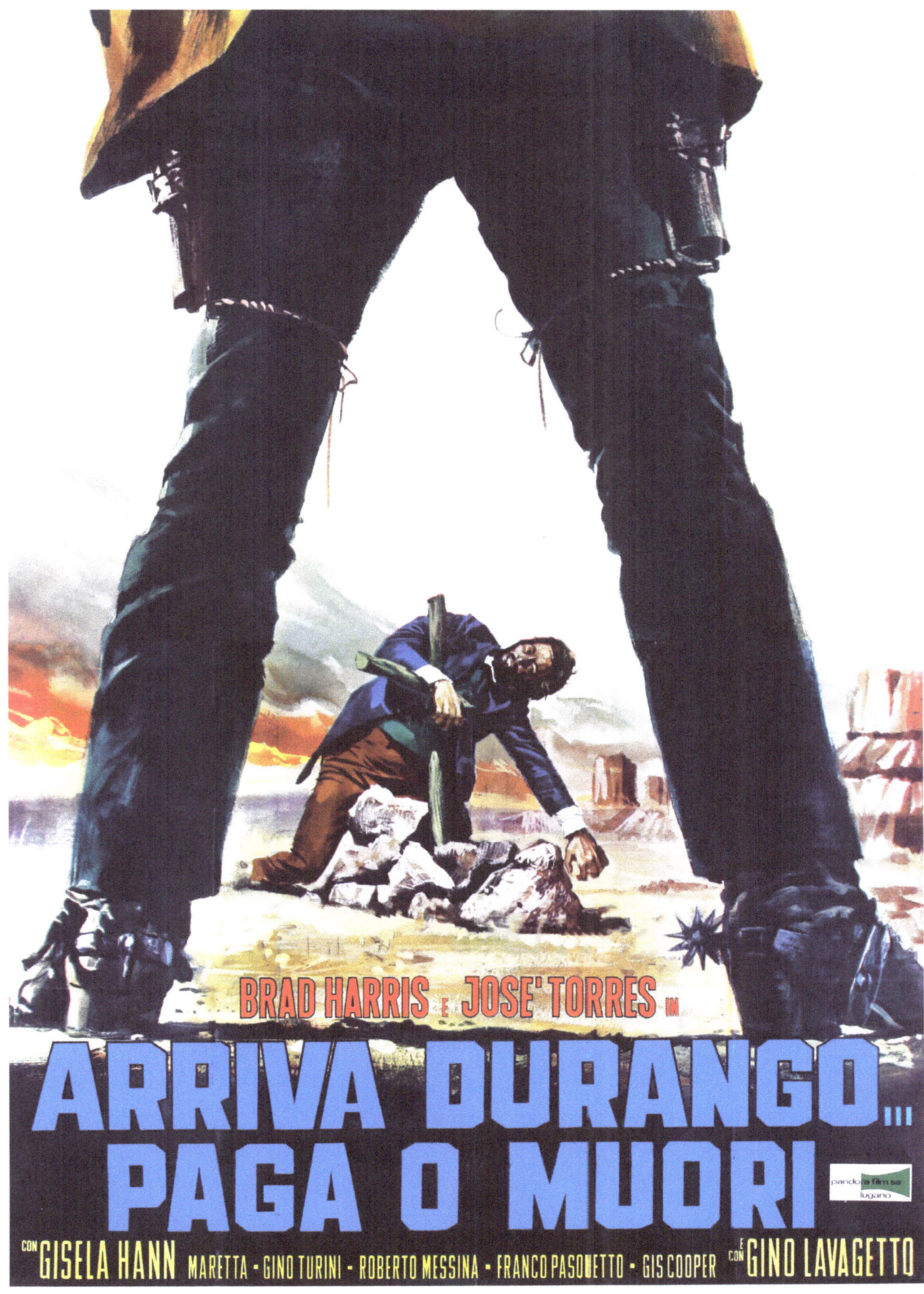

("Durango Is Coming... Pay Up Or Die", 1971, Italy). Artist: unsigned.

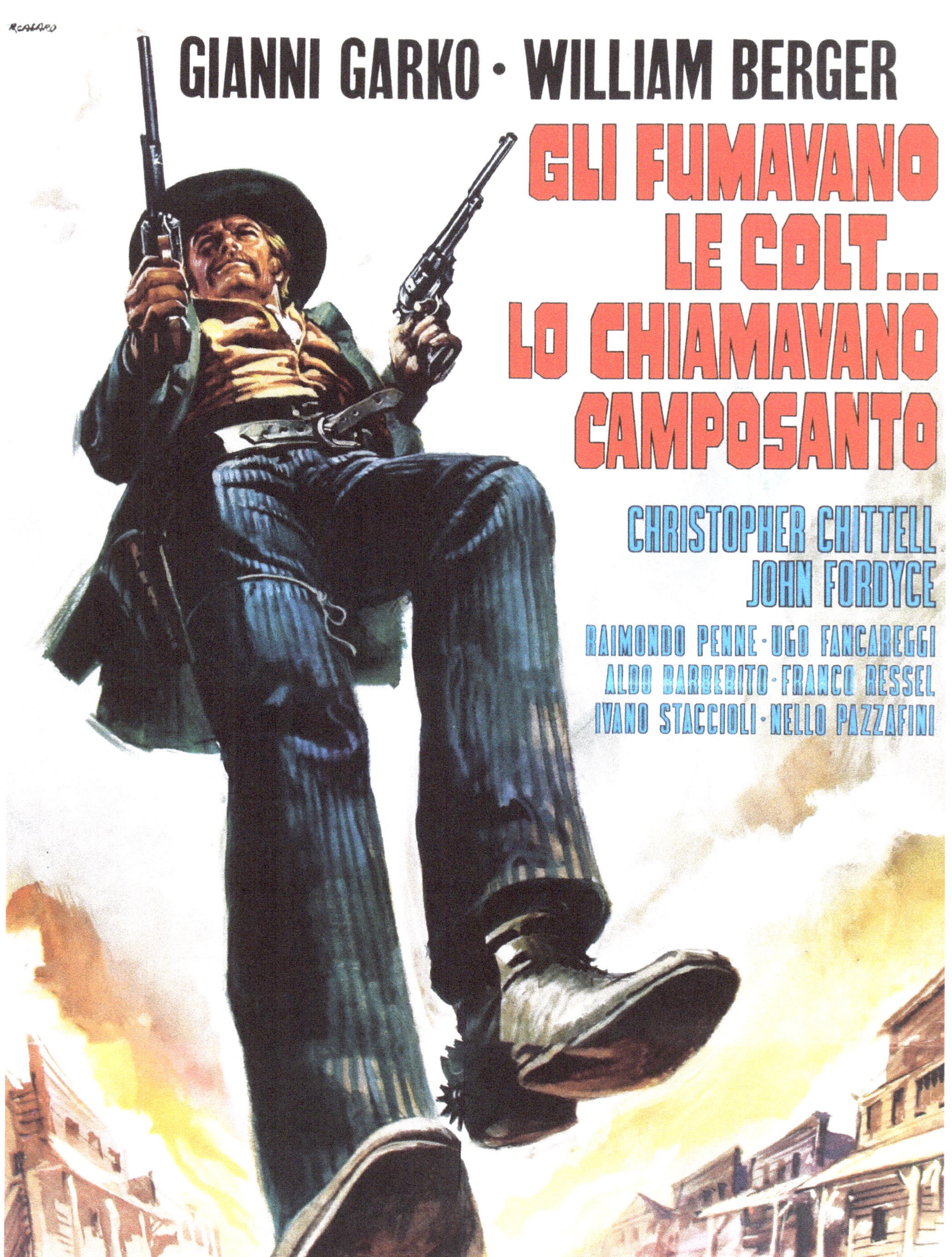

GLI FUMAVANO LE COLT... LO CHIAMAVANO CAMPOSANTO

("His Pistols Smoked... They Called Him Graveyard", 1971, Italy). Artist: Renato Casaro.

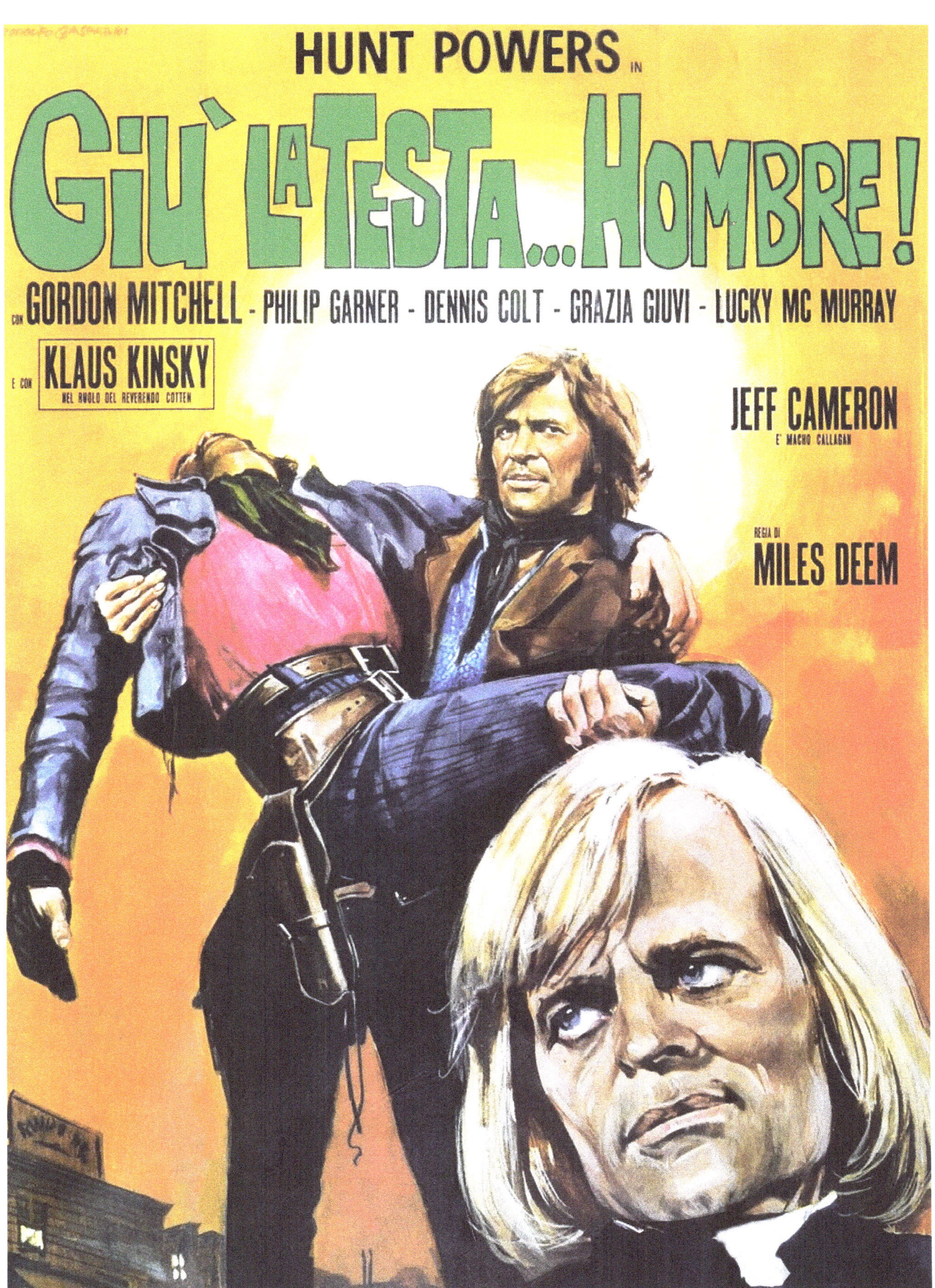

HUNT POWERS IN
GIÙ LA TESTA... HOMBRE!
CON GORDON MITCHELL - PHILIP GARNER - DENNIS COLT - GRAZIA GIUVI - LUCKY MC MURRAY
E CON KLAUS KINSKY
NEL RUOLO DEL REVERENDO COTTEN
JEFF CAMERON
E' MACHO CALLAGAN
REGIA DI
MILES DEEM

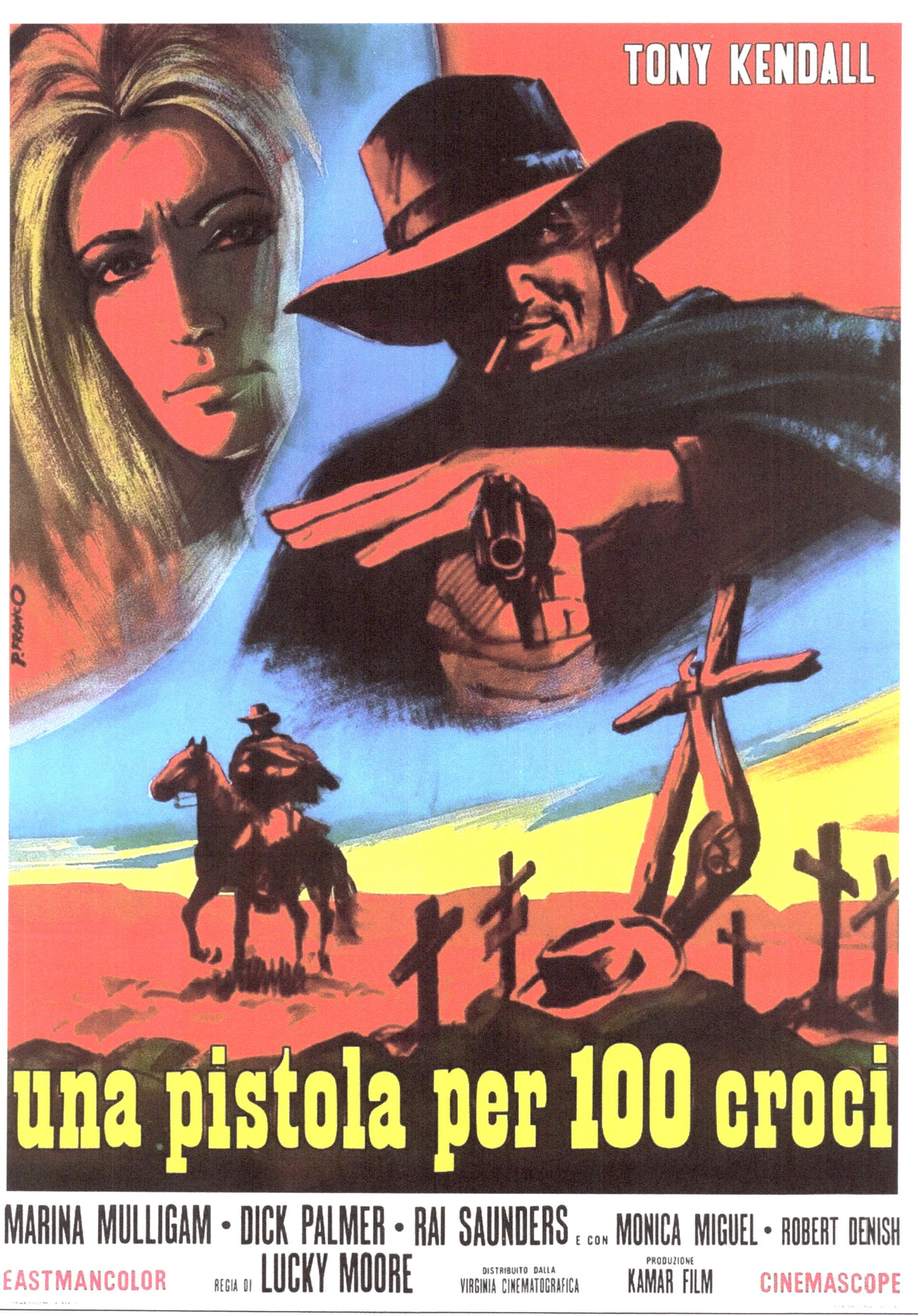

UNA PISTOLA PER 100 CROCI

(''One Gun For 100 Graves'', 1971, Italy). Artist: P. Franco.

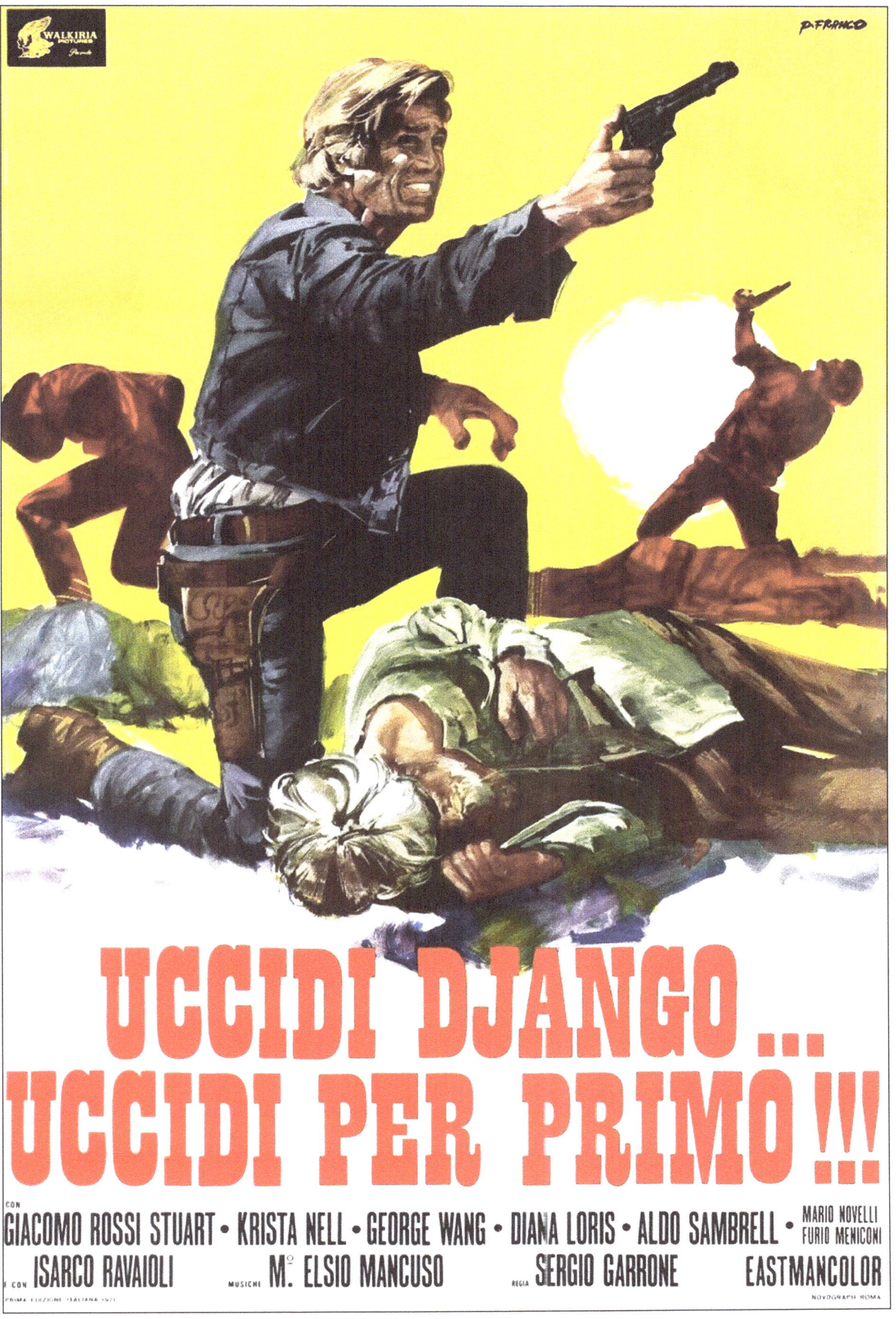

("Kill, Django... Kill First!!!", 1971, Italy). Artist: P. Franco.

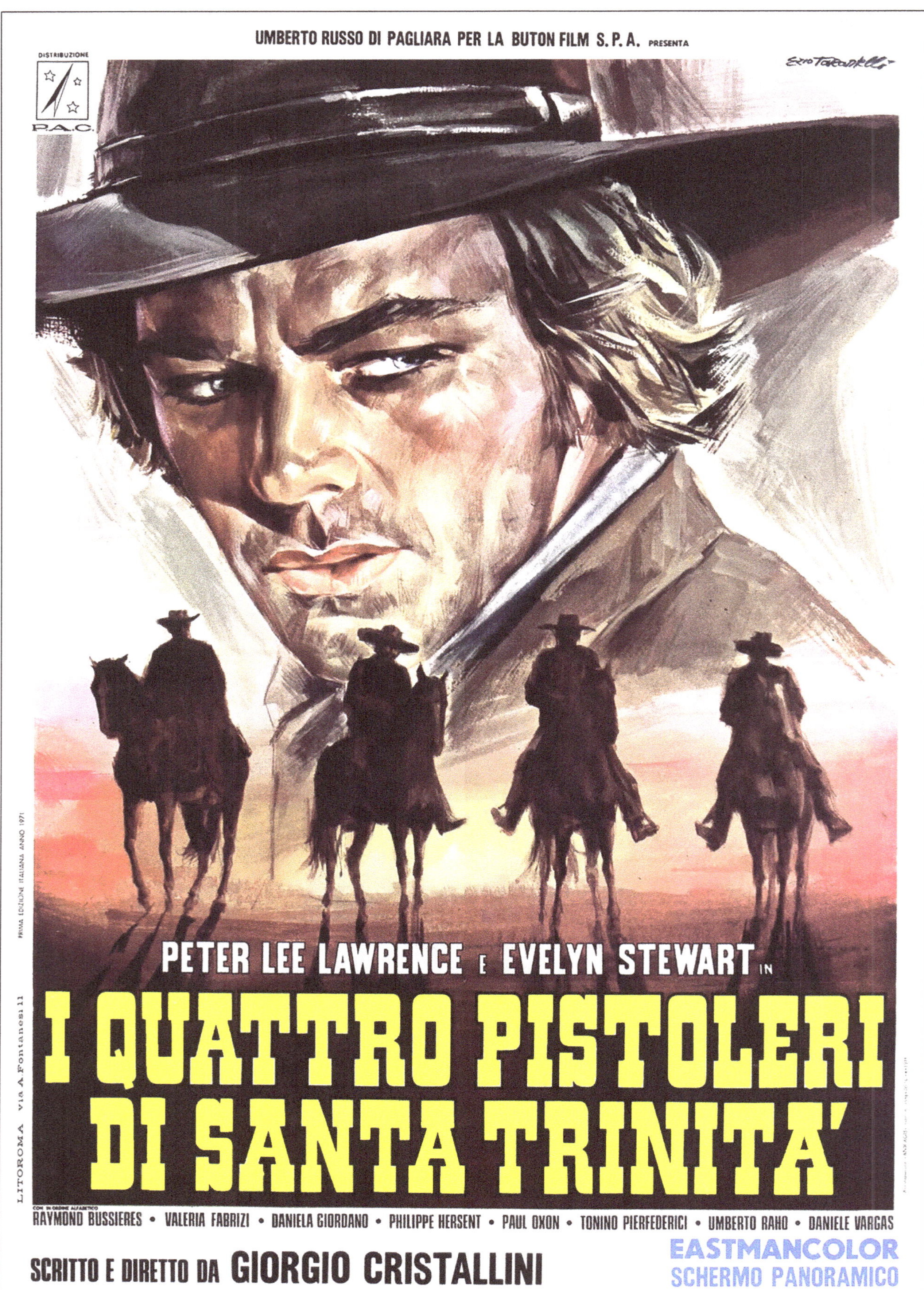

I QUATTRO PISTOLERI DI SANTA TRINITÁ

(''The Four Gunmen Of The Holy Trinity'', 1971, Italy). Artist: Ezio Tarantelli.

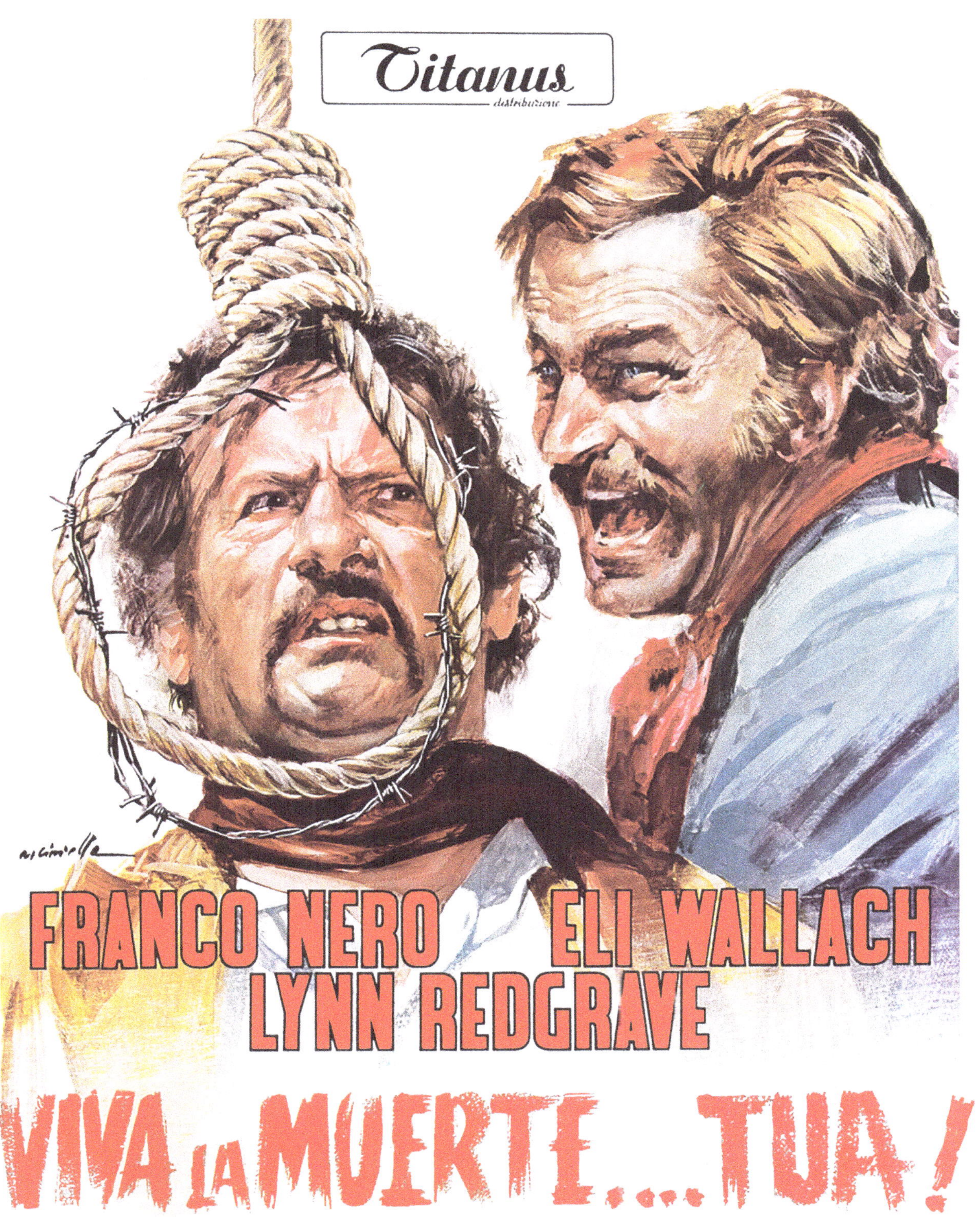

("Long Live Death... Yours!", 1971, Italy/Spain/Germany). Artist: Averardo Ciriello.

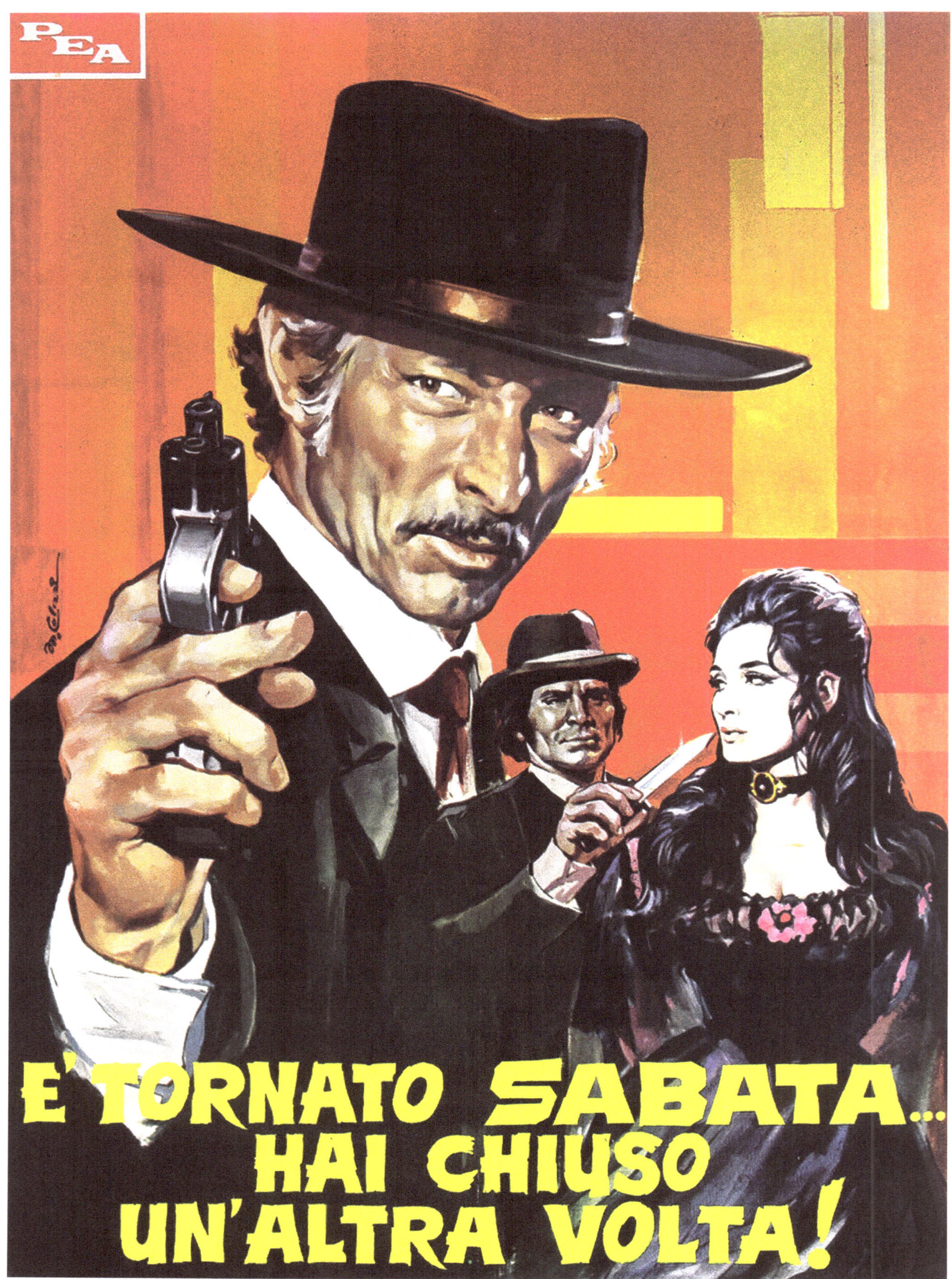

È TORNATO SABATA... HAI CHIUSO UN'ALTRA VOLTA!

("Sabata Is Back... You're Finished Again!", 1971, Italy/Germany/France). Artist: Mauro Colizzi.

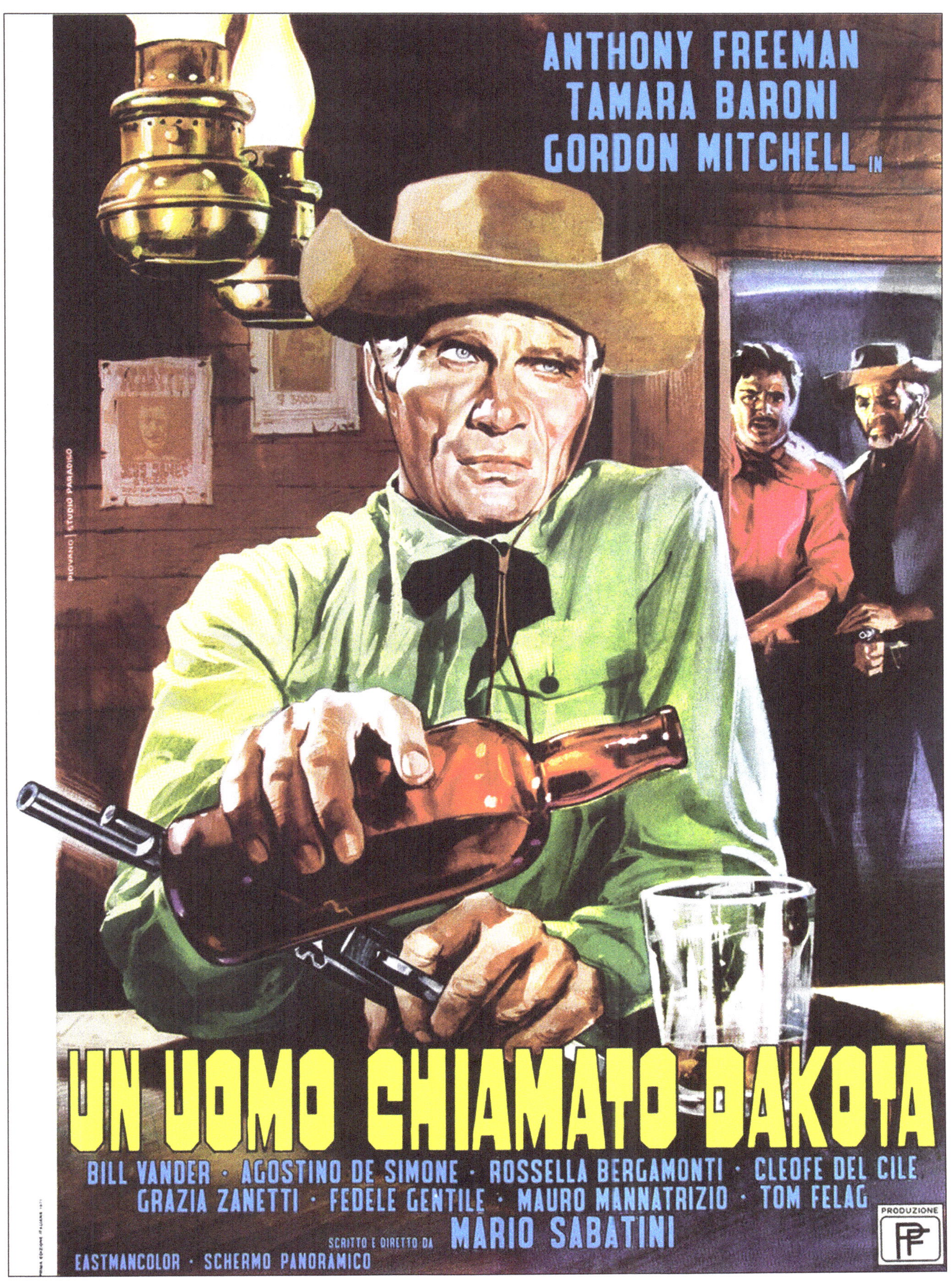

ANTHONY FREEMAN
TAMARA BARONI
GORDON MITCHELL in
UN UOMO CHIAMATO DAKOTA
BILL VANDER · AGOSTINO DE SIMONE · ROSSELLA BERGAMONTI · CLEOFE DEL CILE
GRAZIA ZANETTI · FEDELE GENTILE · MAURO MANNATRIZIO · TOM FELAG
MARIO SABATINI
EASTMANCOLOR · SCHERMO PANORAMICO
SCRITTO E DIRETTO DA
PRODUZIONE

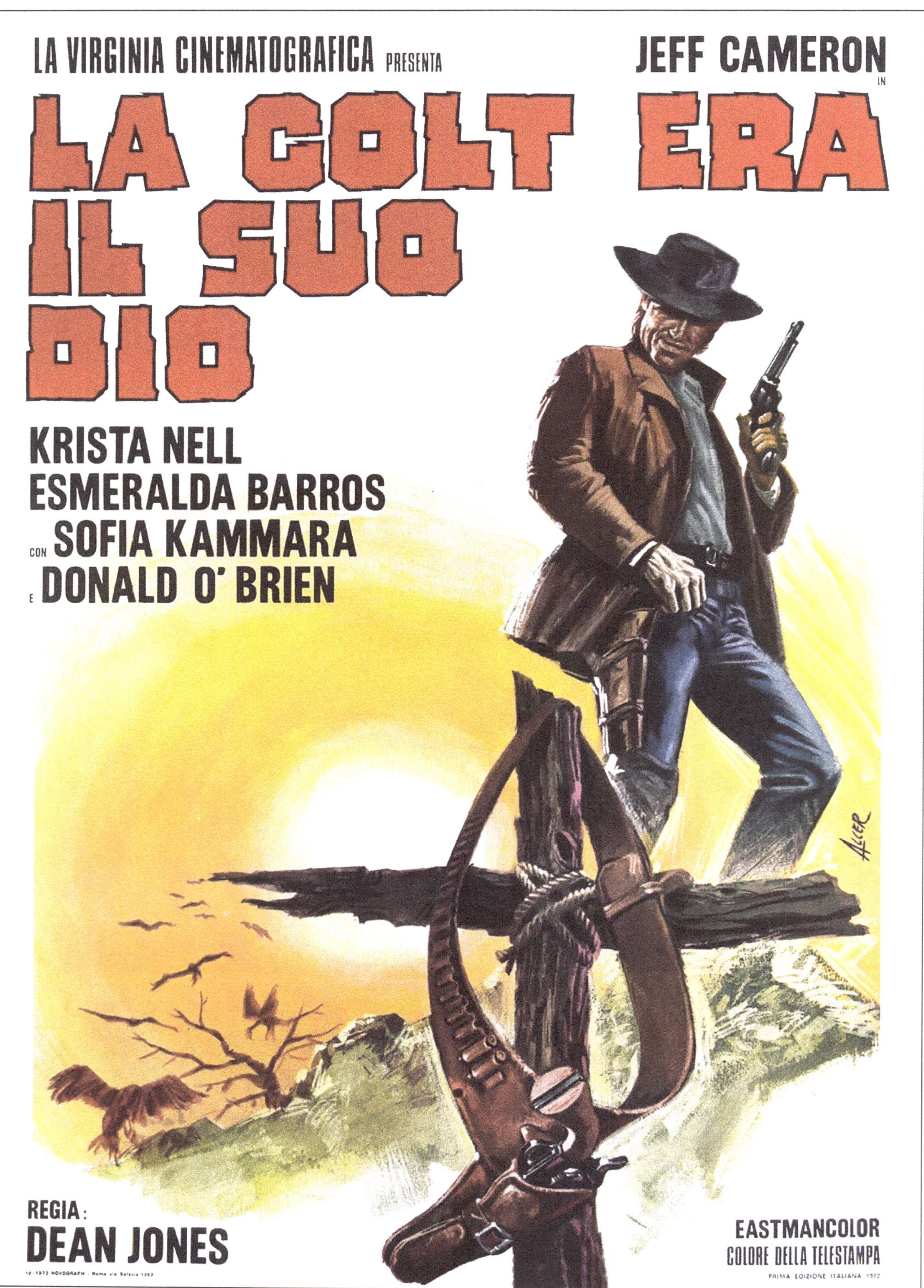

LA COLT ERA IL SUO DIO

("The Colt Was His God", 1972, Italy/Germany). Artist: Aller.

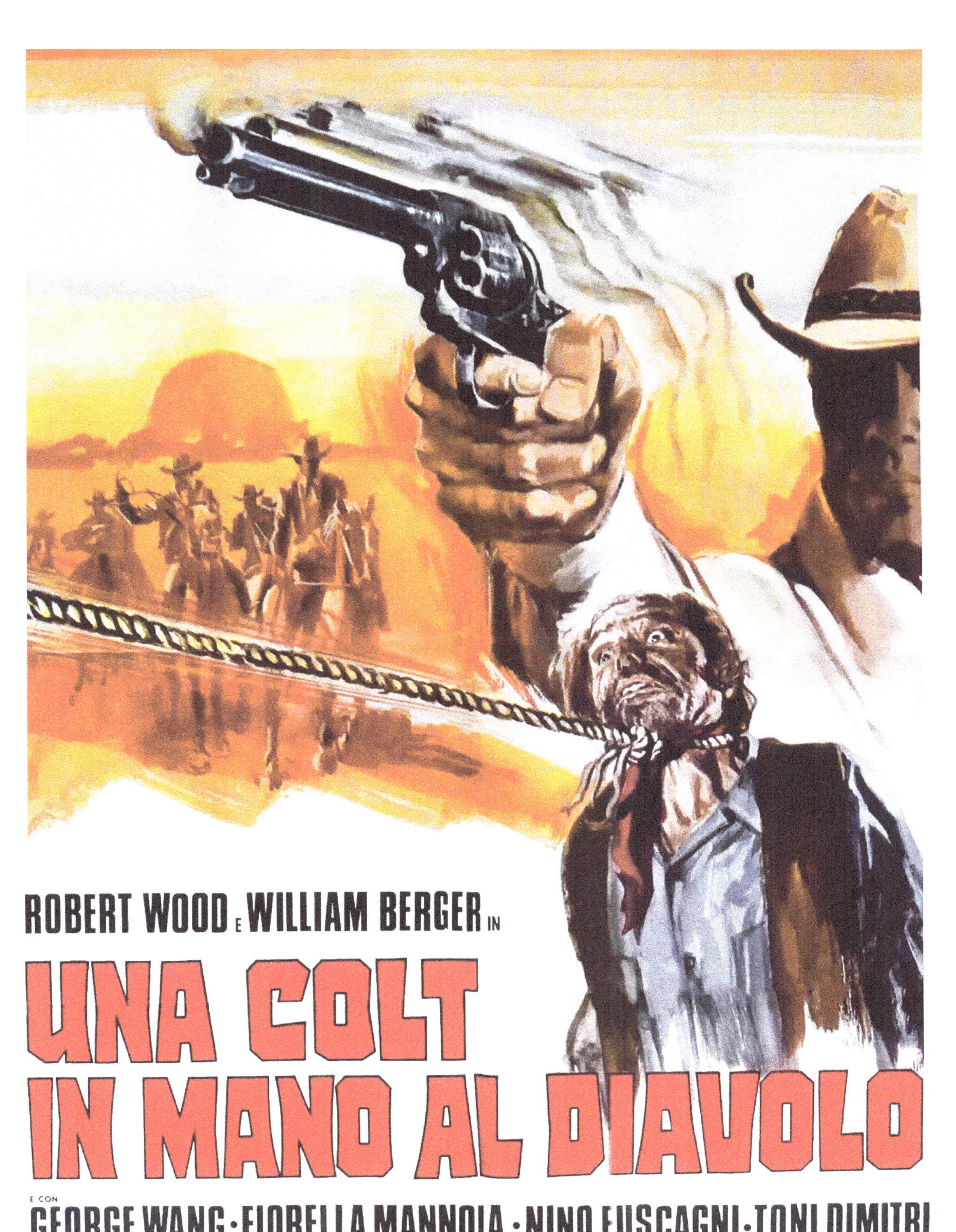

("A Colt In The Devil's Hand", 1972, Italy). Artist: unsigned.

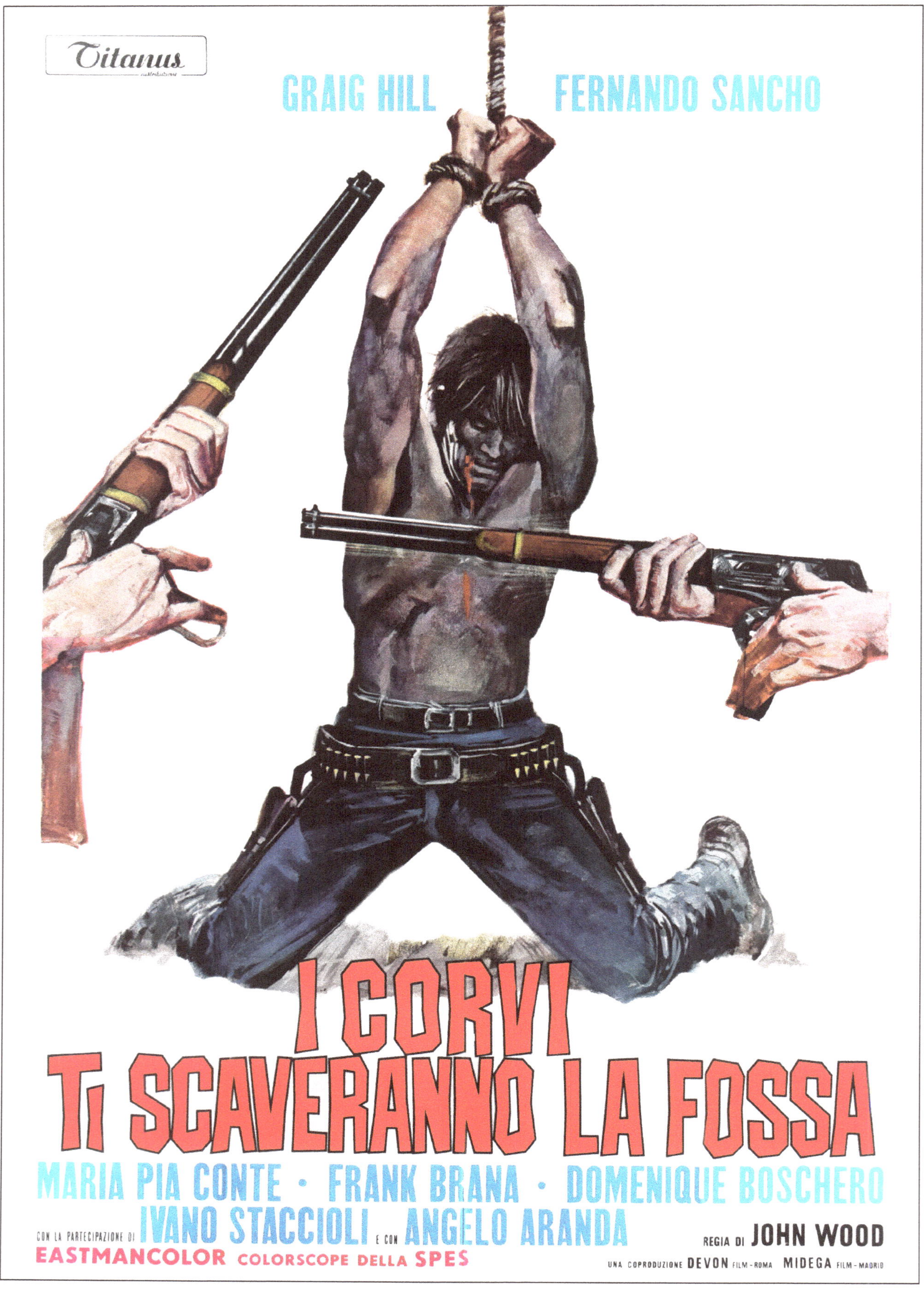

I CORVI TI SCAVERANNO LA FOSSA

(''The Crows Will Dig Your Grave'', 1972, Italy/Spain). Artist: unsigned.

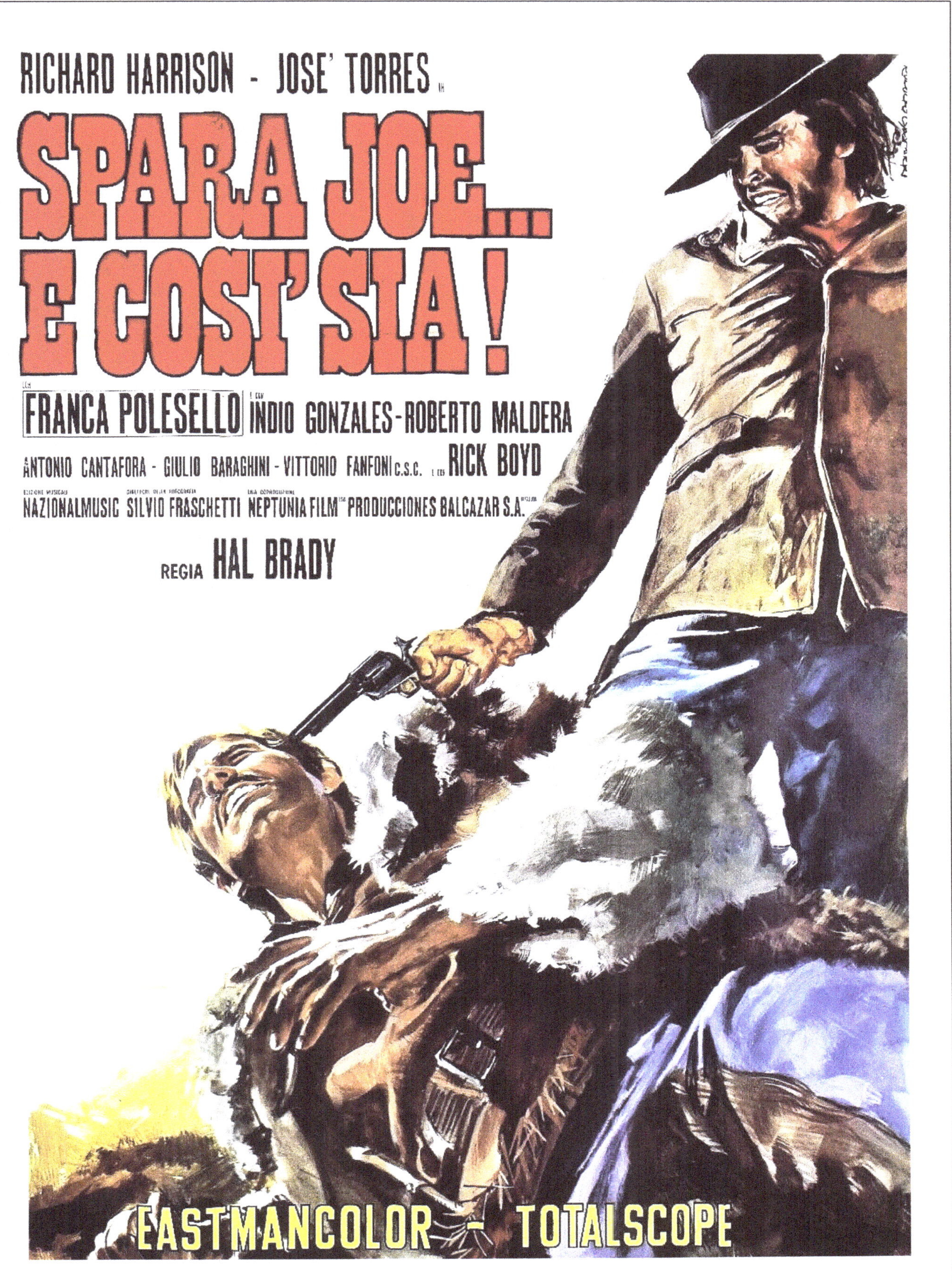

RICHARD HARRISON - JOSE' TORRES in
SPARA JOE... E COSI' SIA !
FRANCA POLESELLO INDIO GONZALES - ROBERTO MALDERA
ANTONIO CANTAFORA - GIULIO BARAGHINI - VITTORIO FANFONI c.s.c. RICK BOYD
NAZIONALMUSIC SILVIO FRASCHETTI NEPTUNIA FILM PRODUCCIONES BALCAZAR S.A.
REGIA HAL BRADY
EASTMANCOLOR - TOTALSCOPE

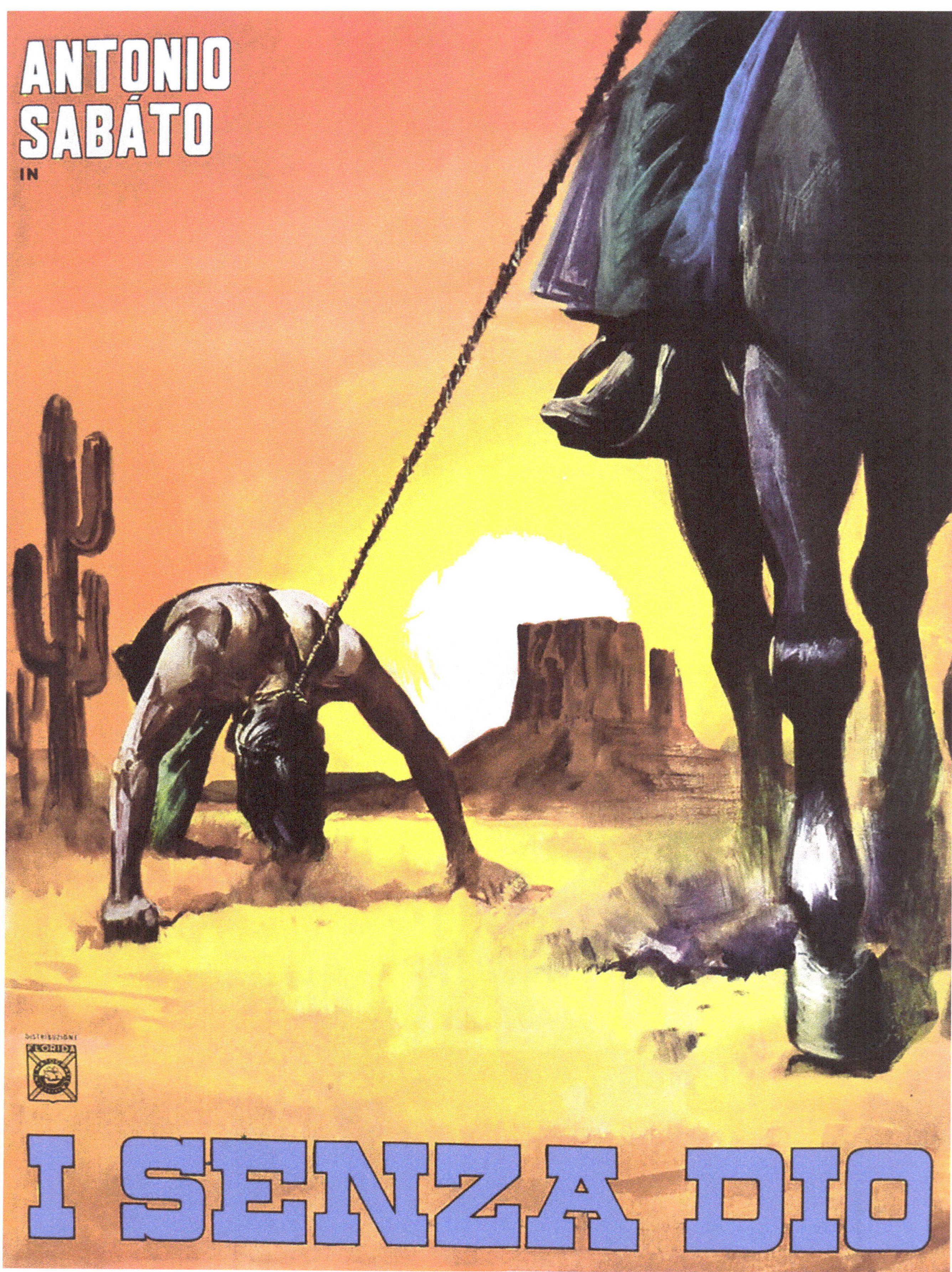

I SENZA DIO

(''The Godless Ones'', 1972, Italy). Artist: unsigned.

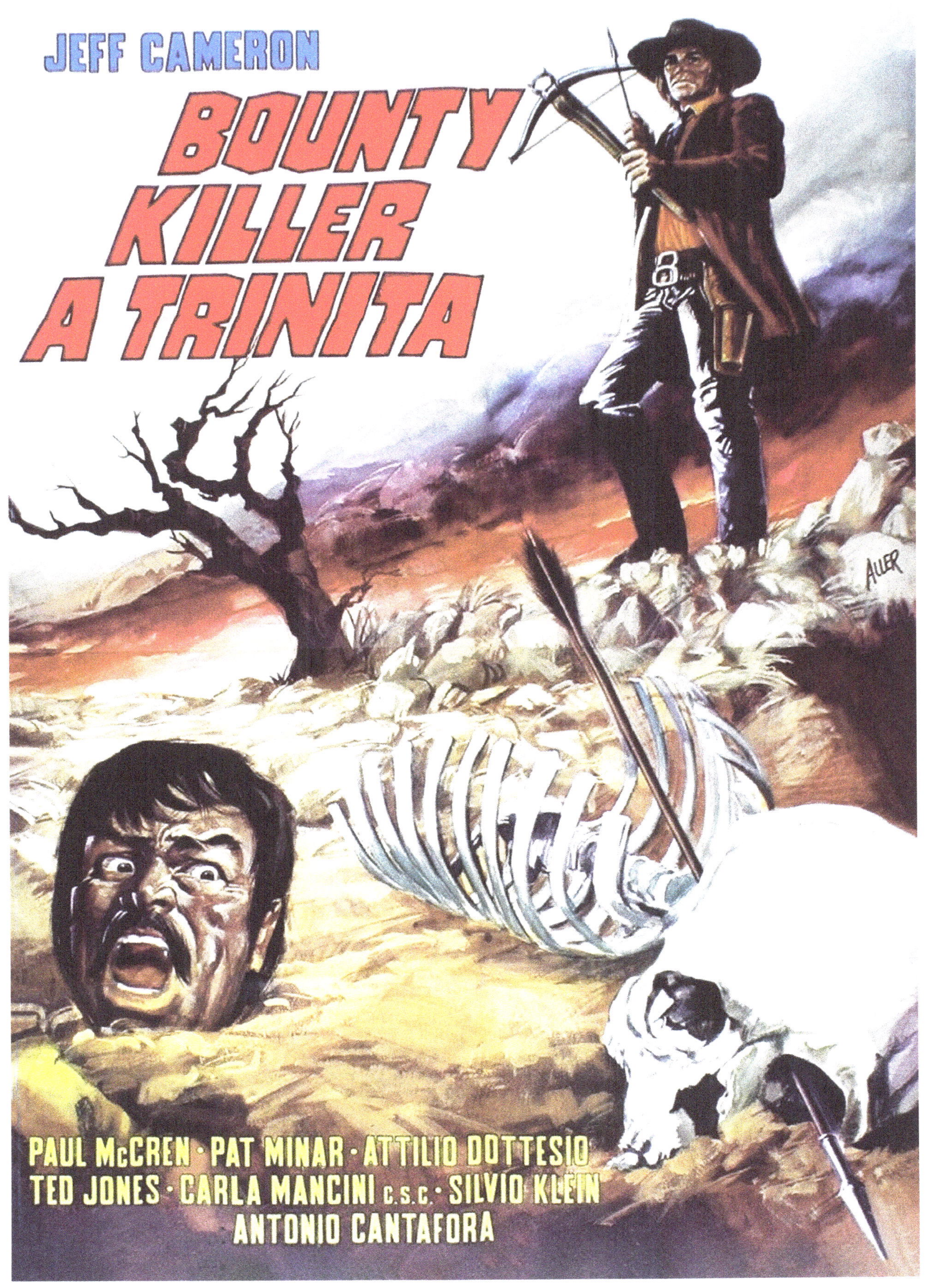

JEFF CAMERON
BOUNTY KILLER A TRINITA
PAUL McCREN · PAT MINAR · ATTILIO DOTTESIO
TED JONES · CARLA MANCINI c.s.c. · SILVIO KLEIN
ANTONIO CANTAFORA

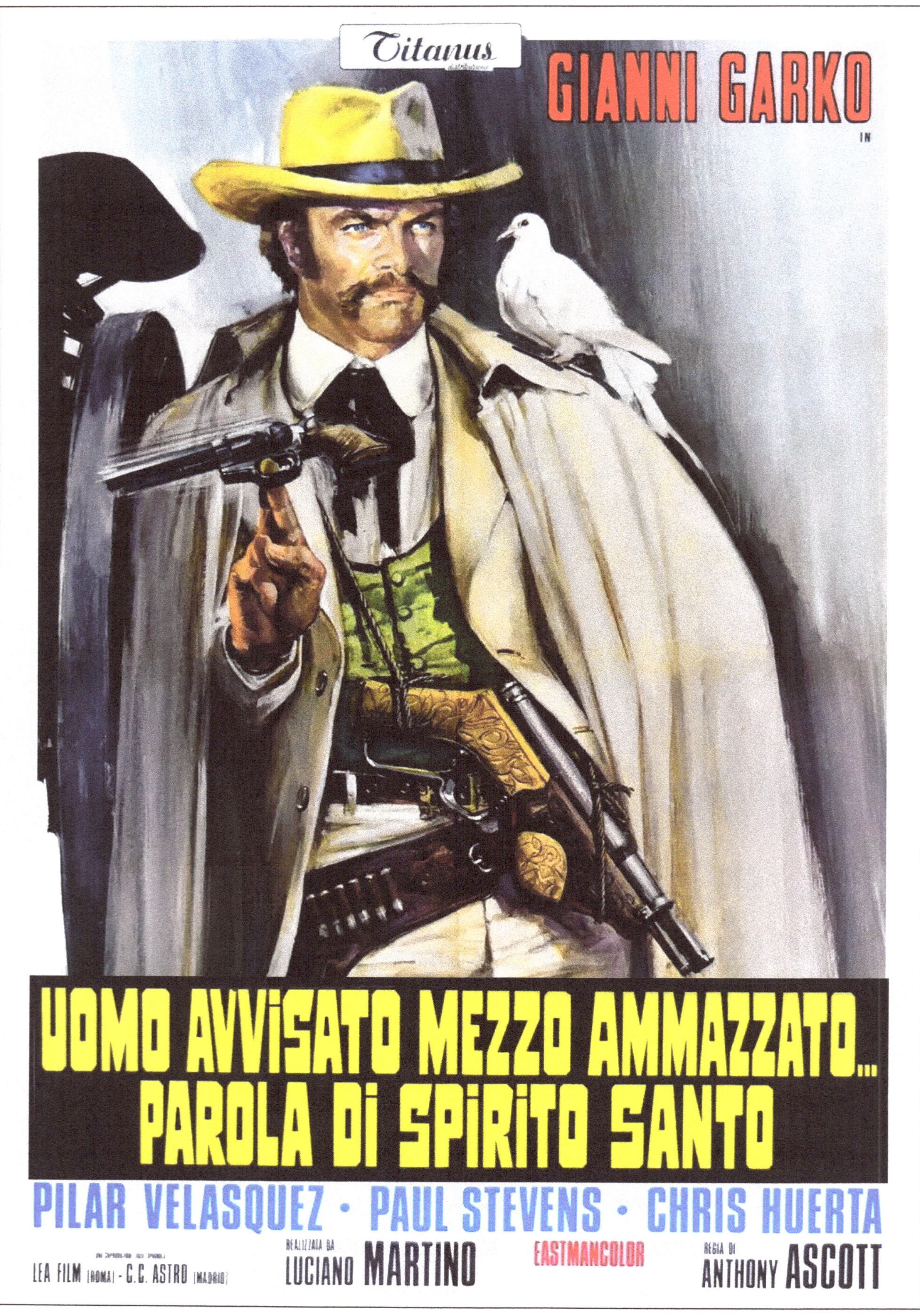

UOMO AVVISATO MEZZO AMMAZZATO... PAROLA DI SPIRITO SANTO

(''Forewarned Is Forearmed... So Says The Holy Ghost'', 1972, Italy/Spain). Artist: unsigned.

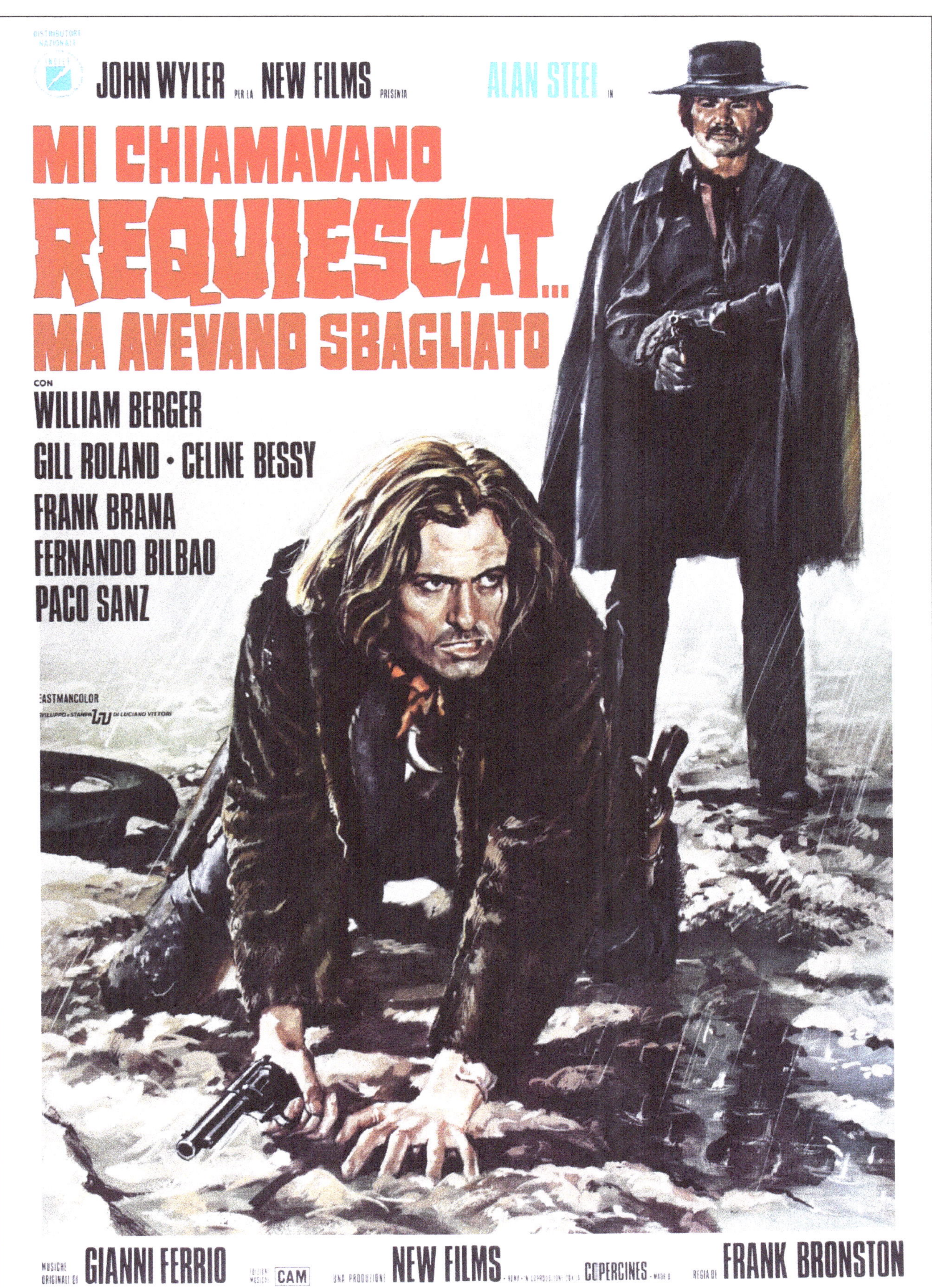

("They Called Me Requiescat... But They Were Wrong", 1973, Italy/Spain). Artist: Renato Casaro.

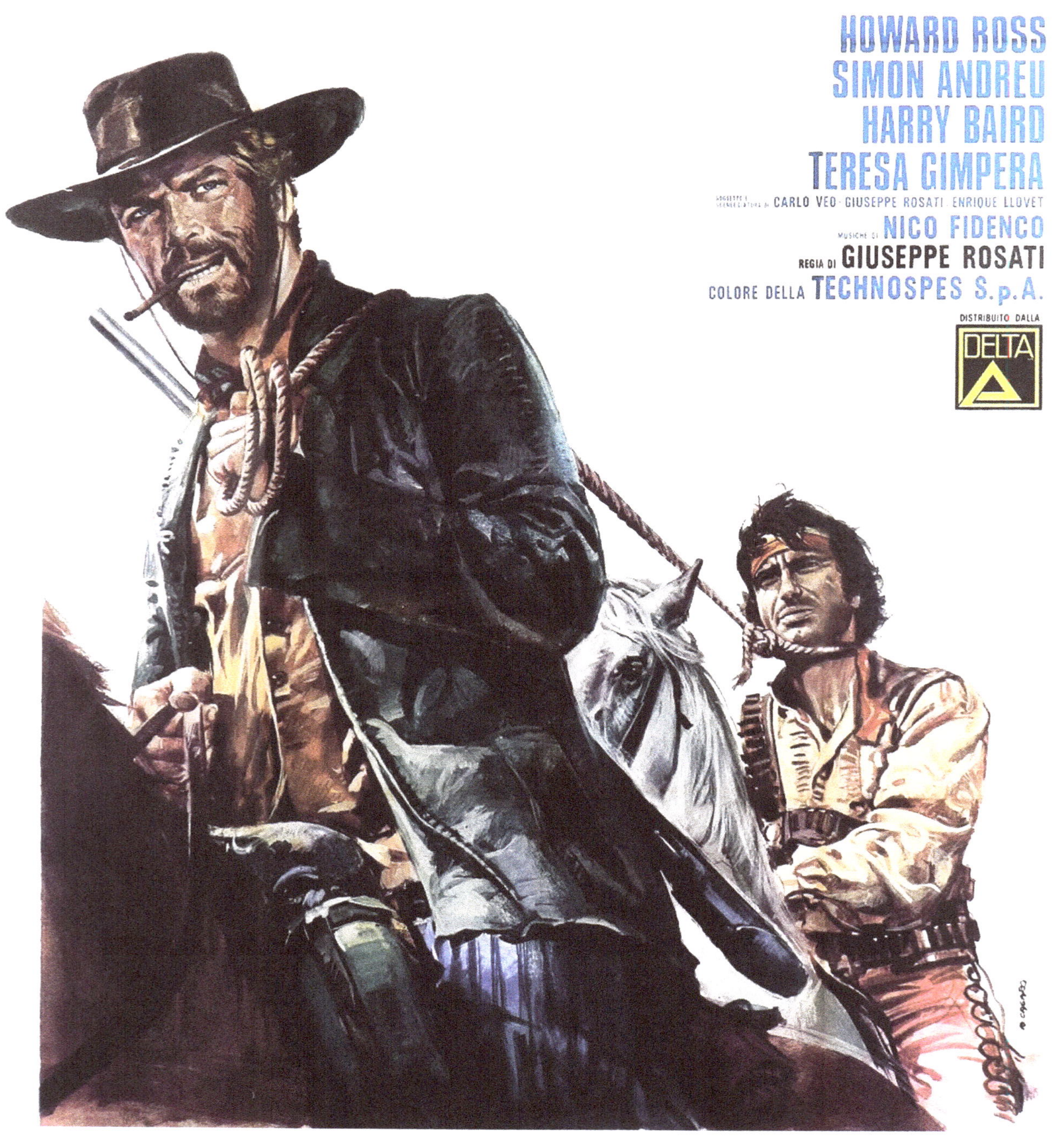

CAMPA CAROGNA... LA TAGLIA CRESCE
("Live, Carrion... The Bounty Grows", 1973, Italy/Spain). Artist: Renato Casaro.

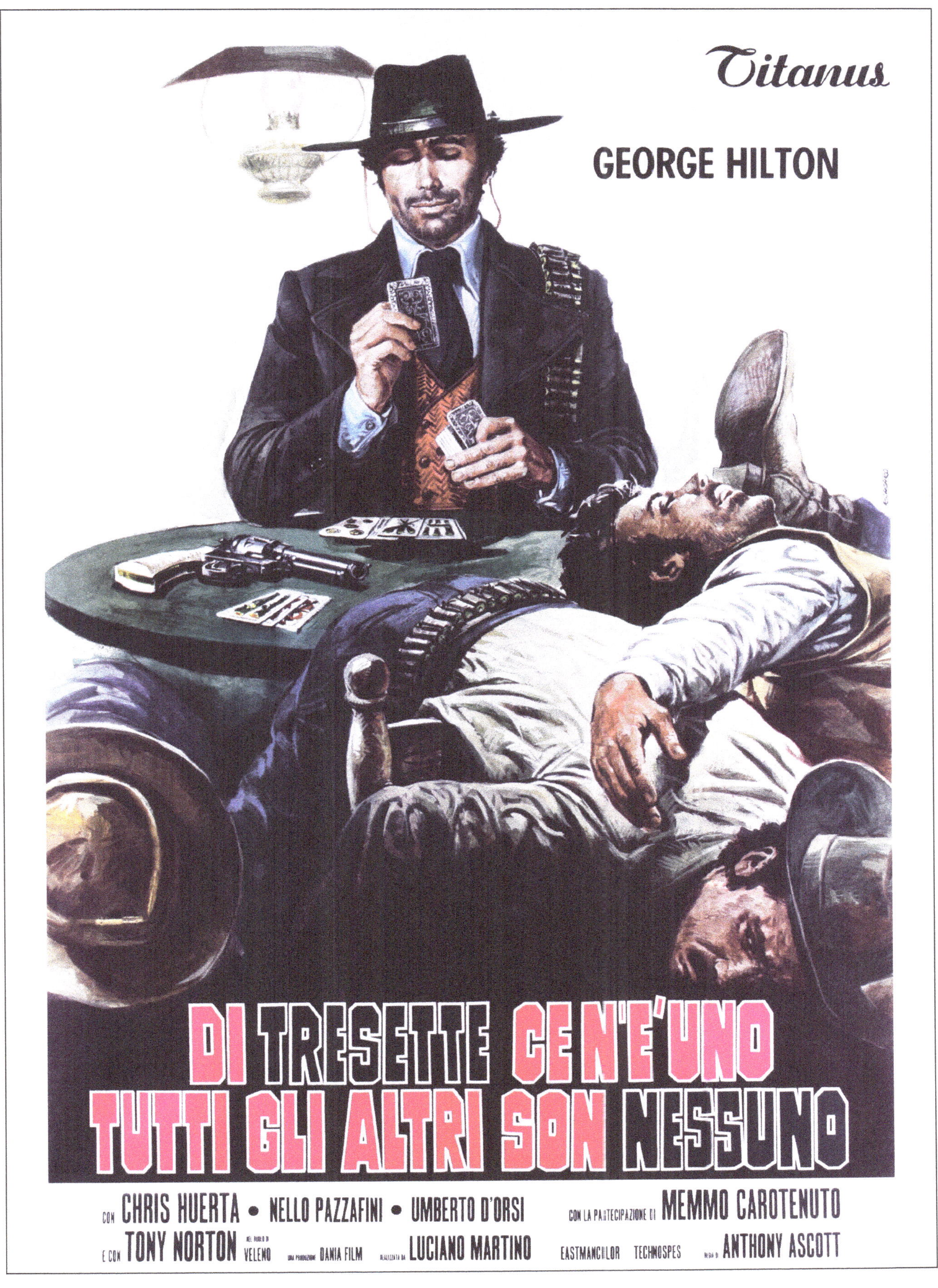

Titanus
GEORGE HILTON
DI TRESETTE CE N'E' UNO
TUTTI GLI ALTRI SON NESSUNO
CON CHRIS HUERTA • NELLO PAZZAFINI • UMBERTO D'ORSI
CON LA PARTECIPAZIONE DI MEMMO CAROTENUTO
E CON TONY NORTON
VELENO
DANIA FILM
LUCIANO MARTINO
EASTMANCOLOR   TECHNOSPES
ANTHONY ASCOTT

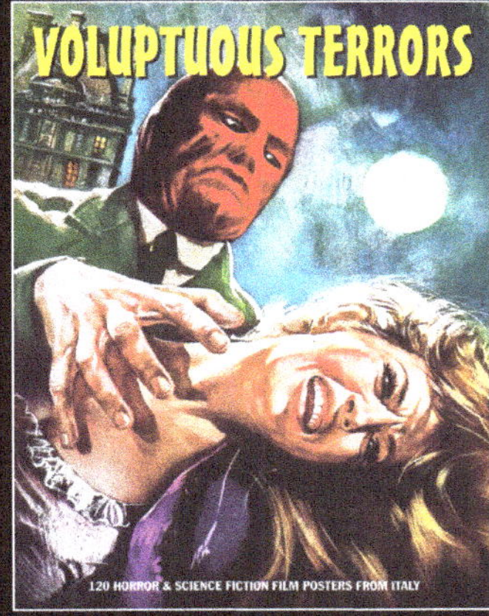
VOLUPTUOUS TERRORS
120 HORROR & SCIENCE FICTION FILM POSTERS FROM ITALY

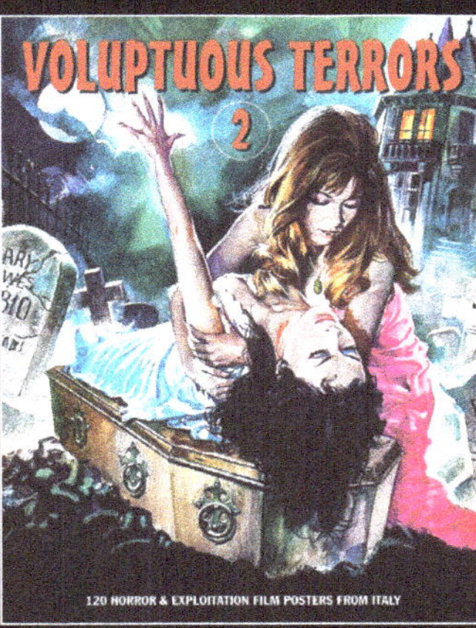
VOLUPTUOUS TERRORS
2
120 HORROR & EXPLOITATION FILM POSTERS FROM ITALY

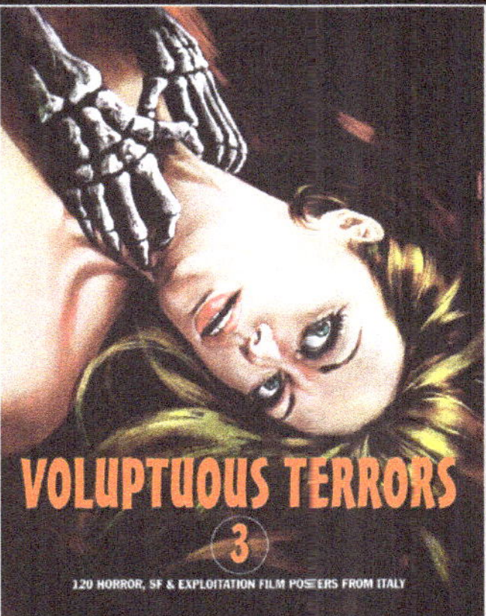
VOLUPTUOUS TERRORS
3
120 HORROR, SF & EXPLOITATION FILM POSTERS FROM ITALY

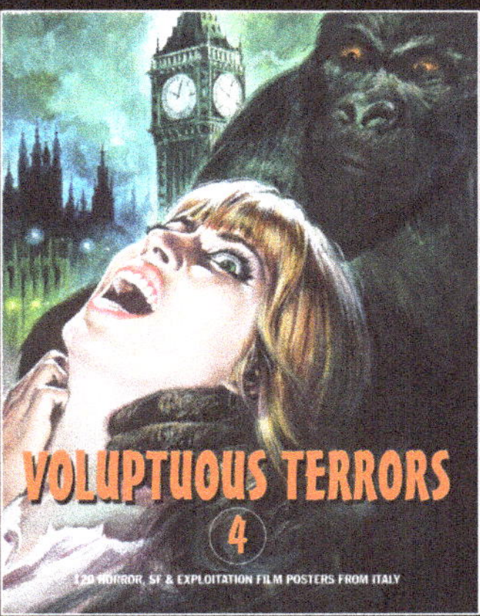
VOLUPTUOUS TERRORS
4
120 HORROR, SF & EXPLOITATION FILM POSTERS FROM ITALY

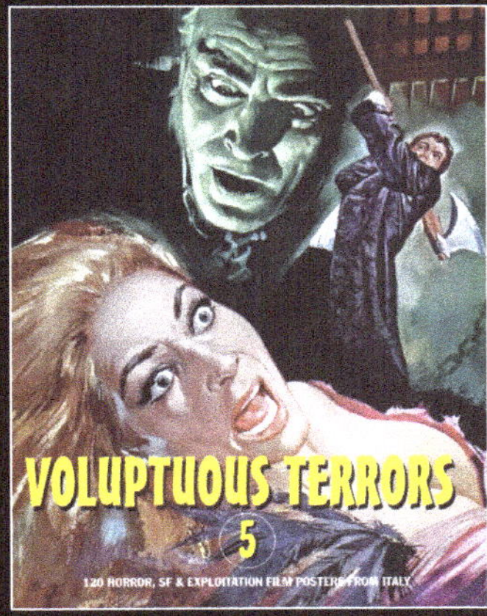
VOLUPTUOUS TERRORS
5
120 HORROR, SF & EXPLOITATION FILM POSTERS FROM ITALY

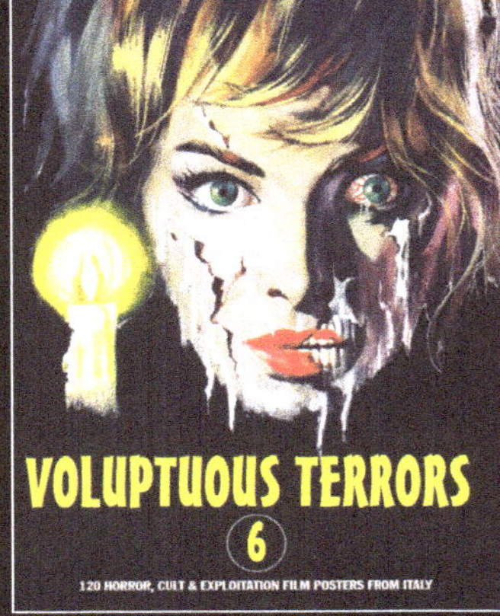
VOLUPTUOUS TERRORS
6
120 HORROR, CULT & EXPLOITATION FILM POSTERS FROM ITALY

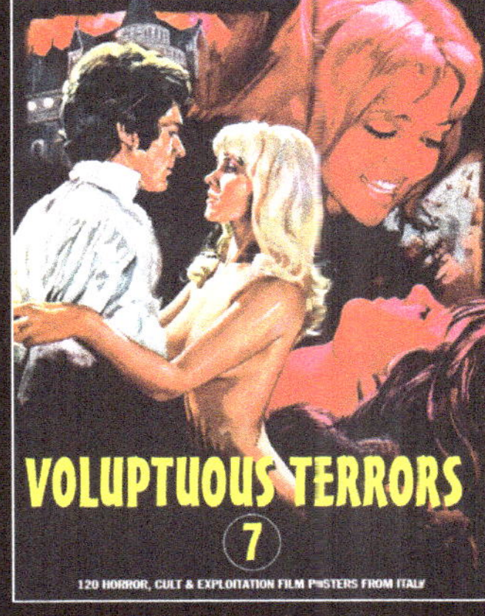
VOLUPTUOUS TERRORS
7
120 HORROR, CULT & EXPLOITATION FILM POSTERS FROM ITALY

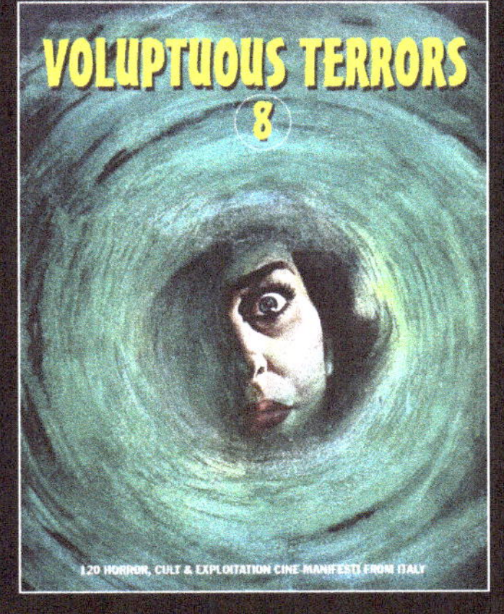
VOLUPTUOUS TERRORS
8
120 HORROR, CULT & EXPLOITATION CINE MANIFESTI FROM ITALY

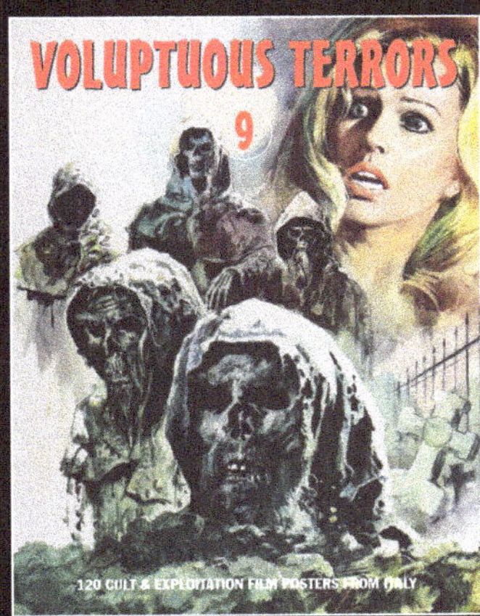
VOLUPTUOUS TERRORS
9
120 CULT & EXPLOITATION FILM POSTERS FROM ITALY

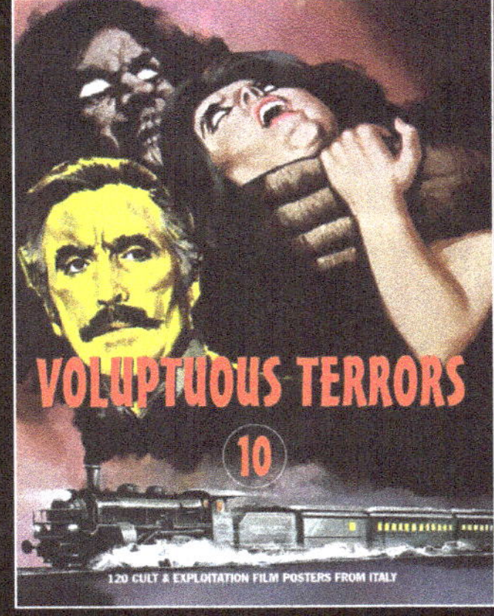
VOLUPTUOUS TERRORS
10
120 CULT & EXPLOITATION FILM POSTERS FROM ITALY

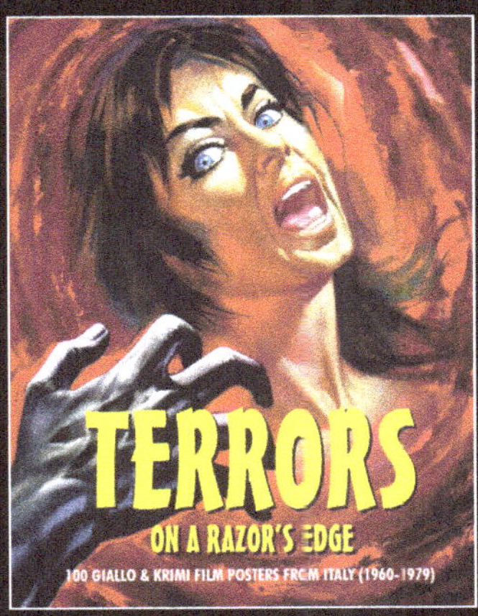
TERRORS
ON A RAZOR'S EDGE
100 GIALLO & KRIMI FILM POSTERS FROM ITALY (1960-1979)

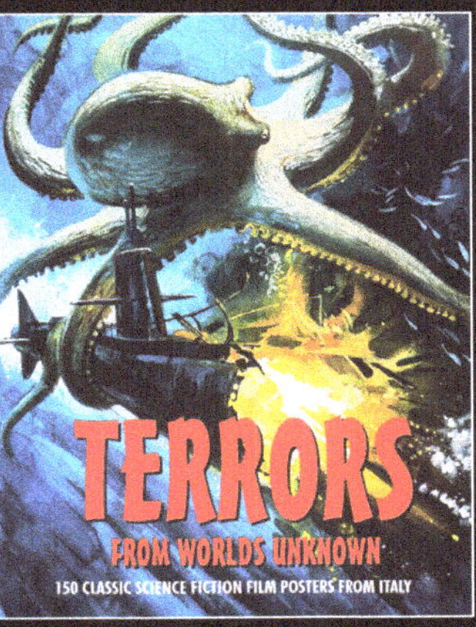
TERRORS
FROM WORLDS UNKNOWN
150 CLASSIC SCIENCE FICTION FILM POSTERS FROM ITALY

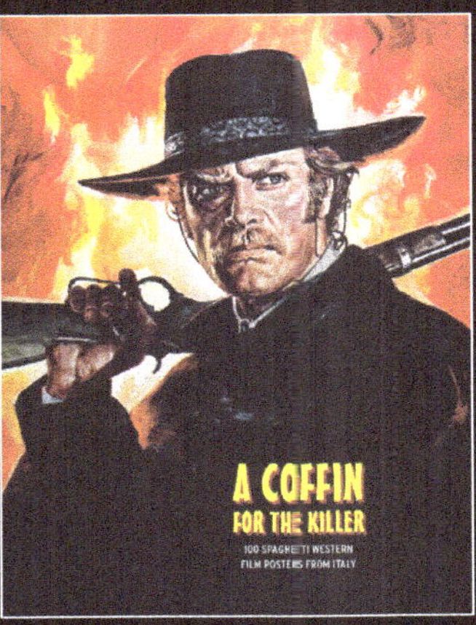
A COFFIN
FOR THE KILLER
100 SPAGHETTI WESTERN
FILM POSTERS FROM ITALY

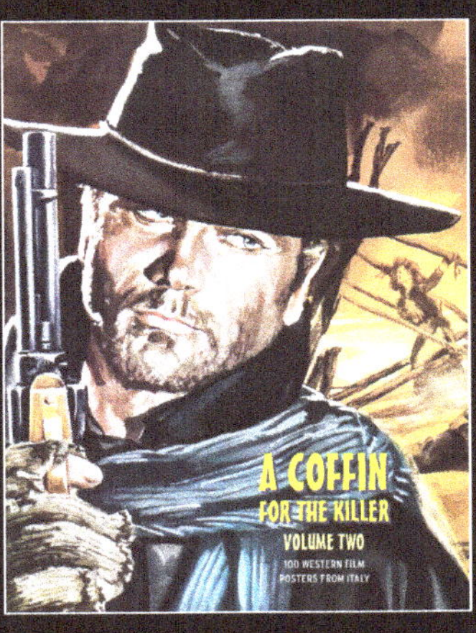
A COFFIN
FOR THE KILLER
VOLUME TWO
100 WESTERN FILM
POSTERS FROM ITALY